Development and the Private Sector

green
press
INITIATIVE

Kumarian Press, Inc. is committed to preserving ancient forests
and natural resources. We elected to print *Development and The
Private Sector* on 30% post consumer recycled paper, processed
chlorine free. As a result, for this printing, we have saved:

8 Trees (40' tall and 6-8" diameter)
3,257 Gallons of Waste Water
1,310 Kilowatt Hours of Electricity
359 Pounds of Solid Waste
705 Pounds of Greenhouse Gases

Kumarian Press, Inc. made this paper choice because our printer,
Thomson-Shore, Inc., is a member of Green Press Initiative, a
nonprofit program dedicated to supporting authors, publishers,
and suppliers in their efforts to reduce their use of fiber obtained
from endangered forests.

For more information, visit www.greenpressinitiative.org

Development and the Private Sector

Consuming Interests

EDITED BY
DEBORAH EADE AND JOHN SAYER

Kumarian
Press, Inc.

Development and the Private Sector: Consuming Interests is based on *Development in Practice* Volume 15, Numbers 3&4 (June 2005), published by Routledge, Taylor & Francis Ltd. *Development in Practice* gratefully acknowledges financial support from affiliates of Oxfam International. The views expressed in this volume are those of the individual contributors, and not necessarily those of the editors or publisher.

Development and the Private Sector: Consuming Interests

Published in 2006 in the United States of America by Kumarian Press, Inc., 1294 Blue Hills Avenue, Bloomfield, CT 06002 USA

The text of this book is set in 10.5/13 Times.

Production and editorial services were provided by Publication Services, Champaign, Illinois.

Printed in the United States of America by Thomson Shore, Inc.
Text printed with vegetable oil-based ink.

∞ The paper used in this publication meets the minimum requirements of the American National Standard for Information Sciences—Permanence of Paper for printed Library Materials, ANSI Z39.48-1984

Library of Congress Cataloging-in-Publication Data

Eade, Deborah.
    Development and the private sector : consuming interests / Deborah Eade and John Sayer.
        p. cm.
    "'Development and the private sector : consuming interests' is based on Development in Practice, Volume 15, Numbers 3&4 (June 2005), published by Routledge, Taylor & Francis Ltd."
    Includes bibliographical references and index.
    ISBN-13: 978-1-56549-218-9 (pbk. : alk. paper)
    ISBN-10: 1-56549-218-8 (pbk. : alk. paper)
1. Economic development. 2. Social responsibility of business.
3. Developing countries—Economic conditions. 4. Globalization. I. Sayer, John. II. Title.
HD82.E22 2006
338.9009172'4—dc22
                                    2006011912

Contents

Part 3
Pressure for Change:
Fair Trade and Ethical Codes of Conduct

Part 4
Resources

Preface

DEBORAH EADE

The relationship between the private sector and development has not been far from the public eye since some of the earliest global campaigns denounced the aggressive or irresponsible marketing strategies of some of the pharmaceutical and agrochemical corporate giants throughout the world's poorest countries. These campaigns and their calls for consumer boycotts coalesced from the 1960s onward into transnational coalitions such as Consumers International (CI), the International Baby Food Action Network (IBFAN), Health Action International (HAI), and Pesticides Action Network (PAN), all of which are still very much alive and kicking today.[1] A number of codes of practice were also developed at that time, by the World Health Organization (WHO) in particular, in relation to the production and pricing of generic drugs and essential medicines, and to the marketing of harmful and addictive products such as tobacco and alcohol. Much of the focus of such initiatives in the 1970s and 1980s was on protecting the interests of consumers, especially those in the global South least able to protect themselves through, for instance, access to impartial—or, indeed, any—information about the drugs and pesticides for sale in their local markets. This was naturally followed by various fair-trade initiatives geared toward consumers in the North, ranging from products for which a new niche could be created on the supermarket shelves (such as coffee, tea, or chocolate) to promoting traditional craft items that could be sold through solidarity networks, charity shops, and stores specializing in handmade artifacts.

More recently, attention has turned to the social and environmental impact of transnational companies on the people in the countries in which their subsidiaries are based, or from which they purchase raw materials or source their products. The corporate social responsibility (CSR) movement has helped bring issues of labor rights and environmental damage to consumers in rich countries, and create pressure on companies to smarten up their act. How successful these efforts have been in achieving real change either in consumer habits or in corporate practice is doubtful, but they have certainly raised the stakes for those companies whose products are at the more visible end of the market. At the same time, however, neoliberal policies have increasingly been associated with the privatization of public utilities and so-called public-private partnerships whereby for-profit private companies take on the delivery of an array of social services, from prison security to pensions and health insurance, from postal and telecommunications systems to residential homes for the elderly. The results of such hybrid partnerships have been mixed, and seem to depend on the capacity of citizens (now recast as "clients" or "customers") to insist on comprehensive coverage of adequate quality. The obvious danger is that those who can afford to do so will opt out of a semi-privatized public system and choose their own supplier, and that the private contractors will gradually abandon (or, in some cases, never offer) any semblance of universal provision. In some cases, corporations and their shareholders have made phenomenal profits; in others, the quasi-privatized companies continue to depend on government handouts, though without the corresponding accountability expected of a publicly owned enterprise. It is paradoxical, therefore, that the Global Compact between the UN and the corporate sector should both underline the critical role of private enterprise in promoting (mal)development, and also give the appearance of conferring a clean— but seldom proven—bill of health on those companies choosing to participate in it.[2]

The private sector has, then, long been recognized as a key determinant of development, whether by facilitating or by undermining it. This book is a compilation drawn from an issue of the journal *Development in Practice*[3] guest-edited by John Sayer. In Chapter 1, Sayer illustrates something of the range and complexity of concerns encompassed by the subject, from bread-and-butter campaign issues such as ethical codes, labor rights, and fair trade to popular responses to the privatization of essential services and the role of small and medium-sized enterprises (SMEs) in generating employment and contributing to economic growth. With contributions from scholars and practitioners from around the world, we trust that these selections and the annotated resources list will together offer something of interest both to readers for whom this is familiar terrain and to those who are newer to the subject.

NOTES

[1] Although innumerable new organizations have emerged in the wake of developments in information technology, these four have gained in strength over their 20–30 years' existence. For instance, CI was founded in 1960 as the International Organisation of Consumers' Unions (IOCU), and today has 250 member organizations in 115 countries, working together to defend the rights and concerns of consumers worldwide. IBFAN was founded in 1979 and now comprises 200 affiliated groups around the world dedicated to promoting healthy infant nutritional practices, particularly breastfeeding. PAN International was founded in 1982, and today encompasses more than 600 member organizations around the globe; its current focus is on the promotion of food security and information about the dangers of adopting genetically modified organisms (GMOs). Established at the May 1981 World Health Assembly, HAI also has a global network working for universal access to appropriate health care and the rational use of drugs; a major focus has been on essential medicines and generic drugs, areas in which it collaborates closely with WHO.

[2] The Alliance for a Corporate-Free UN is a global network of human rights, environmental, and development groups concerned about undue corporate influence on the UN. It supports UN initiatives to hold corporations accountable on issues of human rights, labor rights, and the environment. For more information, see www.earthrights.org. See also Bruno and Karliner (2002) for a critique of how corporate PR is enhanced by involvement with the UN without any obligation for the corporation to make fundamental changes in its behavior.

[3] *Development in Practice* Vol. 15, nos. 3 and 4 (June 2005), published by Routledge, Taylor & Francis Group Ltd. on behalf of Oxfam GB. Summaries of all articles published in the journal are available free of charge in English, French, Portuguese, and Spanish at the journal's website, www.developmentinpractice.org.

REFERENCES

Bruno, Kenny, and Joshua Karliner. 2002. *earthsummit.biz: The Corporate Takeover of Sustainable Development*. San Francisco, CA: Food First.

Abbreviations and Acronyms

AAMA	American Apparel Manufacturers Association
ADB	Asian Development Bank
AGOA	African Growth and Opportunity Act
ASMINDO	The Association of the Furniture Industry
ATPA	Andean Trade Preferences Act
BOP	Balance of Payments
BVQI	Independent Certification Body of Bureau Veritas
CAFTA	Central American Free-Trade Agreement
CAWN	Central American Women's Network
CDD	Community Driven Development
CEP	Community Empowerment and Local Governance Project
CI	Consumers International
CSO	civil society organization
CSR	corporate social responsibility
EIRIS	Ethical Investment Research Service
ENTEL	National Telecommunications Enterprise
ETI	Ethical Trading Initiative
FDI	Foreign Direct Investment
FLA	Fair Labor Association
FSC	Forest Stewardship Council
FTA	Free-Trade Agreement
GMO	genetically modified organism
GMIES	*Grupo de Monitoreo Independiente de El Salvador* (Salvadoran Independent Monitoring Group)
HAI	Health Action International

IBFAN	International Baby Food Action Network
IDB	Inter-American Development Bank
IFI	International Financial Institution
ILO	International Labour Organization
IOCU	International Organisation of Consumers' Unions
ISEAL	Social and Environmental Accreditation and Labelling Alliance
ISO	International Organization for Standardization
ITDC	Intermediate Technology Development Group
JICA	Japan International Cooperation Agency
LDC	Least Developed Countries
LLC	Limited Liability Company
MFA	Multi-Fibre Arrangement
MSI	multi-stakeholder initiative
MSN	Maquila Solidarity Network
NGO	nongovernmental organization
PAN	Pesticides Action Network
PLC	Publicly Listed Company
PPSE	Privatized Public Service Enterprises
SAI	Social Accountability International
SAN	Sustainable Agriculture Network
SGS	Société Générale de Surveillance, an auditing company
SME	Small- and Medium-Sized Enterprise
SOE	State-Owned Enterprises
SRI	socially responsible investment
TFET	Trust Fund for East Timor
TNC	transnational corporation
UK	United Kingdom
UN	United Nations
UNDP	United Nations Development Programme
UNEP	United Nations Environment Programme

UNIDO	United Nations Industrial Development Organization
UNRISD	United Nations Research Institute for Social Development
US	United States
WHO	World Health Organization
WRAP	Worldwide Responsible Apparel Production
WRC	Workers' Rights Consortium
WSSD	World Summit on Sustainable Development
WTO	World Trade Organization

ONE

Do More Good, Do Less Harm:

Development and the Private Sector

JOHN SAYER

No reasoned discussion of equitable growth, the attainment of rights, the effect of globalization on poor people, or the achievement of the Millennium Development Goals (MDGs) can properly take place without considering the role of the private sector. Yet it is surprising how much of the debate on poverty focuses on the roles and responsibilities of governments, NGOs, and international aid bodies. In such discussions, the world of business lurks in the shadows, acknowledged uneasily like a tattooed man at a tea party.

This selection of articles from a special issue of the journal *Development in Practice* (volume 15, numbers 3 and 4) examines some of the debates concerning the role of private business in the development process. These range from accusations that the corporate sector is part of the problem, to arguments that it can, or must, be part of the solution.

Companies are with us for the long haul. The debate over whether or not the private sector should be replaced by some other system of production and distribution has become marginal. Far from being consumed by their own internal contradictions, corporations are expanding and now exert influence on a global scale. The combined sales of the world's top 200 corporations are bigger than the combined economies of all but the 10 largest nations (Anderson and Cavanagh 2000). This vast economic might gives corporations immense political and social influence. While national governments and international institutions have failed to develop governance mechanisms appropriate to a globalized economic system, companies have thrived in this planetary playground.

Today's debates are concerned with the place of companies and markets in society, and with how to control excesses and failures, rather than with the fundamental desirability or possible replacement of private capital. For developing countries, the policy challenge is to create an environment that encourages business growth, trade, and foreign direct investmen (FDI), while ensuring that social policies share the benefits of growth more equitably, in what Andrew Sumner (2005: 269) calls a "precarious trade-off between attracting FDI and maintaining policy instruments to extract the benefits."

This introductory chapter opens with an exploration of the nature of the private sector and its role in relation to economic growth and the distribution of benefits. It goes on to examine the detrimental effects that corporate activity can have on development, followed by a brief look at new forms of opposition to such activities. The business case for corporate social responsibility (CSR) is then outlined, leading into an account of various ways in which some private companies have sought either to mitigate the harmful effects or to enhance the impact of their activities on development. The penultimate section looks at the role of the private sector in achieving the MDGs, and the chapter concludes with some reflections on the need to redirect the dynamism and resources of the private sector to the benefit of humanity.

THE NATURE OF THE PRIVATE SECTOR

In discussing the private sector and development, it is tempting to concentrate entirely on the role of transnational corporations (TNCs) in developing countries. It is here that the most passionate exchanges take place about good and evil, and the humble versus the hegemonic, and where observations about the impact of such corporations have a stark clarity for both admirers and detractors.

In truth, however, most private-sector activity in any economy is small and domestic. The private sector includes the successful local conglomerates, small and medium-sized enterprises (SMEs), and women's cooperatives of the kind praised by those who may condemn larger companies, as well as the amorphous—and vital—informal economy. Even small local companies operate in the marketplace. They too are driven to maximize profit, and are capable of cutting exactly the same corners on responsibility toward the environment or to their employees when they believe they can get away with it. In many respects, the distinction between the TNC and the microenterprise is only one of scale of influence and impact.

Even such apparently clear divisions as local versus foreign business become indistinct when one examines joint ventures, equity investment, licenses, franchises, and subcontracted production. In some cases, the private sector is largely controlled by itinerant members of the nation's diaspora. Trade, finance, and indirect investment do not require a company to put up a nameplate in a given country, but they certainly affect that country's economic development.

Economists differ over whether small or large companies make the greater contribution to national economic growth. Issues of unfair political influence and unwieldy economic impact are less likely to arise in relation to SMEs, though these account for some 90 percent of companies in most market economies, typically employing half the working population (International Finance Corporation 2004). SMEs tend to be favored by those concerned with development because they are usually labor-intensive and so create more employment—often at the lower end of the market, most suited to the poorest people, and in areas where no other job opportunities exist. Significant development assistance goes into fostering conditions to promote the growth of SMEs, and Julian Oram and Deborah Doane make the case in Chapter 7 for supporting these as a path to sustainable development. Moreover, as local companies, SMEs cannot so easily be accused of introducing alien values; indeed, Tim Coward and James Fathers (2005) have highlighted the role that industrial design can play in encouraging indigenous crafts.

SMEs are often more vulnerable than their larger corporate brethren to changes in policy or economic conditions. In Chapter 8, Linda Loebis and Hubert Schmitz offer the example of the furniture exporters of central Java and examine a range of problems facing these producers, along with some possible positive interventions. Turning to Timor-Leste, Ben Moxham warns in Chapter 9 that interventions intended to support the growth of SMEs are likely to fail if they are imposed in a top-down and hurried manner. In developing countries SMEs also face the problem of unequal access to credit, which in turn has given rise to the growing significance of microcredit within overall development spending. Begoña Gutiérrez Nieto (2005) reveals some of the issues surrounding an intervention designed to stimulate the smaller end of the private sector.

The private sector faces very different challenges in open economies than it does, for example, in those that are emerging from decades
of central planning and are now pursuing economic liberalization policies. Private companies that are growing from the ground up confront
problems that are distinct from those faced by companies attempting to
transform state monopolies into private enterprises, in which some of
the immediate growth gains may be characterized as catching up on
unrealized economic potential that had been artificially restrained by
previous systems of economic control. Similarly, some reform economies are simultaneously liberalizing political and social systems, building the political accountability and civil society so important for
controlling the corruption, exploitation, and marginalization that economic liberalization can bring. Others retain centralized political
power, which in turn raises questions about the assumed linkages
between economic and political liberalization. Clearly, a range of policies is needed in order to draw developmental benefits from this complex diversity—and the policies chosen will in turn depend on the
specific historical legacy and on the nature of the enterprise (Kuada and
Sørensen 2005) or international partnership (Jeppesen 2005).

GROWTH AND DISTRIBUTION

Development, in the sense of alleviating widespread poverty and
enabling the great majority of people to gain their rights, involves both
the creation of wealth and its distribution.

All those concerned with such issues therefore look beyond the
achievement of macroeconomic growth. Development in a fuller sense
concerns the lives of all people, particularly the poorest, whose immediate survival is linked more to issues of access to productive resources
and opportunities than to gross national product. Development involves
the achievement of the rights of the whole population to livelihoods and
services, and the creation of sustainable conditions that enable and fur-
nish these.

There is compelling evidence that economic growth is a precondi-
tion for the sustainable alleviation of poverty. In market economies, the
private sector is the main engine of that growth. Corporations play a key
role in the creation of jobs, the contribution of tax revenue, the earning
of foreign exchange, the generation of finance, the achievement of
access to new markets, the transfer or development of technology and

administrative skills, and the provision of more, better, or cheaper goods and services.

Farmers, the informal economy, the self-employed, and remittances from migrant workers do certainly contribute to the creation of wealth in developing countries. But almost all significant cases of countries developing to the point where poverty is dramatically reduced have occurred in situations where larger companies have become a major part of the economy, and more generally, where such companies are involved in international trade and where the private sector has attracted substantial foreign investment.

Clearly, growth does not in itself lead automatically to the reduction of poverty. There are plenty of countries in which a wealthy elite enjoys the benefits of growth while millions live in terrible poverty. There are countries in which companies, particularly extractive industries, make fortunes over the heads of poor communities that see none of the benefits, or worse, are made poorer by the loss of land and the degradation of their surroundings (see Garvey and Newell's discussion of this in Chapter 4).

There is little evidence, though, that development can be achieved on the basis of a decentralized, non-industrial base, unlinked from international trade and investment (Kitching 1982). The most telling examples of countries that have raised impressive numbers of their people out of poverty since the 1950s, most notably in East Asia, have also experienced high growth rates attributable at least in part to the judicious encouragement of international trade and foreign investment. Some would argue that other factors, such as high levels of equitable social investment, provided the impetus for success. China and Vietnam did make such social investment, but while this was accompanied by policies of central planning, economic self-reliance, and market regulation, poverty levels remained unacceptably high. It was when these governments implemented market reforms in their domestic economies and opened the door to international trade and investment that poverty dropped dramatically (see Schaumburg-Müller 2005 for the case of Vietnam).

The contention that East Asian growth took place under conditions of protection and trade opportunities that can no longer be replicated deserves examination. Access to markets in developed countries is becoming easier as two-way trade is liberalized. The case for granting favorable trade terms for the least developed countries is acknowledged by all but the most fundamental free traders. It is now recognized, however, that the types of import and export controls under which the economies of Hong Kong, Malaysia, and Vietnam saw high levels of growth were quite distinct from each other (Watkins 1998; Stiglitz 1996).

The wealth that corporations produce has the potential to propel national growth, but growth itself is not without its critics. Although not presenting a clearly articulated or broadly agreed alternative to business or the market, today's anticapitalist movement incorporates concepts from feminism and environmentalism in addition to socialism, to argue that putting the pursuit of economic growth above other goals is unnecessary and even harmful to the achievement of a just and sustainable society.

Certainly, growth may bring shifts in employment patterns and disrupt the fragile productive opportunities that poor people have managed to establish. People in traditional sectors, overtaken by change, unable to adjust, and facing the increased prices that often accompany growth, can be made still poorer in high-growth economies. The environment, and those who depend on vulnerable ecosystems for their livelihoods, can also fall victim to economic growth. Economic theorists may dismiss the difficulties encountered in rapidly changing economies as purely transitional problems or short-term adjustments. Poor people who face these short-term economic transitions might suggest a variation on Keynes' famous phrase: "in the short term, we are all dead"!

The terms governing the acceptance of foreign investment and trade will underpin the level of benefit they bring. And we look to governments to take measures, for example, through taxation, employment rules, investment rules, and social services, to ensure that growth is related to better distribution of wealth and opportunity, to benefit the whole population.

All this sounds fine: companies produce economic growth, while governments implement social legislation to ensure that the resulting wealth also benefits those most in need. But this scenario overlooks two issues. First, companies also do business in failed states, states at war, and states with weak, corrupt, or incompetent governments. Here, they may actively exploit the situation, bribing government officials, or fueling wars by paying military leaders for rights to minerals or other goods. Second, even where government is adequate, corporations are bound to use all means to shift external conditions in their favor.

Most criticisms of the private sector are concentrated on the unequal distribution of the benefits of growth. The issue for governments, then, is to balance macroeconomic growth with measures to provide for those whose livelihoods are destroyed by the transitional impact of that growth.

THE HARMFUL POTENTIAL OF CORPORATE ACTIVITY ON DEVELOPMENT

Workers: Conditions, Rights, and Wages

Companies are of course criticized on the grounds that they exploit workers, including women and children, in their labor forces. Companies in industrialized countries, while still making a profit, do generally offer wages that provide a standard of living that goes beyond basic needs, enabling workers to participate in society and exercise their rights. In developing countries, people working for the private sector are commonly employed under conditions that fail to bring them adequate housing, health, nutrition, education services, security, and other rights.

Marxists would argue that exploitation takes place in all economies, representing a fundamental, insoluble contradiction between labor and capital. Incidences of growing disparity between ordinary wages and the engorged wealth of the director class, and growing gaps between rich and poor, even in wealthy countries, would seem to support a revival of good old class analysis. But the developmental issue is perhaps more usefully framed in terms of whether companies provide fair and decent wages and conditions rather than whether or not they are exploiting their employees. In addition to the ongoing work of the trade union movement, the ILO has a major program examining the concept of decent work (ILO 2000; Somavía 1999).

The trade union movement is the longest-standing oppositional force to the private sector, functioning in developed and developing countries alike with varying effectiveness. Understandably, unions have tended to focus on achieving improved wages and conditions for their members, and expanding their membership. In doing so, they have often faced repression from governments as well as the private sector.

Fundamental to the issue of workers' rights are the right to organize and freedom of association. However, the very attraction of the free-trade zones established precisely for the purpose of encouraging foreign investment has been the explicit curtailment of union rights within them. China, home to a massive proportion of light industrial manufacturing worldwide, allows only the state-run official trade union. Workers' attempts to organize independent unions or to protest against poor conditions have been dealt with ruthlessly (Human Rights Watch 2002).

If development is viewed as an effort to make people's lives progressively better, then an assessment of the quality of employment must be set against the previous or alternative livelihoods open to workers in the private sector. For instance, conditions faced by rural migrants joining the factory workforce need to be compared to their lives in farms and villages. Despite poor wages, long hours, and poor living conditions, factory employment for young women can compare favorably to the economic and social disempowerment and male domination they experience in the rural household (Kabeer 2000). This is *not* an argument against the struggle to advance workers' rights, but it does suggest that migration in search of industrial employment is now a component of development.

Unfair Competition

Corporate competitiveness, particularly when it involves larger and more powerful companies, is not benign. We see this in many modern societies: big retail chains squeeze out individual local shops, and supermarket purchasing power makes it impossible for small farmers to compete, or for producers to bargain for fair prices.

In developing countries, the problem is a more acute life-and-death issue because the difference in size between big corporations and small producers is far more pronounced. Simply by competing legally within the market, big corporations can have a huge impact on small producers as well as on land and property prices, job opportunities, labor conditions, and migration. In other words, big companies have a profound impact on poor people. Transnational corporations, with all their extra resources, can destroy smaller local competitors and monopolize markets. Massive difference in size between competing firms or producers frequently results in market access being denied to the smallest.

In terms of international trade, as distinct from investment, companies are accused of destroying local business by selling cheap products to developing countries. The greatest criticism focuses on exports of subsidized products, particularly EU and US agricultural produce. But even where products are not subsidized, there is a debate about the fairness of allowing huge foreign companies to compete with small local producers when the former enjoy vast advantages in terms of economy of scale, technology, marketing sophistication, and the reserves necessary to engage in price wars.

Lobbying for Primacy

As well as acting the playground bully, big corporations are capable of handing the shiniest apple to the teacher. Large companies have a successful track record of lobbying national governments and influencing laws, licenses, regulations, and international agreements to their advantage. When a charm offensive fails, companies are quite able to bully governments as well. Threats to transfer production elsewhere can bear such fruit as tax holidays, subsidized infrastructure, relaxed pollution rules, or anti-union legislation.

The power of corporate lobbying extends beyond national governments to international bodies such as the WTO, the IMF, and the World Bank, which can in turn impose trade rules or loan conditions on national governments. Companies also exert huge, often unseen, influence on less high-profile bodies that are engaged in scientific research. Food and pharmaceutical companies have, for instance, influenced the reports and recommendations of UN specialized agencies in ways that favor their sales. Oil and energy companies have sought to influence scientific opinion on the seriousness of global warming (Korten 1995; Oxfam et al. 2002).

When private business activities are shown to be causing environmental, health, safety, or other problems for workers and consumers, a recognizable sequence of responses appears by which companies seek to disrupt and delay any action on the issue:

- Ignoring the reports and speaking of other things
- Disputing the facts and seeking to discredit the research or the researcher
- Calling for further research
- Funding and influencing research bodies and researchers
- Setting up pro-industry advocacy organizations and coalitions
- Calling for voluntary self-regulation
- Lobbying for milder regulation

Such behavior has been witnessed in companies engaged in the production and marketing of pharmaceuticals, tobacco, chemicals, oil, food, automobiles, infant feeding formula, and alcohol, among others.

In some cases, the motivation for such slippery behavior involves fear of massive compensation claims, such as those faced by the asbestos and tobacco industries in Europe and North America. In developing countries, the corporations may be able to modify this strategy, confident that smokers or asbestos victims in the Third World lack the resources to sue successfully.

More encouragingly, we also find some companies taking further steps in their response to criticism, including the following:

- Engaging critics in dialogue about the issue and possible solutions
- Announcing new codes, strategies, engagement in research and innovation, membership of ethical coalitions, and changes to core corporate values
- Marketing a new "caring approach" aspect of the company's identity and products
- Mainstreaming socially responsible policies and practices throughout the supply and distribution chains

Environmental Destruction

Another major criticism of private-sector activity concerns destruction of the natural environment and pollution of the planet. TNCs face accusations of moving dirty, polluting processes to developing countries, where laws are lax or poorly enforced and public scrutiny is weak. That said, it should be recalled that by some measures, the world's most polluted countries lie in the former Soviet bloc. Of course, such pollution was a product of industrialization and not private-sector activity as such. However, since companies are now the unchallenged instruments of industrialization, they are today the cause of massive pollution. Issues of control and regulation are central to solving this problem, but so are debates about the shape and extent of industrialization overall, regardless of whether this involves state-owned or private industry.

For developing countries, the issue is one of competing demands and scarce resources. How far can the environment be allowed to deteriorate in a rush for growth before the human and ecological costs outweigh the benefits and even slow that growth? Should states develop to the point where they can spend their way out of environmental trouble, or is this a huge, irreversible step off a precipice? Are developing countries making the same mistakes as the industrialized countries, but more rapidly? Or can advances in technology enable a more effective cleanup once the economy has grown and before irreversible damage is done? Can we hope that the private sector can become the instrument for solving pollution questions and cleaning up the environmental mess, just as is was the means by which pollution was driven to such levels?

Debt and the Private Sector

Campaigners against Third World debt note that much of the borrowing was encouraged by commercial banks. Many of the debt-relief initiatives involve loans from national governments or multilateral agencies such as the World Bank, while commercial banks have so far avoided much of the wrath of the anti-debt movement.

The financial sector is also attacked for facilitating low tax payments through the fostering of tax havens, including enabling complex corporate and financial structures that minimize tax liability. Financial companies are charged with exposing developing countries to huge risks by speculating aggressively on currencies, commodities, and share prices. The 1997 East Asian financial crisis was held responsible for a massive rise in poverty in countries such as Indonesia, wiping out years of social improvement. Many attacked international speculation and the financial institutions and structures for causing the problem.

Privatization of Vital Services

Worldwide, companies are increasingly contracted to deliver services formerly considered the responsibility of the state or local government. In developing countries, this may not necessarily be a response to the government's belief in the effectiveness of privatization, but to outside pressure to liberalize and deregulate the service sector. Regardless of the motives, the trend is toward private-sector involvement in water supply, education, transport, communications, and health care. As a result, the private sector is ever more involved in essential components of the development process, which can bring companies into direct dealings with poor people and needy communities.

When a commercial company is providing a service, it will often concentrate on those aspects offering the best returns. The desire to make a profit may result in cutting back services to areas where people are less able to pay, and to more remote areas where overhead costs are higher. In both cases, this means reduced services to poor people (Tati 2005).

The privatization of service provision takes different forms. In some cases, the private sector becomes engaged in large-scale infrastructure development. In many cases, however, the newly privatized companies depend on foreign investment, a phenomenon that brings its own risks, as illustrated by Leopoldo Rodríguez-Boetsch in his detailed analysis of Argentina (Chapter 6). David Hall, Emanuele Lobina, and Robin de la Motte illustrate in Chapter 5 how civil society and political opposition have challenged top-down approaches to privatized water and sanitation utilities. Overall, experiences around the world have shown that the key to responsible privatization is, paradoxically, effective government involvement. Both the terms set out when services are privatized and the ongoing management of the activity by statutory regulatory bodies are equally crucial to the success of the privatization process.

The Social Impact of Products and Processes

For companies producing weapons or tobacco, the core business and main product can be said to have a negative impact on development. The campaign against the promotion of infant feeding formula in developing countries is the best-remembered example of targeting a product considered to have such an impact. But when the main product itself is intrinsically or potentially damaging, this raises fundamental questions about what corporate social responsibility (CSR) should look like for such companies.

In addition to environmental destruction, companies stand accused of destroying cultures, traditions, and ways of life as they rush about their business. The impact of extractive industries on the use or ownership of traditional lands is a controversial issue, as is the wider impact of the rapid opening up of remote areas on the indigenous people who live there.

The introduction and promotion of new products seek to alter people's tastes and styles. Older and more traditional societies, processes, and products can be particularly vulnerable to the aggressive marketing of new products, which are often targeted at women. Traditional garments, medicines, or foods and the practices associated with them often embody important cultural and social values. Hence there may be far more at stake than simply the adoption of a modern replacement for an item that is rooted in culture.

More extreme is the social impact of companies doing deals with one of the warring factions in the context of armed conflict, for instance in order to gain mineral or other business rights. In such instances, companies have been accused of bankrolling violence and destruction.

PRESSURES FOR CHANGE

Shareholder Power

The old division of roles, in which companies concentrated purely on growth, within the law, while the government paid attention to questions of equity, through the law, is drawing to an end. Parallel to the growth of corporate power is a growth in demands and expectations that companies be accountable on a global scale for the impact of their actions on the environment, on labor, and on human rights.

Shareholders can be stakeholders, and different types of stakeholders can be shareholders (as illustrated, for instance, by Hayes and Walker 2005). A company's shareholders may now include the type of people who would willingly join a consumer boycott or choose a fair trade product (Simpson 2002). Such shareholders don't want to hear that their investment is harming the environment or exploiting children in the developing world.

The concentration of power and wealth represented by globalization is confronted by a growing opposition movement, which is also global in scope. High-profile protests are now focused on multilateral bodies such as the WTO, the World Bank, the OECD, the EU, and the G8 meetings. Protesters argue that these organizations are controlled by big business and use their global authority primarily in its interest (Juniper 1999; Newell 2000). The spectacular collapse of Enron and WorldCom due to financial dishonesty, and shareholder revolts in the UK against massive executive pay packages, have focused attention on the ethics and social responsibility of giant international corporations. The more radical critics view TNCs as an antisocial force that is responsible for pollution and poverty. Several popular campaigns target specific companies, such as those involved in the production of genetically modified (GM) seeds or branded sportswear produced by

poorly paid workers (Canadian Democracy and Corporate Accountability Commission 2002).

NGOS AND SOCIAL ACTIVISM

Many governments have come to believe that privatization, deregulation of markets, tax reduction, and looser environmental and labor laws
are the only way to maintain international competitiveness (Marsden
2004). In developing countries, such deregulation was not necessarily a
fondly embraced economic strategy, but was a condition for the receipt
of much-needed assistance from the international financial institutions
or to qualify for WTO membership. Whereas governments in the North
may make the choice not to exert adequate controls over companies as a
means of attracting investment, governments in the South often lack the
capacity and the resources to play a more effective regulatory role,
whether or not they wish to do to so.

Into the space left by less capable governments have stepped
NGOs. Like the corporate sector, NGOs have grown in size and influence in the era of globalization. They have expanded their role into that
of a countervailing force to unbridled corporate power. Through their
capacity to influence the media and public opinion, and even to mobilize people on the streets, NGOs have exerted pressure on the corporate
sector. Some believe they have gained the power to grant or withhold a
"social licence" (Warhurst 2001) and represent a form of "civil regulation" (Bendell 2000), though others underline that an agency's integrity
demands that it observe the standards demanded of companies (Frame
2005).

Social activism against corporate excesses has been aided by the
rapid transformations in information technology. News of corporate
malpractice reaches the public almost immediately, and those adversely
affected can communicate and campaign internationally more easily
and cheaply than ever before. With the intermediation of trade union
structures or NGO networks, villagers who find the fish dying in a river
due to upstream mining, or garment workers whose punch cards are
confiscated before overtime begins, can bring their problems swiftly to
the attention of industrialized-world consumers and fellow-workers at
the head office.

The engagement of two upwardly mobile sectors of globalized
society—TNCs and NGOs—on questions of equitable and sustainable

development carries profound significance for the fortunes of the development process as a whole. The resolution of this relationship will be a determining factor in achieving the goal of alleviating mass poverty in this interdependent world.

THE BUSINESS CASE FOR PRO-DEVELOPMENT ACTION

There are three broad areas in which companies can pay attention to their impact on the development process: core business activity, philanthropic programs, and policy advocacy (Nelson 1996). The most important and immediate of these involves changes to a company's core business activity, and much of the recent literature discusses the successes and failures of CSR programs.

The business case for corporate responsibility toward poverty and development is built on several pillars. First is the proposition that robust societies enable successful business. Any legal organization hoping to operate in the marketplace will benefit from stable, well-governed societies containing healthy, educated workers and consumers. There is a generalized interest in rule-based, open, and predictable financial and trading systems. Operating in a society with a decayed environment, high levels of disease, vulnerability to climate change, and poor security incurs increased personnel, security, and insurance costs. Business cannot boom in societies that are failing. The human waste and social conflict that result from poverty undermine market potential.

The problem with appealing to the private sector to invest in a society that would be conducive to its own success is that companies tend to behave like prisoners in the classical dilemma. They would love for every other company to pay high wages to their workers, who are their own potential customers, and to pay for a clean and healthy environment in which they could then operate. But to maximize their own profits, they would like to politely make their excuses, externalize as many costs as they can, and pay their workers the lowest possible wages. Improving society in general is a long-term investment, while so much business behavior is short-term.

A second aspect of the business case for CSR concerns reputational risk management. There are market and financial risks associated with operating in a society with poor labor, environmental, and social conditions. But there is also a reputational risk associated with making profits and hiring cheap labor in a country in which parents cannot afford to send their children to school, and in which people are dying for lack of adequate medical attention, housing, or food. In an era of increased public scrutiny of corporate conduct, greater campaigning, and more effective media coverage of critical NGOs and trade unions, companies cannot so comfortably do business in poor countries without being seen to do so in a way that addresses inequality. As pressure grows for tighter controls over business conduct in developing countries, those who move voluntarily will gain "first mover" advantage. Companies that are forced to react to legislation or criticism risk greater costs and a poorer reputation. A company that is seen as part of the problem rather than part of the solution will suffer damage to its reputation or its brand, and this may turn off consumers.

A good reputation carries internal as well as external benefits. Companies that command public respect will find it easier to recruit and retain the best and brightest workforce and maintain buoyant morale. Workers and managers alike, the argument goes, are increasingly disinclined to separate their personal and professional morality.

Third, the development of products and services that address social and environmental challenges presents new business opportunities. As a market, poor people make up for their relative lack of spending power by their weight in numbers. Focusing on meeting the needs of poor people can, some would argue, both address important developmental needs and open up profitable new markets. For instance, Prahalad and Hart (2002) hold that business can discover lucrative new markets at "the bottom of the pyramid" among the poorest people in society (now renamed "the base of the pyramid" by the politically prudish). In their view, TNCs are particularly well placed to create the conditions for such markets as they have the resources, managerial skills, and knowledge necessary to build commercial infrastructure, and are the best positioned to unite NGOs, communities, local governments, and local entrepreneurs to meet the needs of the poorest sector of the market. In making these arguments, Prahalad and Hart challenge five fundamental corporate assumptions: the poor are not the corporate target; the poor cannot afford products; only developed markets will pay for new technology; the bottom of the market is not important for long-term corporate interests; and the intellectual excitement is in the developed markets (Waddell 2000).

An additional case for general social responsibility is that a company that is seen as having a beneficial effect in the South will be able to increase sales to ethically aware consumers and attract ethically sensitive investors in the North. This is particularly true for clothing and sportswear brands that are selling image above utility, an argument presented by Carolina Quinteros in Chapter 11 as key to the survival of the Central American garment-manufacturing industry.

LIMITS TO THE BUSINESS CASE FOR CSR

Companies that do not deal directly with the public, or have a brand-name image to sell, are correspondingly less exposed to consumer scrutiny. The public does not usually buy machine tools, polystyrene granules, ships, or cattle feed. Similarly, many local companies and even TNCs based in developing countries where civil society and the media are less advanced may avoid the scale of scrutiny or criticism faced by Northern TNCs.

In certain sectors, at certain periods of corporate evolution, various elements of the business case for active responsibility toward developing countries may apply. But the business case for CSR goes only so far. Skeptical commentators suggest that most CSR activity is in fact motivated far more by the need to reduce risks than by the wish to enhance reputation. Some very hard-nosed cost-benefit analysis goes on before companies decide to pay out for improved environmental and social conduct, or even to abide by the law. If the penalty is less than the cost of installing cleaner equipment, companies have been known to pay the fine and carry on polluting.

Despite the many articulations of a business case for responsible corporate behavior, companies frequently face trade-offs between profits and ethics. There is money to be made by squeezing past, wriggling under, papering over, diverting attention from, minimizing, or simply flouting environmental, labor, and social standards. This is all the more easily done in less-developed countries where governments, trade unions, and consumer associations are all less able to discover and denounce transgressions.

Critics of market-based solutions to poverty are blunt: the logic of the market is immutable, and it is right to turn its back on Africa, and in fact on any poor, remote, underdeveloped area. The market will concentrate sales where customers are concentrated, accessible, and prosperous. The market will concentrate production where costs are cheapest in terms of appropriately skilled labor, raw materials, regulations, taxes, and the necessary technical, managerial, and financial structures, or where production leads to better access to consumers. There may be some minor markets worth developing among the very poor, but these are limited. Endogenous accumulation and standard theories of capital accumulation do not apply to poor, remote, sparsely populated, disease-ridden parts of the planet (Sachs 2004). The market has never been the mechanism for addressing serious social problems, nor can it be.

Joel Bakan (2004) refers to corporations as institutional psychopaths, required by law to externalize as many of their costs as possible. As such, he argues that it is absurd to expect them voluntarily to give priority to social responsibility, or to behavior motivated by ethical concerns.

Skeptics of reform argue that any company that makes a move toward assuming more social responsibility will be viewed as inefficient and become susceptible to a takeover by companies skilled in mergers and acquisitions. As equity investments operate internationally, companies that invest in environmental and social concerns can be accused of inefficient management and gobbled up by ruthless raiders from over the horizon. Proponents of regulation argue that in these circumstances, it is only through the imposition of mandatory international standards that companies will become simultaneously socially responsible and profitable.

Ultimately, however, if the business or economic case for good corporate conduct is insufficient, citizens and their governments must continue to assert the moral, social, and political case for corporate responsibility.

CORPORATE INITIATIVES: DO MORE GOOD, DO LESS HARM

The impact of a company's operations involves both the goods and services it produces, and the labor, environmental, and social impact of the way it organizes itself to produce them. It is possible to conceive of a company producing cheap eyeglasses for the African market while polluting local rivers with heavy metals, or one that aggressively markets powdered baby milk in the Third World while maintaining an excellent record of labor relations and employee welfare.

Historically, philanthropy was the chief manifestation of corporate social concern, and this still plays a major role in the definition and analysis of CSR in the United States, where the philanthropic tradition is strong. In recent years, major companies have recognized that social responsibility must first and foremost concern their core business, and must infuse the entire organization from boardroom to boiler room. To differentiate the philanthropic and internal dimensions of CSR from the more proactive social role companies can play as part of core strategy, some have proposed the terms "corporate social investment" and "corporate social leadership."

"Social entrepreneurship" is another area of growing interest. The definition of a social enterprise is far from fixed, but is in general an organization bearing some characteristics of both NGOs and businesses. A company with strongly articulated social values and a commitment to providing goods or services that contribute to the needs of a disadvantaged section of the community can be considered a social enterprise. So too can NGOs that are financed more through fees and sales than by grants, and that bear some of the organizational and managerial characteristics more common to the private sector. There is a great deal of energy and enthusiasm for this new approach to social progress, particularly in North America, and among NGOs rather than the corporate sector. Although there is clearly space for growth, the social enterprise movement has yet to meet challenges of scalability, entrenched economic and political interests, and the tendency of NGOs, let alone social enterprises, to put organizational financial health ahead of mission and values by equating and confusing the two.

The term "corporate social responsibility" remains a useful catchall for the requirement of corporations to pay heed to environmental and social issues. Among most of the massive TNCs, the debate about the form, extent, and sincerity of CSR remains vibrant and significant. When a major corporation makes an incremental change in its policies and practices, this has a more profound impact on the lives of more people than do the more spectacular stands of smaller companies that create a niche market based on their high-profile ethical approaches to producing or sourcing their products, such as Ben & Jerry's (which sells ice cream) or The Body Shop (which sells cosmetics). Such companies may nevertheless point the way, or provide inspiration that may one day be picked up by the oil majors.

For every keen exponent of CSR programs, however, there is a skeptical and articulate critic. Critics of the voluntary nature of CSR, and the dangers of this becoming shallow window-dressing, call for "corporate social accountability" emphasizing the need for externally determined standards, generally of a mandatory nature.

It is therefore necessary to review current thinking on the capacity of corporate philanthropy, codes of conduct, fair trade and ethical trade, and the case for regulation versus voluntarism.

Corporate Philanthropy

Although the current CSR debates center on the impact of core business practices, we should not discount the philanthropic contributions corporations can make to equitable development. Philanthropic and social programs are also beginning to reflect a greater awareness of the social and environmental impact that a company's main business might have. Certain car manufacturers and electricity-generating companies have introduced programs offsetting the carbon emissions of their activities and their products through funding of, for example, reforestation projects. Several mining companies have focused their health and environmental programs more directly on the communities affected by their mining.

Other companies, rather than donating funds to uncontroversial traditional charities, have realized that their philanthropy can reflect their particular skills and capacities. Telecom and information companies are increasingly making technical staff and equipment available to relief agencies. Pharmaceutical companies have earmarked manufacturing inventories for donation and have helped with relief agencies' contingency planning. Banks and other financial companies are looking at issues of microcredit for poor producers, remittances, and other pro-poor financial services as well as corruption-reducing transfer systems.

Codes of Conduct

Until the 1990s, CSR was considered to involve paying taxes, delivering a quality product, providing employment, and abiding by the law. Today, codes of conduct address an array of issues addressing corporate responsibility toward the environment, workers, and society as a whole. Codes have proliferated at various levels. Global initiatives include the UN Secretary-General's Global Compact and the OECD guidelines. Industry-wide initiatives include the timber and DIY industries' Forest Stewardship Council, and the Marine Stewardship Council covering fishing and seafood. Beyond these lie a multitude of individual in-house company codes.

The relationship of codes of conduct to development requires examination of the intended and the actual beneficiaries. As Sumi Dhanarajan shows in Chapter 10, codes with fine-sounding standards on the environment and working conditions do not necessarily directly address issues of fair wages, poverty, or inequality in the host country. Too often, suppliers pay for the implementation of environmental standards and workplace facilities in the code, and pass this extra cost on to the workforce in the form of lower wages. Even where the codes ensure the well-being of the employees in the company's factory or supply chain, these workers can come to represent an elite part of the workforce amidst widespread poverty.

It is easier for larger producers to meet the requirements of codes, just as it is far easier and more cost efficient for a buyer to audit and monitor larger producers. Even here, the cost of auditing is sometimes borne by the supplier. There are also economies of scale in such things as the safe handling and storage of materials, so that the costs of compliance again favor larger producers. There is a danger, therefore, that codes of conduct will lead to a concentration of production in larger supplier factories or bigger plantations. Small workshops, family farms, and homeworkers are likely to lose orders from companies with comprehensive, well-monitored codes of conduct. Yet they are among the very poorest workers, whom codes of conduct are designed to benefit.

It has been argued that codes are the creation of corporations based in industrialized countries, often overrepresenting the concerns of consumers, social activists, and more responsible company executives in those countries, rather than the needs expressed by the people they are intended to assist (Nelson et al. 2005). In Chapter 13, Anne Tallontire, Catherine Dolan, Sally Smith, and Stephanie Barrientos explore the impact of codes of conduct on the position of women, concluding that codes alone do not necessarily bring about the intended improvements, and that it is work in society, beyond the realm of corporate codes of conduct, that will improve women's employment situation. Jem Bendell suggests in Chapter 2 that stakeholder democracy offers a more representative approach to defining what constitutes socially responsible corporate behavior, and in Chapter 4 Niamh Garvey and Peter Newell examine the demand for corporate accountability and contend that more power should originate in the affected communities.

Although codes of conduct may not contain all the solutions, greater understanding and the growing adoption of codes signal changing perceptions of what constitutes acceptable corporate conduct.

Fair Trade and Ethical Trade

The fair trade movement has had more impact than most other recent initiatives to raise public awareness about injustices and inequalities in the trading system. It has also spearheaded a debate on fairer alternatives. The movement has managed to build up fair trade businesses to the point where they now compete with mainstream companies in certain products, such as coffee and chocolate. The movement is benefiting a growing number of small producers worldwide and increasing the commodities eligible for fair trade status. The importance of NGOs in advocating and publicizing fair trade among consumers is examined by April Linton in Chapter 12.

The movement faces several dilemmas and crucial choices, however, as it grows in scale and recognition. Do the trading arms of the fair trade movement want an ever larger share of the market, or should they seek greater influence over all trade? How significant is the danger that the growth and strengthening of fair trade companies will become an end in itself, obscuring the original mission of making all trade fairer?

The process of developing international standards for what constitutes fair trade in a given product is increasingly complex, requiring agreement between the many companies and NGOs that constitute the international fair trade body that arbitrates these standards. Once standards are defined, a process of training, auditing, and accreditation is required before that product can bear the fair trade mark. Both the development of standards and their implementation represent transaction costs for the fair trade movement. Even though producers often receive a preset, minimum guaranteed price for their products, a great deal of the premium charged to the final consumer of fair trade products needs to be earmarked to cover the costs necessary to ensure that proper standards are achieved and upheld. This is an awkward issue for a movement that speaks of cutting down on the intermediary costs of international trade.

Producers in the developing world invest in structures, knowledge, and facilities to enable them to gain certification as suppliers of fair trade products. On occasion, the market for such products is not big enough for all their output to be sold to fair trade organizations, especially at the guaranteed price. NGOs and fair trade companies alike received substantial grants and subsidies to cover the early development of the movement. Grant-making organizations still put a lot of money into helping producers raise standards to meet the fair trade criteria.

Fair trade NGOs, some engaging in trading and others promoting and publicizing the idea, are funded organizations rather than for-profit businesses. Some see this as pump priming for a sustainable market system, and others view it as a subsidy supporting the entire fair trade project. The bottom line, however, is whether these fair trade initiatives have improved the lives of ordinary people in the face of pressures such as debt, volatile commodity markets, and inadequate government services. In the case of Nicaraguan coffee producers, Karla Utting-Chamorro (2005) found that such constraints undermine the impact of even the best-designed initiatives.

Several major retailers worldwide, particularly those that have been the butt of critical campaigns such as garment, sportswear goods, and food retailers, are involved in initiatives with trade unions and NGOs to find ways to make their trading more ethical. Ethical trade activities aim to improve the labor rights of workers in the supply chain as well as the environmental and social impact of international trading activities. Learning from the policies, procedures, and standards of the fair trade movement, criteria for ethical trade usually represent targets and aspirations. Taking account of the current pressures and conditions confronting the major retailers, they confront practical questions such as "How do we move from where we are now to where we would like to be?" This work therefore seeks ways to advance and measure improvements with a view to making all mainstream trade more ethical.

Voluntarism versus Regulation

The encouragement of good behavior on a voluntary basis is not an alternative to national governments holding corporations to account, and international regulatory frameworks upheld by strong international institutions can also prevent the environmental and labor equivalent of tax havens. Voluntary codes are an immediate way of reducing environmental harm and the suffering caused by the negative social impact of business. But they are also a method of designing and testing the benchmarks, feasible ideas, norms, and standards for more ethical business conduct that will, in the future, inform the regulatory frameworks and mechanisms. There is too much at stake to pursue the long-term goal of better corporate regulation while harm continues to be caused, or to believe that voluntary approaches to these problems will lead to sustainable solutions. We do not have the luxury of choice; we must do both.

Peter Utting elaborates such a case for voluntary CSR and mandatory regulation of corporations in Chapter 3. Co-regulation, involving trade unions, NGOs, and companies in multisector initiatives to develop, implement, and measure CSR programs, lies somewhere between self-regulation and binding laws on corporate conduct.

There are other gray areas between voluntary and mandatory controls. Certain stock markets, and official business service agencies such as governmental export credit guarantee services, require adherence to international codes of practice. Although this is not mandatory regulation in the sense that a business could continue to operate without registering on a particular stock market or seeking certain government benefits, these initiatives certainly go beyond self-regulation.

There is a body of belief that companies leading the way in CSR will eventually be motivated to ally with NGOs and trade unions to lobby for mandatory codes of corporate conduct, a case argued by Peter Williams (2005). As market leaders in CSR deepen their own programs, they will develop an increasing aversion to losing business to rogue companies and free-riders who have failed to make the same kinds of social investment. If laws are introduced, the pioneering companies will have the advantages of first movers.

CORPORATIONS AND THE MILLENNIUM DEVELOPMENT GOALS

At the Millennium Summit in September 2000, political leaders from around the world established the MDGs. In many ways, these goals are a test of our collective humanity, our common morality, and our political will. They will stand or fall as milestones on the path toward genuine human civilization.

Virtually nobody could disagree with the intent of the MDGs. They aim to halve extreme poverty and hunger, achieve universal primary education, eliminate gender inequality in education, reduce child mortality by two thirds, reduce the maternal mortality rate by three quarters, reverse the spread of AIDS, reverse the incidence of malaria and other diseases, and halve the proportion of people without access to safe drinking water by 2015.

Although governments have committed to these goals, civil society—local and international NGOs—have embraced them as a concrete set of targets to which they could contribute, and to which they could hold governments accountable.

The interim results are not good, even if you believe some of the dodgier state statistics from self-aggrandizing regimes. Governments and civil society are well behind target as the clock runs down. The goals will not be achieved without more participation and coordination by governments, civil society, and most importantly, an injection of energy, ideas, and support from the private sector.

Business can develop affordable and accessible products and services. Food companies can offer products that address nutritional deficiencies. Pharmaceutical companies can focus on basic medicines. Utilities can bring cleaner water and cheaper power to poor and remote communities. Programs to reduce child labor can get kids into school. Technology can foster education. Women can be employed and trained in ways that empower them (Nelson and Prescott 2003).

There is a perverse way in which governments sometimes seem to need wars to crystallize political will and bring them to their senses. Will corporations need more protests, more scandals, more collapses, and more Bhopals, before they realize the role they must play to earn a place at the table in a world aspiring to the MDGs? If we fall short of these goals in 2015, the community of ordinary people around the world who question the meaning of globalization will swell. Frustration and anger will grow at the failure to provide food, schooling, and health care for the children to whom we feel increasingly close—all the world's children. Our economic systems, political institutions, and social structures will be up for review in the eyes of a disillusioned population. People will point the finger of blame not only at political leaders, but also at the world's big companies.

ECONOMIC IMPACT AND BEYOND

The influence of companies on the development of our societies raises questions that extend into the heart of our behavior and our human relationships. Corporate culture cannot be defined simply as the imposition of the interests of a ruling class, or even some alpha-male managerial class, on the rest of us. Corporations have evolved their own behavioral norms and values irrespective of whether their owners are robber barons or trade union pension funds.

Is this the corporate culture we deserve—a reflection of the current state of human civilization, a manifestation of our cruder survival instincts? Or has it taken on a certain autonomy, driven by its non-human institutional imperatives? Put differently, are corporate needs shaping society, or is society able to shape corporate behavior? If the truth lies in the middle, with some kind of iterative process, how balanced is that reciprocity? Do we, in fact, want corporate culture to influence our personal culture at all?

Does the impulse to compete and to grow that essentially drives the market system necessarily limit our own imagination of a world where cooperation, modesty, and balance would play a dominant role? Has corporate culture dazzled us with a frenzied multiplicity, breadth, and diversity, leaving us unable to perceive the true narrowness of its purpose?

If corporations represent a worldview that the accumulation of wealth should reign supreme, can the lone individual possibly resist? Do trade unions, consumer groups, and the rest of civil society represent a robust, collective, and organized counterweight to corporate hegemony, or are they only capable of a desperate, token reaction?

Cultural identity is a potent motivating social force. The corporate world is fairly clumsy when it comes to its cultural footprint. Will the new opposition to corporate power come not from those necessarily economically impoverished or exploited by corporate action, but from those who also feel culturally or spiritually disenfranchised, marginalized, or humiliated by the changes to their lives most tangibly represented by the hegemonic marketing of the TNCs?

The challenge is to put companies in the service of society and create wealth for it, not to concentrate wealth. Private companies and development agencies have distinct motivations and functions, but it is possible to imagine new forms of ownership and control that retain the power and dynamism of corporations to innovate and mobilize resources efficiently without their need to adopt a ruthless character and attempt obscene concentrations of wealth. In the end, companies are programmable machines, and we the people, through our moral principles, expectations, demands, and laws, must write the program. We must ensure that we do not create machines with such a narrow mission on such an unwieldy scale that they trample on their creators, on the weak, and on the vulnerable. We must program them to operate in the service of us all, particularly those who are dying for their goods and services.

REFERENCES

Anderson, Sarah, and John Cavanagh. 2000. *Top 200: The Rise of Corporate Global Power.* Washington, DC: Institute for Policy Studies.

Bakan, Joel. 2004. *The Corporation: The Pathological Pursuit of Profit and Power.* New York: Free Press.

Bendell, Jem. 2000. "Civil Regulation: A New Form of Democratic Governance for the Global Economy?" In Jem Bendell (ed.), *Terms of Endearment: Business, NGOs and Sustainable Development.* Sheffield, UK: Greenleaf.

Bendell, Jem, and Rob Lake. 2000. "New Frontiers: Emerging NGO Activities to Strengthen Transparency and Accountability in Business." In Jem Bendell (ed.), *Terms of Endearment: Business, NGOs and Sustainable Development.* Sheffield, UK: Greenleaf.

Canadian Democracy and Corporate Accountability Commission. 2002. *The New Balance Sheet: Corporate Profits and Responsibility in the 21st Century.* Ottawa: Canadian Democracy and Corporate Accountability Commission.

Coward, Tim, and James Fathers. 2005. "A Critique of Design Methodologies Appropriate to Private-Sector Activity in Development." *Development in Practice* 15(3&4):451–462.

Frame, Bob. 2005. "Corporate Social Responsibility: A Challenge for the Donor Community." *Development in Practice* 15(3&4):422–431.

Gutiérrez Nieto, Begoña. 2005. "Private Funding of Microcredit Schemes: Much Ado about Nothing?" *Development in Practice* 15(3&4):490–501.

Hayes, Barbara, and Bridget Walker. 2005. "Corporate Responsibility or Core Competence?" *Development in Practice* 15(3&4):405–412.

Human Rights Watch. 2002. *Paying the Price: Worker Unrest in Northeast China.* New York: Human Rights Watch.

International Finance Corporation. 2004. *2004 Annual Review: Small Business Activities.* Washington, DC: World Bank Group.

ILO. 2000. *Decent Work: International Labour Conference 87th Session 1999.* Geneva: ILO.

Jeppesen, Soeren. 2005. Enhancing Competitiveness and Securing Equitable Development: Can Small, Micro, and Medium-Sized Enterprises (SMEs) Do the Trick? *Development in Practice* 15(3&4):463–489.

Juniper, Tony. 1999. "Planet Profit." *Guardian Weekly,* 25 November.

Kabeer, Naila. 2000. *The Power to Choose: Bangladeshi Women and Labour Market Decisions in London and Dhaka.* London: Verso.

Kitching, Gavin. 1982. *Development and Underdevelopment in Historical Perspective: Populism, Nationalism and Industrialisation.* London: Methuen.

Korten, David. 1995. *When Corporations Rule the World.* London: Earthscan.

Kuada, John, and Olav Jull Sørensen. 2005. "Facilitated Inter-firm Collaboration in Ghana: The Case of Danida's Private-Sector Development Projects." *Development in Practice* 15(3&4):475–489.

Marsden, Chris. 2004. "Dealing with Joel Bakan's Pathological Corporation: A Strategy for Campaigning Human Rights and Environmental NGOs." London: Business and Human Rights Resource Centre. [Available at www.global policy.org/soccecon/tncs/2004/07pathological.htm (retrieved 26 January 2005).]

Nelson, Jane. 1996. *Business as Partners in Development: Creating Wealth for Countries, Companies and Communities.* London: The Prince of Wales Business Leaders Forum.

Nelson, Jane, and Dave Prescott. 2003. *Business and the Millennium Development Goals: A Framework for Action.* London: International Business Leaders Forum.

Nelson, Valerie, Adrienne Martin, and Joachim Ewert. 2005. "What Difference Can They Make? Assessing the Social Impact of Corporate Codes of Practice." *Development in Practice* 15(3&4):539–545.

Newell, Perel. 2000. "From Responsibility to Citizenship? Corporate Accountability for Development." *IDS Bulletin* 33(2): 91–100.

Oxfam, Save the Children, and VSO. 2002. *Beyond Philanthropy: The Pharmaceutical Industry, Corporate Social Responsibility and the Developing World.* Oxford: Oxfam GB, Save the Children, and VSO.

Prahalad, C. K., and Stuart Hart. 2002. "The Fortune at the Bottom of the Pyramid." *Strategy + Business* 26:54–67.

Sachs, Jeffrey. 2004. "The End of Poverty." 2004 OXONIA inaugural lecture, delivered at the Said Business School, University of Oxford, 13 October. [Summary available at www.oxonia.org/events_2004_sachs.html (retrieved 24 February 2006).]

Schaumburg-Müller, Henrik. 2005. "Private-Sector Development in a Transition Economy: The Case of Vietnam." *Development in Practice* 15(3&4): 349–361.

Simpson, Anne. 2002. "Money Talks: The Rise of Socially Responsible Investors." In R. Crowe (ed.), *No Scruples? Managing to Be Responsible in a Turbulent World.* London: Spiro Press.

Somaría, Juán. 1999. "Decent Work." Report of the ILO Director-General, 87th Session of the International Labour Conference, Geneva, 1–7 June.

Stiglitz, Joseph E. 1996. "Some Lessons from the East Asian Miracle." *The World Bank Research Observer* 11(2):151–177.

Sumner, Andrew. 2005. "Is Foreign Direct Investment Good for the Poor? A Review and Stocktake." *Development in Practice* 15(3&4):269–285.

Tati, Gabriel. 2005. "Public-Private Partnership (PPP) and Water-Supply Provision in Urban Africa: The Experience of Congo-Brazzaville." *Development in Practice* 15(3&4):316–324.

Utting-Chamorro, Karla. 2005. "Does Fair Trade Make a Difference? The Case of Small Coffee Producers in Nicaragua." *Development in Practice* 15(3&4):584–599.

Waddell, Steve. 2000. "Complementary Resources: The Win-Win Rationale for Partnerships with NGOs." In Jem Bendell (ed.), *Terms of Endearment: Business, NGOs and Sustainable Development.* Sheffield, UK: Greenleaf.

Warhurst, Alyson. 2001. "Corporate Citizenship and Corporate Social Investment: Drivers of Tri-sector Partnerships." *Journal of Corporate Citizenship* 1(1):57–73.

Watkins, Kevin. 1998. *Economic Growth with Equity: Lessons from East Asia.* Oxford: Oxfam GB.

Williams, Peter. 2005. "Leveraging Change in the Working Conditions of UK Homeworkers." *Development in Practice* 15(3&4):546–558.

PART 1

Calling Business to Account: Beyond Corporate Social Responsibility

TWO

In Whose Name?

The Accountability of Corporate Social Responsibility

JEM BENDELL

INTRODUCTION

The concept of accountability has become a mainstream issue within international development policy and research, as exemplified by UNDP's Human Development Report 2002 (Goetz and Jenkins 2002). The focus has generally been on how accountability deficiencies in governmental and intergovernmental organizations have led to poor development outcomes. The nonprofit NGOs that ostensibly pursue pro-development goals have been recognized for their useful role in holding governments to account, through domestic and international channels. However, their increasing power in this regard has been subject to some criticism, and such organizations are now finding their own accountability questioned. This is part of an unfolding "new accountability agenda" concerning those non-state actors that affect development (Goetz and Jenkins 2002). A key part of that agenda is to address the accountability of increasingly large, and international, corporations, particularly when they appear to be responsible for or complicit in human rights abuses, stunted social development, and environmental degradation. For more than 10 years NGOs have played a key role in highlighting such problems and putting pressure on corporations to change (Bendell 2000). This has led to an explosion of voluntary efforts by companies, often in collaboration with those same NGOs, to develop policies concerning, and processes to address, their relationship to society—efforts that have given rise to terms such as "corporate social responsibility" (CSR) and "corporate citizenship," which are now in widespread use.

Much work done in this area relates to issues in the global South, such as child labor, sweatshops, pollution, and deforestation. For this reason, the people and environments of "developing" countries are often intended as the beneficiaries of more responsible corporate practice. There is often an underlying assumption, therefore, that the development of the global South will be supported by such CSR activities. More recently, it has been suggested that corporations can be conscious agents of development by identifying opportunities to source from or sell to disadvantaged people in ways that improve their quality of life (Prahalad 2004). This marks a change from previously established views of corporations as the enemies, unconscious engines, or ungrateful beneficiaries of development. Consequently, the role of corporations, and CSR in particular, in international development requires more systemic analysis.

The terms "participation" and "partnership" are often heard in relation to CSR, along with the assertion that many different "stakeholders," including corporations, should be engaged in responses to development challenges. This resembles the emphasis on participation and partnership in public policy discourse since the early 1990s. Just as stakeholder dialogue, participation, and partnership have often been regarded uncritically in public policy, many actors who are involved in CSR initiatives see these as inherently positive approaches. As a consequence, multi-stakeholder initiatives (MSIs)—often called "partnerships" between governments, business, and civil society—have become mainstream on the international development policy scene, as illustrated by the 2002 Johannesburg World Summit on Sustainable Development (WSSD), which elevated such initiatives to the level of intergovernmental agreements (calling MSIs "Type II" outcomes and the latter "Type I").

The justifications for MSIs have tended to stress the importance of combining the different skills and resources of different organizational types—government, civil, and private—in order to deliver change (Waddell 2000). They have also pointed to the learning that can arise from interactions between individuals and institutions that would not otherwise engage in communication, and the new assets this can create in terms of skills, understanding, and trust. Many such initiatives arise out of a situation of prior conflict between government, business, and civil society. Multiple companies have been adopting standards for their social and environmental performance that are developed by, or in consultation with, some civil society organizations (CSOs), and often after pressure from other such organizations, manifested either directly or through pressure on corporate buyers and, increasingly, investors. This situation could be described as the quasi-regulation of business by civil society, or "civil regulation" (Bendell 2000). This leads to a different justification for MSIs based on how they create new avenues for people to hold companies accountable for their actions. As I have argued elsewhere, "In providing a means by which people can hold corporations accountable for their actions and change their policies and operations, civil regulation offers a novel channel for the democratic governance of the global economy by civil society" (Bendell 2000: 249).

However, the opportunity for MSIs to provide new mechanisms for accountability and, therefore, democratic governance does not necessarily result in the achievement of such. Various analyses have suggested that the (supposed) intended beneficiaries of CSR activity and MSIs have had only a limited influence on them (Bendell 2000; Bass et al. 2001; Utting 2002). "There are tensions and contradictions between the Northern-driven CSR 'movement' and developing country interests," argues Peter Utting (2002: 96) of UNRISD. Questions have been raised about whether the concerns of Northern NGOs, and the responses of the companies they target, are always appropriate. For example, initial responses to campaigns on child labor in the sporting goods industry in Pakistan led to many children losing their jobs and working in more hazardous or abusive industries (Save the Children 2000). Others have pointed out how Northern NGOs can marginalize the interests and role of local groups in the South. For example, environmental NGOs such as Conservation International have been criticized for arranging deals with governments and multinational companies that exclude local groups, particularly on issues such as bioprospecting (Choudry 2003). From a different perspective, some have argued that the trend toward higher voluntary social and environmental standards is protectionist, in effect if not in intent. For example, the Colombian government raised a complaint with the WTO concerning a voluntary CSR standard relating to imports of cut flowers, which it felt was reducing the country's competitiveness, especially as auditors of the standard were not available locally (WTO 1998).

Given these questions, the growth of voluntary corporate initiatives on aspects of international development, as well as the role of stakeholder participation, dialogue, and partnership in them, should not be assumed to represent an expansion of opportunities for affected communities to hold companies accountable. Rather, the accountability of various initiatives to those who will (presumably) benefit needs to be examined, as does the appropriateness of the discourse they help to create about international development challenges. This chapter thus focuses on two initiatives that bring together a variety of companies to address aspects of their social and environmental impacts. The limited amount of multistakeholder participation from the global South is highlighted, along with the implications of this for discourse and practice. In particular, the chapter demonstrates how the way in which the problems and solutions are defined serves the commercial interests of Northern participants, to the detriment of Southern stakeholders and intended beneficiaries. Reasons for this situation are identified and suggestions made for what can be done about it. Ultimately, the current enthusiasm for stakeholder participation and partnership needs to evolve toward a closer consideration of accountability and democracy. "Stakeholder democracy" is offered as a conceptual framework to help in this process.

INITIATIVES ON WORKPLACE PRACTICES

The conditions of workers in the global South who make many of the products sold in the West have been a particularly high-profile CSR issue for large retailers and branded-products companies since NGO campaigns in the mid-1990s called on them to take responsibility for their supply chains. A variety of MSIs addressing working conditions have since been launched. In 1997 the Ethical Trading Initiative (ETI) was established in the UK to bring together companies, NGOs, and labor unions to improve practices in corporate supply chains. Two years later a similar initiative was launched in the United States, called the Fair Labor Association (FLA). Two further such initiatives, the Worldwide Responsible Apparel Production (WRAP) and Social Accountability International (SAI), are the focus of this chapter.

Worldwide Responsible Apparel Production (WRAP)

Originally the initiative of the American Apparel Manufacturers Association (AAMA),[1] WRAP proclaims its dedication to "the promotion and certification of lawful, humane and ethical manufacturing throughout the world."[2] In 1998 the AAMA developed the "Worldwide Responsible Apparel Production Principles," described as "basic standards that address labor practices, factory conditions, and environmental and customs compliance," and two years later launched a nonprofit organization to oversee their implementation: WRAP (www.wrapapparel.org). By 2002 WRAP covered 700 companies responsible for 85 percent of clothing sales in the United States, and more than 615 factories in 56 countries had earned the "WRAP Good Factory Seal of Approval."

The organization claims that its intended beneficiaries are workers in the clothing and footwear manufacturing industry, most of whom are in the global South. The participation of Southern stakeholders is, however, limited. All but 1 of the 12 board members appear to be US citizens. Apart from one business consultancy in El Salvador, *Reducción de Riesgos* (Risk Reduction), all of the auditors accredited to inspect and award this seal were US accounting firms (Prieto 2002). The only way Southern stakeholders can relate to this initiative is by endorsing its principles, as opposed to having some say in the organization's work.

The lack of Southern participation in and governance of this MSI, developed in the name of workers in the global South, has major implications. As Marina Prieto of the Central American Women's Network (CAWN) has noted, "Many activists in Central America and elsewhere have pointed out serious flaws in the initiative's approach" (Prieto 2002). In April 2000 the NGO Maquila Solidarity Network (MSN) (www.maquilasolidarity.org) identified the following problems with WRAP:

- A lack of independence in its board, essentially giving businesses the right to veto decisions.
- Very weak standards in terms of hours of work, minimum wage, freedom of association, and discrimination; issues specific to women, such as maternity leave and specific forms of harassment, including sexual, are not even mentioned.
- Public disclosure is not considered.
- *Maquilas* must pay for the cost of monitoring (US$1500–3000) themselves.
- Monitoring appears to be carried out only by private firms, excluding NGOs and trade unions.
- The interview process for workers is unclear, and because visits are pre-arranged, companies can "clean up" in advance.[3]

WRAP is not the only game in town, and its existence threatens to marginalize the work of Southern stakeholders on labor rights issues. For example, WRAP began working in El Salvador, directly competing with a local civil society initiative headed by the nonprofit Salvadoran Independent Monitoring Group (GMIES) (www.gmies.org.sv), which was established in 1996. This was the first such program ever to conduct external monitoring of labor conditions in the *maquila*, and it has since monitored factories supplying major companies, such as Liz Claiborne and Gap (Prieto 2002). In contrast to WRAP, GMIES emphasizes the importance of maintaining a regular presence at the factory, stresses the need for workers to get to know and trust the monitors and understand their role, and insists on the right to publish at least some of their monitoring reports and to share information on practices such as forced overtime and harassment. Lack of employer cooperation is also documented. Prieto therefore has argued

> The WRAP system should not . . . become the standard . . . across Central America because it would lead to major labour rights violations being completely ignored. Confidential reports by private-sector monitors often fail to convey an accurate picture of conditions in the Maquilas, meaning that consumers in the North would be unable to discriminate between companies on ethical grounds. (Prieto 2002: 13)

In the presence of such concerns, the director of GMIES, Carolina Quinteros,[4] is skeptical of the intent of WRAP and similar initiatives that are dominated by commercial interests in Northern countries:

> Initiatives like WRAP reflect the intention of the big corporations to appropriate a concept that was created from activist movements in favour of human and workers' rights. The struggle for a code of conduct that reflects the responsibility of companies towards their workers . . . and the demand for a monitoring process that contributes to improving workers' conditions have been transformed into a business discourse. This discourse is closer to corporate public relations than to real undertakings towards workers and consumers. (quoted in Prieto 2002: 13)

Social Accountability International (SAI)

Industry-led initiatives such as WRAP face a credibility problem with the Western NGOs that put the issue on the companies' agendas in the first place. Consequently, there has been a strong impetus for companies to enlist in either an NGO-led process or one involving NGOs as partners (Murphy and Bendell 1997). Various MSIs on workplace practices have appeared since the mid-1990s. Social Accountability International is not an MSI but a New York–based NGO that in 1997 developed a standard called SA8000 against which workplace conditions world-wide could be assessed and certified. The organization consults with stakeholders regarding their opinions on the standard and upgrades it, and the associated guidance material, as it deems appropriate. It also accredits auditing firms offering companies SA8000 certification.

SAI emphasizes that its standard is authoritative on two fronts: it integrates a number of ILO and human rights conventions, and its system of independent verification and accreditation draws on the processes defined by the International Organization for Standardization (ISO). In contrast to many initiatives in this field that ignore fundamental workers' rights, such as freedom of association, and leave the monitoring of implementation largely to self-declarations, these attributes of the SA8000 system make it a credible operation.[5]

However, on closer inspection these two attributes are not uncomplicated, and some of the problems that arise cast doubt on any assumption that an MSI or an NGO-led process such as this is accountable to the intended beneficiaries. The ILO conventions were written with governments in mind, and adapting them for direct application to companies is a process that provides scope for debate and disagreement—it is not merely a technical exercise. This is tacitly accepted by SAI through its effort to seek legitimacy through multi-stakeholder consultation over the SA8000 standard. However, the processes of standard implementation, monitoring, certification, and accreditation are portrayed as technical, not political, exercises. Further, the ISO standards and guidelines on these matters have been developed by the private sector with an eye on the interests of the conformity assessment industry, and were not initially intended for application to social issues. The influence of ISO and the conformity assessment industry has been key to the way SAI works. Thus, in its publications, presentations, and conversations, SAI and its accredited auditing companies stress objectivity, confidentiality, neutrality, reasonableness, internationality, and speed as hallmarks of their professional approach to monitoring compliance with workplace codes of conduct.

Recent research on the application of these approaches to monitoring banana plantations in Costa Rica highlighted how each of these hallmarks of "professionalism" can actually undermine the ability of the monitoring process to effect change as well as marginalize alternative approaches (Bendell 2005).

The first issue is speed. Most commercial social auditing companies try to do their audits in two to three days, with a team of two to three people. The short amount of time available is a result of the high day rates charged by certification companies. In just a couple of days, auditors have to cover a range of issues, so the considerable constraint of time significantly influences the nature of the audit. It means that auditors seek to reduce the potential complexity that could be faced during an audit in order to automate the process. It also means that important research techniques such as off-site interviews are often ruled out, although they could provide crucial information. Yet the speed is marketed as a positive attribute of these auditors, in contrast to local monitoring organizations that could both have a more regular presence at the workplace and take more time to make the assessments.

Then there is the emphasis on international application. SAI emphasizes that SA8000 is global and can be applied to a factory or plantation anywhere in the world, and audited by accredited companies like SGS and BVQI anywhere in the world. These auditors point to their international presence as a demonstration of their ability to provide clients with a global solution, if one is required. However, at the time of this research, these offices did not have staff trained in social auditing, and much of the auditing has been conducted by staff from UK or US offices, who have limited knowledge of the local culture and politics, and who face language barriers. Local monitoring groups may not be able to provide Western retailers with a "global solution" but may well prove invaluable in providing one that is sensitive to local realities.

Third is the question of confidentiality. This is considered important in that a company might not want stakeholders to know that it is being assessed, in case it fails the audit. However, their confidential nature means that audits cannot be verified by other researchers or NGOs. Many local monitoring groups are open about which workplaces they examine, and publish all or part of their findings. However, SA8000 borrows from ISO approaches requiring auditors to act confidentially.

A fourth issue concerns objectivity. Positivist approaches have been challenged within the social sciences for 20 years, given an understanding of how the social realm is socially constructed. "Evidence" is never "objective" in that the person viewing it is involved in deciding what it means and whether it counts as evidence in the first place. One auditor's "evidence" is another auditor's clutter. Despite the rhetoric of professional objectivity, all auditing decisions are discretionary, at every moment of the audit process, from the decision of whom to talk to, to what to ask, how to ask it, what to follow up on, and what to recommend. Yet SAI-accredited auditors argue that they are more "objective" than local NGOs, presenting their lack of knowledge and experience of local contexts as a positive attribute. Attendance at SA8000 training courses revealed the pro-client biases of commercial auditors on issues such as freedom of association (Bendell 2001).

Fifth—and ironically, given their claim to objectivity, but understandably, given their financial concerns—auditors like SGS made a feature of their favorable disposition toward commercial clients. "There is the problem that compliance with the letter of the standard might not mean compliance with the spirit of the standard. You need to approach these issues objectively," said one SA8000 course tutor (Bendell 2001). Therefore, the "objectivity" claimed by commercial auditors is really their "reasonableness," or their flexible and unsuspicious subjectivity.

A sixth issue is neutrality. Like a number of other groups in the emergent profession, SAI presents the monitoring of workplaces by accredited companies as a neutral test of labor conditions. Companies pass or fail audits; officially, management does not receive help from auditors on improving compliance, nor do workers receive help in improving their situation. However, this restriction is rooted in the practice of auditing management systems, not performance standards. For the latter, it is an undesirable restriction as it prevents the provision of constructive advice to improve the situation. In addition, the idea of a neutral test is methodologically illogical. SA8000 inherited a methodology that is suited to the inspection of "things," such as light bulbs and financial accounts, and not people or social relations. People's representations of their situation cannot be treated as concrete, immovable "facts."

Evidence from focus groups concerning sexual harassment illustrates this. At first, women workers on the banana plantations said that they did not suffer sexual harassment. After more discussion, it emerged that they didn't see the abuse they received as harassment, as it was "normal" for men to behave in the ways they did. Once it was suggested that just because it was "normal" did not mean that it was not harassment, they agreed that, in fact, they did suffer sexual harassment (Bendell 2001). Thus, evidence of "sexual harassment" was produced by the team of researchers helping the women to explore the issue. Other auditors may not have decided to pursue the matter, being content to ask the yes/no question "Do you suffer sexual harassment?" and check the "no" box accordingly. That "objective" evidence of the absence of sexual harassment from a "neutral" test would have been produced by the auditors' use of uncommon terminology and the consequent lack of communication with the workers. By striving to maintain neutrality, auditors accept the power relations that exist in a workplace; but the capability of passing workplaces as acceptable is in fact far from neutral, since it actually reinforces those power relations. This is a very different approach from that of groups such as GMIES, which do not aim for their monitoring to be a neutral test, but rather see it as a mechanism for driving change.

The monitoring methodology promoted, and in many ways required, by SAI can be challenged on the grounds of its appropriateness and its effects on the efforts of Southern stakeholders, particularly local monitoring initiatives. SAI's accreditation process is also problematic in its effects on these groups; the organization subscribes to the ISO guideline that all accredited organizations be treated the same, so that the same paperwork and financial arrangements are required of a small NGO operating in only one region as are required of a major multinational inspection company.

Any initiative, policy, or mechanism will have its drawbacks. However, the problem is whether a particular approach, such as that of SAI, marginalizes alternatives that might offer increased accountability to intended beneficiaries. Participatory methods of workplace appraisal are being tried but do not receive the same corporate support. The ETI has gone some way in promoting these more engaged processes of monitoring, yet the emphasis on the visit by an external expert remains, in a way that parallels the industrializing and depoliticizing of participatory public-policy processes by development consultants.

The focus on producer certification can also be questioned. Not only does SAI define the problem as stemming from producer practices rather than buyer-supplier relations, but it also allows the risks associated with improving labor standards and obtaining certification to be borne by producers. In times of economic stress, companies could cancel their contracts with some farms, and reduce the terms and conditions on other farms, but still retain one or two as SA8000 certified, if they so wished. SAI is not alone in this approach. WRAP, the FLA, and the ETI all identify the problem of poor working conditions as something to be dealt with "over there," in the factories and plantations across the global South, rather than "over here," in the offices of large corporations that monopolize access to markets, drive down prices, require higher quality, and place short-notice "just-in-time" orders for products. This is in contrast to the fair trade movement, which sees changed buyer-supplier relations as key to any process of improving workers' conditions. The fact that Southern stakeholders do not have a voice in the governance of organizations based in London, New York, and Washington may help to explain why these organizations do not deal with these difficult issues.

Initiatives on Sustainable Development

Although it is distinguished from purely environmental matters, much of the impetus for a renewed focus on CSR came from the environmental movement. In the early 1990s many environmental groups turned their attention to companies, calling on them to address their impact on society, on issues such as deforestation, climate change, and overfishing (Murphy and Bendell 1997). The environmental consulting industry grew and grew, and began to theorize its work in terms of helping companies address their sustainability—involving their economic and social as well as their environmental impacts. Within this context, many people with an environmental background began working on issues such as workplace conditions and human rights. The problem was that their expertise in these issues was limited, and they often lacked any mandate from organizations with a long history in these areas, such as trade unions. Relations between environmental NGOs and trade unions, or other NGOs working on development and human rights, are seldom extensive. The issue of CSR has provided some points of contact, but participation is often poorly balanced between these different types of organizations.

Environmental NGOs working on an expanding range of CSR issues therefore often find their accountability challenged. One illustrative initiative is the Better Banana Project, developed by the New York NGO Rainforest Alliance. This project established a standard against which plantations could be assessed, initially using environmental criteria, but gradually incorporating a range of provisions on working conditions. The quality of these criteria, the expertise of the auditors, and the organization's independence from the main client of certification, Chiquita Brands International, were all challenged by trade unions and environmental organizations in Latin America. Now administered by a

variety of NGOs from across the continent, all members of the Sustainable Agriculture Network (SAN), the project has made efforts to
improve relations with unions and others, although its accountability to
intended beneficiaries is still limited (Bendell 2000, 2005).

The experience of the Forest Stewardship Council (FSC) may also
be instructive here. Established in 1993, the initial impetus for the FSC
came from concern about the role of the timber trade in tropical deforestation. FSC oversees a sustainable forest management standard and
accredits auditors to certify companies that manage forests in accordance with the standard. It has paid close attention to balancing the
interests of different stakeholders in business and civil society, North
and South, on issues of social, environmental, or economic importance,
and is democratically accountable to its membership (Murphy and Bendell 1997). Despite this, only about one-quarter of the FSC's 300-plus
members are from the global South (Blowfield 2004), though members
have equal voting rights. By 2002 over 345 logging operations and 23.8
million hectares of forests had been certified under the FSC system, yet
84 percent of these forests were in the global North (Bass et al. 2001).
Tropical deforestation had increased (Worldwatch Institute 2003). One
problem is that the method of certification used for the FSC is more
suited to large companies with auditable management systems, which
can afford certification and do not have complex relations with local
communities. This makes certification in the North generally easier
than in the South (Bass et al. 2001; Blowfield 2004). This demonstrates
that even if accountability issues are addressed in the organizational
governance of an MSI, a particular discourse of standards and certification can structure the possibility for uptake within the global South,
leading to questions about trade distortion and protectionism.

The future of CSR is often thought to lie in how the financial
world responds. Similar problems to those just outlined may beset the
world of socially responsible investment (SRI), including inadequate
attention to social issues and the global application of a Northern
interpretation. In 2002 the "London Principles" were launched by the
UK financial industry, setting out conditions under which financial
market mechanisms can best promote the financing of sustainable
development.[6] In the workshop of 120 people who helped develop the
principles, no human rights organizations or trade unions and only
one development charity were represented. Of the 26 individuals and
institutions consulted, none was from human rights, development, or
labor organizations (Corporation of London 2002). Thus, the principles

failed to address health, human rights, transparency, corruption, bribery, political lobbying, good governance, trading structures, or market regulation. At the 2002 WSSD a memorandum of understanding was signed with the United Nations Environment Programme (UNEP) declaring that the London Principles are applicable to all cities and markets, despite the absence of any Southern consultation.

Reasons and Responses

The initiatives profiled in this paper are by no means the worst or the most criticized; on the contrary, they are considered leaders in the field of CSR, and their promotion of stakeholder participation is widely welcomed by various policymakers and funders. For this very reason, if the accountability of these initiatives can be questioned, that of most CSR initiatives might be questioned even more. The constituencies in whose name CSR is promoted are not yet able to hold most CSR initiatives accountable.

This situation is due in part to the fact that a key impetus for CSR comes from a corporation's need to manage the risk of its reputation being damaged due to the influence of Northern NGOs on the media, consumers, investors, staff, and regulators. Thus, the concerns of Northern NGOs were the initial impetus for CSR. The relationship between these NGOs and other opinion formers in the North, and the intended beneficiaries of their work in the global South, is therefore key.

One implication for NGOs is how they manage their own downward accountability to the constituencies they are meant to serve. "Few NGOs active in ethical trade are accountable to the people they claim to represent, and where they have adequate international networks they do not manage these to systematically understand and present the views of their so-called constituencies," argues Mick Blowfield (2004: 87). This statement echoes existing debates about NGO accountability in public policy advocacy and service provision (Edwards and Hulme 1996). For example, NGOs have sometimes been found to exclude representative people's associations, membership organizations, and trade unions from various social reforms (Uphoff 1996). Some Southern NGOs that pay closer attention to maintaining good relations with funding bodies compared with the constituencies they are meant to be serving have also been critiqued (Hudock 1999).

Another reason for the limited accountability of CSR is that once issues have been raised, responses are implemented in accordance with

the interests and capabilities of large companies and commercial service providers. Thus we see large retailers focusing their attention not
on their own buying practices but on suppliers, preferring the "global"
solutions offered by corporate-friendly auditors, who themselves seek
to define and promote practices in ways that suit their own priorities.

The implication for those NGOs who participate in voluntary MSIs
on CSR is that they must recognize the dangers of co-optation and the
inherent limitations of this area of activity. As their collaborations with
industry become more "successful" in terms of funding, participation,
reach, and recognition, they must consider which groups they might be
marginalizing or competing with, and whether those groups are less
attractive to corporate interests and why. Then they should engage with
them. This is essentially about managing the paradox of power that
arises when apparent success in working with powerful organizations
undermines one's effectiveness (Bendell 2005). It is also important for
NGOs to see beyond their specific issues, whether they be child labor,
deforestation, or other concerns, and recognize how processes of globalization have engendered challenges to corporate legitimacy, which
have in turn prompted companies to work with NGOs. NGOs must realize that these collaborations may have an effect on that broader political
context.

There are also reasons why corporate executives should be concerned about the limited accountability of CSR. In terms of reputation
management, unless the intended beneficiaries are engaged, it is not
certain that the challenges they face will be addressed. The failure to
resolve underlying problems may provide material for future reputa-
tionally damaging campaigns. In addition, certain issues pose challenges beyond concerns about one's reputation; HIV/AIDS, climate
change, poverty, and social conflict all present risks to the future expansion of business in the global South, and thus to the long-term strategies
of international companies. Institutional investors such as pension
funds should also be interested in this, as they invest across whole sectors and need to be assured that the threats to their long-term portfolios
arising from problems such as AIDS, poverty, and climate change will
be effectively tackled. These problems can be addressed more effectively through the exchange of information with intended beneficiaries,
and ensuring that activities have credibility with, and a mandate from,
those beneficiaries.

Finally, there is the question of corporate power. Activities such as
child labor and deforestation, two leading CSR issues, have been with

us since humans first walked on the earth, yet only since the early 1990s have they become issues of corporate responsibility. This is because people woke up to the growth of corporate power and started to target companies directly. If CSR does not address the imbalance of corporate power, then it is unlikely to reduce growing criticisms. Indeed, if it is seen to consolidate corporate power, those companies involved in CSR will become even bigger targets.

Governments and intergovernmental institutions should also act on this. MSIs need guidance and encouragement to address their accountability issues. Although early discussions about the role of the UN Global Compact included the possibility of its role in forming guiding principles for MSIs, this did not materialize. Some MSIs and NGOs have formed the International Social and Environmental Accreditation and Labelling (ISEAL) Alliance, which has developed a code on standard setting. The code stresses the need for stakeholder participation, but this is not conceived in terms of democratic accountability to intended beneficiaries. The code says that those who might be "materially affected" by a standard should be consulted, but this includes groups that might be making significant amounts of money from a process, rather than being limited to organizations representing the interests of those whose rights are not being upheld by it. The code represents an uncomfortable compromise between maintaining an appearance of a technical approach to the issue addressed, and the politics that are inherent in MSIs. ISEAL was founded in particular to help its members achieve credibility in future WTO processes, which through the triennial reviews of the Agreement on Technical Barriers to Trade have placed the corporate-dominated ISO and the commercial auditing community in the position of defining legitimate processes for standard setting and conformity assessment. Thus, the current involvement of governments and intergovernmental institutions leaves much to be desired. Instead, leadership will be required to establish criteria for the validity of claims about social phenomena that do not serve purely commercial interests, and then to have these recognized by the institutions that govern international trade.

CONCLUSION: TOWARD STAKEHOLDER DEMOCRACY

"The increase of corporate power and the rise of influential NGO movements presents a great challenge for democratic systems," argues

Minu Hemmati (2002: 265) in a review of the growth in MSIs on sustainable development prepared for the WSSD. Some have warned of a new and antidemocratic global corporatism arising from the growing interest in partnerships between corporations, NGOs, and intergovernmental bodies (Ottaway 2001). Evidence from the field of CSR presented in this chapter adds to this concern about the unaccountability of MSIs, while at the same time suggesting that they could be important new mechanisms for people to influence the corporations that affect their lives. To promote their positive function, we need to be clearer about what it is that is good about MSIs. We need a shift in discourse away from stakeholder dialogue, participation, and partnership toward an articulation of policy and practice that places democratic principles at the center.

Concepts of democracy are, of course, contested, with historical debates between advocates of representative versus participatory democracy. Modern twists to this debate involve cosmopolitan, deliberative, and associative concepts of democracy, among others. Engaging with concepts and techniques of democracy poses a significant challenge.

One popular view is that in a democratically governed society, a community of people should have meaningful participation in decisions and processes that affect them and should not be systematically adversely affected by another group of people without being able to rectify the situation (Dahl 1961). This means that any organization can be assessed in terms of democracy: organizations should be accountable to those they affect—particularly those who are negatively affected. There are various mechanisms for such accountability, some that an organization itself can attend to and others that require external bodies, such as state regulators and courts, which in turn should be democratically accountable. Because the "demos" or people who make claims for the democratic control (directly or indirectly) of an organization are also affected by it, this can be understood as "stakeholder democracy." The concept of stakeholders is useful as it groups people on the basis of an interest in an organization—the unit central to this conception of democracy. The ability of a system of democracy by stakeholder groups to deliver individual democratic rights depends on those stakeholder groups themselves being democratic. As most stakeholder groups form organizations themselves, their accountability is a valid question in terms of the ideal of stakeholder democracy. Thus, we could define a stakeholder democracy as an ideal system of governance of a society where all stakeholders in an organization or activity have the same opportunity to govern that organization or activity. Stakeholder groups are key to this process, as well as being the subjects of democratic governance.

The term is already being used in activism and international development advocacy. For example, Tim Concannon of a small human rights group called the Stakeholder Democracy Network argues that "stakeholder democracy means empowering grassroots stakeholders."[7] He uses the term to introduce human rights principles into the mainstream discourse on "stakeholder dialogue" and "stakeholder participation." The popularity of these two terms is illustrated by the combined total of 77,800 websites they generated on the Google search engine in July 2004, even more than the 71,400 generated by the classical concept of "participatory democracy," and far outnumbering terms describing more recent theoretical developments ("associative democracy," 1510; "deliberative democracy," 24,800).

The concept of stakeholder democracy has not been discussed widely in academia, although there has been some work on democracy and corporations in the field of management studies: "industrial" or "workplace democracy" appears in literatures on organizational behavior and human resource management, for example, and the idea of "shareholder democracy" in works on finance and corporate governance. Some management theorists have mentioned the concept in terms of all of a company's stakeholders, external as well as internal, although they have shied away from venturing a specific definition (Turnbull 1994; O'Dwyer 2004).

Meanwhile, Nottingham University Business School has initiated discussions about stakeholder democracy, understood as a topic of inquiry that "focuses on the question of how far stakeholders have certain democratic rights in governing the corporation."[8]

Future research on stakeholder democracy will need to consider the dynamics of power in stakeholder relations. Consideration of the power of discourse production, and how it is shaped by particular interests, will be key to this. The examples in this chapter of how MSIs set the boundaries of participation, by defining the agenda for problem solving, illustrate that democracy is not promoted merely by increasing participation but by ensuring that stakeholders having an equal opportunity to shape agendas that create the boundaries of that participation (Bendell 2005).

Another vital area of analysis is the relationship between deliberation and action, or compulsion. Deliberation cannot be divorced from issues of compulsion: if a state had a parliament that was ignored by the monarch, then it would not be considered a democracy; nor, by the same token, should a stakeholder process that has limited powers of implementation be considered democratic. Further, if the existence of that stakeholder process actually undermined processes of compulsory regulation, then its democratizing credentials could also be questioned. Given the growing recognition of the patchiness of the commercial rationale for CSR, the truest responsibility of one company may actually be to work for the accountability of *all* companies, thereby backing improved regulations nationally and internationally (Bendell 2004).

Until now, the international development and management professions and academies have largely ignored each other (Wong-MingJi and Mir 1999). However, to inform progressive policy and practice in the field of CSR and MSIs, these schools of thought and practice will have to engage with and learn from each other.

ACKNOWLEDGMENTS

I would like to thank Virginia Rodríguez and Desirée Abrahams for research assistance and the Aspen Institute's Non-profit Sector Research Fund for supporting my doctoral research. Some of my findings there are incorporated in this paper.

NOTES

[1] In August 2000 the AAMA merged with the Footwear Industries of America and the Fashion Association to become the American Apparel and Footwear Association.

[2] The statements quoted in this section are from www.wrapapparel.org/infosite2/index.htm (retrieved 18 October 2002).

[3] See www.cawn.org/newsletter/16/us_monitoring.html (retrieved 28 October 2004).

[4] Carolina Quinteros has also contributed a chapter to this volume (see Chapter 10).

[5] For more information on the SA8000 standard and workers' rights, see Kearney and Gearhart (2004).

[6] See www.cityoflondon.gov.uk/living_environment/sustainability/ (retrieved 18 January 2005).

[7] See www.stakeholderdemocracy.org (retrieved 12 July 2004).

8 Program of the 2nd Annual ICCSR Symposium, "Stakeholder Democracy—Perspectives from across the Business Disciplines," Nottingham, 28 November 2003.

REFERENCES

Bass, Steven, Xavier Font, and L. Danielson. 2001. "Standards and Certification: A Leap Forward and a Step Back for Sustainable Development." In Tom Bigg (ed.), *The Future Is Now: Equity for a Small Planet*. London: IIED.

Bendell, Jem (ed.). (2000) *Terms for Endearment: Business, NGOs and Sustainable Development*. Sheffield, UK: Greenleaf.

———. 2001. *Towards Participatory Workplace Appraisal: Report from a Focus Group of Women Banana Workers*. Occasional Paper. Bristol: New Academy of Business.

———. 2004. *Barricades and Boardrooms: A Contemporary History of the Corporate Accountability Movement*. Geneva: UNRISD.

———. 2005. *In Our Power: The Civilisation of Globalisation*. Sheffield, UK: Greenleaf.

Blowfield, Mick. 2004. "Implementation Deficits of Ethical Trade Systems: Lessons from the Indonesian Cocoa and Timber Industries." *Journal of Corporate Citizenship* 13:77–90.

Choudry, A. 2003. "Beware the Wolf at the Door." *Seedling*, Genetic Resources Action International (GRAIN), October.

Corporation of London. 2002. *Financing the Future: The Role of the UK Financial Services in Sustainable Development*. London: Corporation of London.

Dahl, Robert A. 1961. *Who Governs? Democracy and Power in an American City*. New Haven, CT: Yale University Press.

Edwards, Michael, and David Hulme (eds.). 1996. *Beyond the Magic Bullet: NGO Performance and Accountability in the Post-Cold War World*. West Hartford, CT: Kumarian Press.

Goetz, Anne-Marie, and Rob Jenkins. 2002. *Voice, Accountability and Development: The Emergence of a New Agenda*. Background Paper for the UNDP Human Development Report 2002. New York: Oxford University Press.

Hemmati, Minu. 2002. *Multi-Stakeholder Processes for Governance and Sustainability: Beyond Deadlock and Conflict*. London: Earthscan.

Hudock, Ann. 1999. *NGOs and Civil Society: Democracy by Proxy?* Cambridge: Polity Press.

Kearney, Neil, and Judy Gearhart. 2004. "Workplace Codes as Tools for Workers." *Development in Practice* 14(1–2):216–223.

Murphy, David F., and Jem Bendell. 1997. *In the Company of Partners: Business, Environmental Groups and Sustainable Development Post-Rio*. Bristol: Policy Press.

O'Dwyer, Brendan. 2004. *Stakeholder Democracy: Challenges and Contributions from Accountancy.* ICCSR Research Paper No. 18. Nottingham: University of Nottingham.

Ottaway, Marina. 2001. "Corporatism Goes Global: International Organisations, NGO Networks and Transnational Business." *Global Governance* 7(3):265–292.

Prahalad, C. K. 2004. *The Fortune at the Bottom of the Pyramid: Eradicating Poverty through Profits, Enabling Choice through Markets.* Philadelphia: Wharton School Publishing.

Prieto, Marina. 2002. *US Monitoring Sees No Evil.* Central America Report, Autumn. London: CAWN (available at www.cawn.org/newsletter/16/us_monitoring.html).

Save the Children. 2000. *Big Business, Small Hands: Responsible Approaches to Child Labour.* London: Save the Children Fund.

Turnbull, Shann. 1994. "Stakeholder Democracy: Redesigning the Governance of Firms and Bureaucracies." *Journal of Socio-Economics* 23(3): 321–360.

Uphoff, N. 1996. "Why NGOs Are Not a Third Sector: A Sectoral Analysis with Some Thoughts on Accountability, Sustainability and Evaluation." In M. Edwards and D. Hulme (eds.), *Beyond the Magic Bullet: NGO Performance and Accountability in the Post-Cold War World.* West Hartford, CT: Kumarian Press.

Utting, Peter. 2002. "Regulating Business by Multistakeholder Initiatives: A Preliminary Assessment. In *Voluntary Approaches to Corporate Responsibility.* Geneva: UNRISD/UN-NGLS.

Waddell, Steve. 2000. "Complementary Resources: The Win-Win Rationale for Partnership with NGOs." In J. Bendell (ed.), *Terms for Endearment: Business, NGOs and Sustainable Development.* Sheffield, UK: Greenleaf.

Wong-MingJi, Diana, and Ali Mir. 1997. "How International Is International Management?" In P. Prasad, A. Mills, M. Elmes, and A. Prasad (eds.), *Managing the Organizational Melting Pot: Dilemmas of Workplace Diversity.* Thousand Oaks, CA: Sage.

Worldwatch Institute. 2003. *Winged Messenger: The Decline of Birds.* Worldwatch Paper 165. Washington, DC: Worldwatch Institute.

WTO. 1998. *Environmental Labels and Market Access: Case Study on the Colombian Flower-Growing Industry.* WT/CTE/W/76 (G/TBT/W/60), 9 March. Geneva: WTO.

THREE

Corporate Responsibility and the Movement of Business

PETER UTTING

INTRODUCTION

Terms such as "corporate social responsibility" (CSR), "corporate citizenship," and "partnership" have become buzzwords in international development discourse. This reflects the fact that an increasing number of transnational corporations (TNCs) and large domestic companies, supported by business and industry associations, are adopting a variety of so-called voluntary initiatives that aim to improve their social, environmental, and human rights records. Such initiatives include, for example, codes of conduct; measures to improve environmental management systems and occupational health and safety; company triple bottom line reporting on financial, social, and environmental aspects; participation in certification and labeling schemes; dialogue with stakeholders and partnerships with NGOs and UN agencies; and increased support for community development projects and programs.

This chapter considers why the CSR agenda has taken off since the 1980s, examining in particular the role of both civil society and business actors in mobilizations concerned with CSR. The title is meant to convey the idea of a dual movement: big business (a) is being moved by social, political, and market pressures associated with civil society, consumer, and shareholder activism, as well as regulatory threats; and (b) is not simply responding or reacting to pressure but is itself mobilizing to influence, control, and lead the agenda of institutional reform.

CIVIL SOCIETY AND CSR ACTIVISM

The history of progressive institutional change under capitalism suggests that new policies, norms, and regulations often reflect changes in the balance of social forces, activist pressures, and regulatory threats, as well as occasional crisis conditions. The rise of welfare legislation in postwar Europe, for example, occurred in a context in which the labor movement and other ideological and political forces associated with social democracy were relatively strong, and big business had been weakened through previous decades of depression and war (Gallin 2000). The adoption of nonbinding international standards for TNCs by the ILO and the OECD in the 1970s, and of UN codes of conduct related to specific products in the 1980s, was due largely to influences and pressures associated with civil society activism, regulatory threats of binding international regulation of TNCs, and calls from developing countries and others for a new international economic order (Hansen 2002; Richter 2001).

Civil society engagement with CSR issues has expanded considerably since the 1980s, with numerous NGOs and NGO networks, as well as consumer groups and trade unions, mobilizing around issues such as child labor, sweatshops, fair trade, the rights of indigenous peoples, the release of toxic chemicals, oil pollution, tropical deforestation, and other forms of environmental degradation. Various factors account for the upsurge in CSR activism and the involvement of NGOs in advocacy, economic, and regulatory activities.

First, the NGO sector was expanding rapidly, gaining legitimacy as a development actor and seeking new areas of engagement. The rise of so-called civil regulation,[1] involving myriad forms of confrontation and collaboration between civil society organizations (CSOs) and business, reflected broader changes that were occurring in global governance, where rule making and implementation, and the exercise of power, have become more diffused and multilayered (Held 2003).

Second, not only neoliberals but also some activists and NGOs were critical of what were—in reality or perception—the failed attempts by government and international organizations to regulate TNCs. They sought a "third way" centered on voluntary approaches, collaboration, and partnerships. Changes in tactics and strategies, involving both service delivery and advocacy, also supported this approach. As NGOs were drawn increasingly into service-delivery functions and market relations, an increasing number became part of a growing CSR industry of service providers. The third-way approach was also reinforced by pressures and incentives that encouraged NGOs to move beyond confrontation and criticism, and to propose solutions and engage constructively with mainstream decision-making processes. And in a context in which certain regulatory roles of government and trade unions were being constrained by both the ideology and impact of neoliberalism, and where some forms of regulatory authority were, in effect, being privatized, NGOs assumed regulatory functions by designing and administering new institutions associated, for example, with codes of conduct, certification and labeling schemes, and activity monitoring and reporting.

Third, to traditional concerns about the negative developmental impacts of TNCs was added another set of issues. There was growing recognition that globalization and economic liberalization were altering the balance of rights and obligations that structure the behavior of corporations (Chang 2001). TNCs were enjoying new rights and freedoms as a result of economic liberalization and globalization without commensurate obligations and responsibilities, most notably in developing countries. Increasing international trade, foreign direct investment (FDI), and other financial flows were seen to be benefiting TNCs and finance capital while, in many countries, labor and environmental conditions deteriorated, the number of people living in extreme poverty failed to decline, and inequality increased (UNRISD 1995, 2000). Global awareness of such imbalances and regulatory deficits, and of the need for institutional reform, was reinforced through a series of UN summits and commissions, as well as through the antiglobalization movement.

Fourth, several environmental and social disasters and injustices, linked to large corporations or specific industries, became high-profile international issues around which activists mobilized. They included, for example, the Union Carbide toxic gas leak in Bhopal, India; the *Exxon Valdez* oil spill; Shell's activities in Nigeria and elsewhere; sweatshop conditions in factories supplying Nike and other brand-name companies; tropical deforestation linked to companies including Aracruz, Mitsubishi, and McDonald's; Monsanto's promotion of genetically modified organisms (GMOs) and their impacts on small farmers, food security, and consumer health; child labor in the football industry; fires in Asian toy factories; environmental disasters associated with mining companies; and the spread of HIV/AIDS, particularly in migrant-labor systems structured by the mining industry.

As civil society engagement with CSR issues intensified, activism not only expanded but also assumed more diverse forms.[2] Particularly prominent are the following types of activism and relations with big business.[3]

Watchdog activism, which involves identifying and publicizing corporate malpractice by naming and shaming specific companies, is undertaken by organizations including CorpWatch (United States), Corporate Watch (UK), Greenpeace,[4] Human Rights Watch, International Baby Food Action Network (IBFAN), Maquila Solidarity Network, Minewatch, Norwatch (Norway), Oilwatch, Pesticide Action Network (PAN), Project Underground, and PR Watch.

Consumer activism and the fair trade movement, which involves efforts to inform consumers about specific products or companies, organize consumer boycotts, and ensure that companies and consumers in the North pay a fair price to small producers in the South, are undertaken by, for example, Consumers International, Equal Exchange, Fairtrade Foundation, Fairtrade Labelling Organisations International (FLO), Infact, Max Havelaar Foundation, Traidcraft Foundation, and Transfair.

Shareholder activism and ethical investment, in which CSOs or individuals buy shares in companies and use the format of annual general meetings of shareholders to raise complaints and propose changes to corporate policy and practice, is undertaken, for example, by Actares, Ethical Investment Research Service (EIRIS), Ethical Shareholders, Interfaith Center for Corporate Responsibility, Shareholder Action Network, and Social Investment Forum.

Litigation, including what has been called transnational litigation or foreign direct liability (Newell 2001; Ward 2001), is a form of protest in which activists and victims use the courts to prosecute corporate malpractice, as in recent cases involving Shell and Coca-Cola. Organizations involved include the Center for Justice and Accountability, EarthRights International, and the International Labor Rights Fund.

Critical research, public education, and advocacy involves generating and disseminating knowledge on the developmental impact of TNCs, corporate malpractice, and North-South trade and investment relations, and attempting to influence public and academic opinion, as well as policy makers, through campaigns and other strategies. Examples include the activities of Amnesty International, Centre for Research on Multinational Corporations (SOMO, the Netherlands), Corporate Europe Observatory, Friends of the Earth, Health Action International, Institute for Policy Studies, International Institute for Sustainable Development, Nautilus, New Economics Foundation, Oxfam International, People-Centered Development Forum, Programa Laboral de Desarrollo (PLADES, Peru), Third World Network, Transnationale (France), and World Vision.

Collaboration and service provision is when nonprofit organizations engage with corporations and business associations to identify, analyze, and disseminate knowledge on good practice; raise awareness of corporate responsibility issues; engage in partnership programs and projects; provide training and advisory services; promote and design improved standards, as well as socially and environmentally sensitive management and reporting processes; and carry out monitoring and auditing. Examples include Fair Labor Association, Forest Stewardship Council, Global Reporting Initiative, Institute for Social and Ethical Accounting, International Institute for Environment and Development (IIED), New Academy of Business, Partners in Change (India), and Social Accountability International.

Eclectic activism is simultaneous engagement by CSOs in both collaboration and confrontation. This might involve, for example, providing technical assistance to companies, participating in stakeholder negotiations or dialogues, and simultaneously promoting "naming and shaming" actions or demanding legalistic regulation of TNCs. Examples include: Centre for Science and Environment (CSE-India), Clean Clothes Campaign (CCC), IBASE (Brazil), International Federation of Human Rights (FIDH), International Union of Food and Allied Workers (IUF) and other international trade union organizations, Worker Rights Consortium (WRC), and WWF-International.

BUSINESS AS A MOVEMENT

History teaches us that progressive social change occurs not only in response to social and political pressures from below, but is also related to institutional reforms engineered from above. Indeed, capitalism and its elites have shown a remarkable capacity to accommodate opposition and resistance, and to deal with crisis conditions and contradictions by developing new institutions, and reforming or strengthening existing ones (Utting 2002a).

This brings us to the second dimension of the movement of business. Big business has proved very capable of organizing, networking, and mobilizing around CSR issues. An important sector of business is not simply reacting to pressure or engaging in defensive posturing or "greenwash"; it is a proactive player that is shaping and disseminating the CSR agenda. It does this through various institutional or organizational forms.

First, a group of high-profile TNCs and large national companies have placed themselves at the forefront of the CSR agenda through sponsorship,

PR, advertising, dialogues, networking, and participation in partnerships, as well as by making concrete changes in business policies, management systems, and performance. These include, among others, ABB, Backus (Peru), BP, Carrefour (France), Dow Chemicals, Dupont, Eskom and Sasol (South Africa), Ford, IKEA, Levi Strauss, Merck, Migros (Switzerland), Novo Nordisk, Rio Tinto, San Miguel (Philippines), Shell, Suzano and Aracruz (Brazil), Tata Iron and Steel (India), Toyota, and Unilever.

Second, the CSR agenda such businesses promote has been supported both by traditional business and industry associations (such as the International Chamber of Commerce (ICC), the International Employers Organization (IEO), and the World Economic Forum) and by chemical, mining, and other sectoral associations. A relatively new set of business-interest NGOs and foundations with close ties to TNCs and corporate philanthropists also actively promotes CSR. They include, for example, the Bill and Melinda Gates Foundation, Business for Social Responsibility (BSR), Business in the Community, CSR Europe, the Global Business Council on HIV and AIDS, Instituto Ethos (Brazil), the International Business Leaders Forum (IBLF), Peru 2021, Philippines Business for Social Progress, and the World Business Council for Sustainable Development (WBCSD).

Third, the financial services industry, including some banks, investment funds, insurance companies, accountancy and auditing firms, and rating and index agencies, has also become a more proactive CSR player, primarily through the promotion of socially responsible investment, reporting, and certification. Relevant companies include, for example, Calvert, Domini Social Investments, Dow Jones, FTSE Group, KPMG, SGS, and UBS.

Fourth, TNCs, large national companies, industry associations, business-interest NGOs, and corporate foundations are entering into a range of collaborative CSR initiatives with NGOs, trade unions, academic centers, governments, the UN, the World Bank, and other international organizations. Such collaborative arrangements include, for example, the following:

- The participation of the International Chamber of Commerce (ICC) and various TNCs in the United Nations Global Compact
- WBCSD's promotion of arm's-length studies of the paper, pulp, and mining sectors

- Chiquita, Danone, and IKEA's involvement in Global Framework Agreements signed with global union federations (previously called international trade secretariats)[5]
- Numerous UN-business partnerships, such as UNDP's activities with Cisco Systems; UNICEF's fundraising efforts with British Airways; WHO's initiatives with pharmaceutical, mining, and food and beverage companies, and the Global Alliance for Vaccines and Immunization (GAVI)
- Participation of TNCs (for example, BP, Nike, and Novo Nordisk) in recently established multistakeholder initiatives, which promote standard setting, reporting, monitoring, certification, stakeholder dialogues, and so-called best practice learning

TNCs and business organizations are also actively lobbying governments and international organizations on CSR issues and participating in global summits and other public policymaking processes and governance structures. A number of large corporations, for example, mobilized to influence the 1992 Earth Summit process, creating in 1990 the Business Council for Sustainable Development. In 1995 this forum was strengthened when it merged with the World Industry Council on Environment to form the WBCSD, whose membership now includes 170 large international companies (Schmidheiny et al. 1997). In the buildup to the 2002 World Summit on Sustainable Development, the WBCSD and the ICC formed Business Action for Sustainable Development, which, according to the ICC website, "creates a network to ensure that the world business community is assigned its proper place at the world summit . . ." (www.iccwbo.org).

Understanding the Mobilization of Big Business

While civil society pressures and influences of the type outlined above have constituted crucial drivers of CSR, there are other reasons behind the engagement of big business with the CSR agenda. The corporate CSR discourse is structured around a series of propositions that tie in with new theories and thinking associated with modernization, neoliberalism, global governance, new institutional economics, and business management.

The Business Case for CSR

An influential body of business and academic opinion emphasizes the win-win proposition that good social and environmental performance is also good for profits (Holliday et al. 2002; Porter and van der Linde 1995). Evidence for this aspect of the business case is, in fact, mixed. Nevertheless, it figures prominently in the discourse of some business leaders and management gurus. Four claims, in particular, are made:

- CSR can enhance a company's competitive advantage.
- Some forms of CSR, such as eco-efficiency or recycling, can actually reduce costs.
- CSR is good for staff morale and motivation.
- CSR is a proxy for competent management and associated qualities related to innovation, the ability to anticipate and deal with risks, and learning and using knowledge effectively.

The role of CSR in risk management is a crucial aspect of the business case. Globalization and the strengthening of civil society imply new risks for TNCs. It is often said that high-profile brand-name corporations can run but they cannot hide. Instances of malpractice in their supply chains can be detected and publicized internationally. Consumer campaigns and boycotts can harm a company's or product's image, sales, and competitive advantage, particularly in the case of brand-name companies. And in some countries, such as the United States and the UK, TNCs are also becoming more vulnerable to litigation related to social, environmental, and human rights issues. Such risks to profits, market share, and reputation can, to some extent, be managed through CSR. Engaging in CSR through voluntary initiatives can also be a way of diminishing regulatory threats from government.

Structural changes in the way production is organized internationally, notably the growth of global value chains and outsourcing, mean that the business activities and standards that are of concern to CSOs and consumers relate not only to the core enterprises of TNCs but also to other firms involved in their supply chains. TNCs, therefore, need to put in place institutional arrangements to control the activities of the enterprises with which they have contractual relations but which they do not own. Various CSR initiatives, including codes of conduct, monitoring, auditing, certification, and labeling can facilitate such control (Ascoly et al. 2001). Some forms of collaboration between TNCs and

CSOs, such as Global Framework Agreements and certain multistake-holder initiatives, can provide information and feedback to the corporate center regarding the activities of both affiliates and suppliers on the corporate periphery (Utting 2000).

The Theoretical Underpinnings of CSR

The business case for CSR extends beyond the micro level of the firm to the macro level of the capitalist system, which is periodically threatened by crisis and instability. As Gramsci noted, the longevity of capitalism has to do with the ability of ruling elites to govern not through force but through consensus, exercising moral, cultural, and intellectual leadership, and entering into relations with civil society that cultivate certain values and opinions conducive to stability and the rejection of alternatives that are perceived as radical. Corporate engagement with CSR issues can also be seen in these terms (Levy 1997; Bendell and Murphy 2002). Business elites are not only responding defensively; they are proactively trying to influence, control, and lead the agenda of institutional reform and social and economic change (Utting 2002a).

The voluntary approaches that are central to the CSR agenda have a powerful ideological and theoretical grounding. Neoliberalism, which has guided the process of economic liberalization since the late 1970s, critiques certain forms of command-and-control regulation and state intervention on the basis that they interfere with both individual freedom and efficiency. In relation to social, labor, and environmental standards, the implication is that private enterprise can, to some extent, regulate itself through corporate self-regulation and voluntary initiatives, and that it will do so largely in response to a variety of market and societal signals, given its innate capacity to innovate.

Stakeholder and governance theory suggests that modern business should no longer be preoccupied exclusively with the interests of shareholders and relations with the state and trade unions, but must respond to the concerns of multiple stakeholders, including NGOs, consumers, environmentalists, and local communities. According to this perspective, we live in a globalizing world that is now more interdependent, complex, and risky. Knowledge and power are dispersed among multiple actors, including CSOs and networks. Such trends and contexts suggest that decision making needs to engage multiple stakeholders, actors, and interests (Freeman 1984). Corporate responsibility should not be simply a reactive response to confrontational activism and command-and-control regulation. Business can be proactive and work in partnership with CSOs, government, and multilateral institutions.

Furthermore, modern institutions, including corporations, have the capacity to reflect critically on their role and performance, engage in organizational or social learning, and reform themselves. In today's world a successful business must be able to adapt to rapidly changing circumstances. Interaction and dialogue with stakeholders constitute crucial mechanisms for learning and adaptation. From the perspective of both good governance and good management, business-NGO collaboration and public-private partnerships (PPPs) are, therefore, important (Zadek 2001). Indeed, there is a strong body of theoretical opinion and historical analysis that suggests that such forms of interaction, based on dialogue and networking, are fundamental for regulatory reform (Braithwaite and Drahos 2000).

These approaches are reinforced by theoretical positions, currently in vogue, that emphasize the role of institutions—or formal and informal rules of the game. Drawing on the writings of Karl Polanyi (1944), various proponents of CSR, voluntary approaches, and partnerships stress the importance of "embedded liberalism" (Ruggie 2001), the notion that if capitalism and economic liberalization are to have a human face and deliver socially inclusive development, and if the stability of the system is to be maintained, then markets need to be regulated by institutions that limit the concentration and abuse of economic power. Voluntary initiatives and partnerships are seen as an important element in this broader strategy. New institutional economics (NIE) has revived interest not only in the role of regulatory institutions but also in the role of the firm as an administrative organization (as opposed to a purely economic actor) that must take steps to reduce both production costs and transaction costs (Toye 1995). Various CSR initiatives that are conducive to stability, predictability, and risk management, and that provide information about suppliers and other stakeholders, are relevant in this regard.

EMERGING TRENDS AND FUTURE CHALLENGES

How are these dual CSR movements likely to evolve? Which actors and coalitions will dominate the agenda of regulatory change associated with social and environmental conditions and labor and other human rights?

To answer these questions it is important to refer to two recent developments in both civil society and corporate activism. The first involves a degree of convergence in business and civil society approaches to development and regulation, and the strengthening of multistakeholder initiatives or co-regulation. The second involves new forms of civil society activism centered on corporate accountability.

Convergence and Co-regulation

The emerging forms of NGO-business collaboration referred to in the previous section have been consolidated and institutionalized since the turn of the millennium. This is apparent in several respects. First, the trend of NGOs becoming active players in the CSR industry through various forms of service provision and commodified activities has intensified, to such an extent that the distinctions between civil society and business, NGOs and companies, or "not for profit" and "for profit" are becoming increasingly blurred (Deacon 2003; Stubbs 2003). This convergence of functional roles is evident in the case of NGOs and small firms that provide technical assistance, research, auditing, and other CSR services. A more structural shift may also be occurring as some NGOs or activists constitute themselves as companies.[6]

Second, a new set of regulatory institutions has emerged, involving so-called multistakeholder initiatives or nongovernmental systems of regulation (O'Rourke 2002). As the limits of codes of conduct and other CSR initiatives associated with corporate self-regulation became apparent, some TNCs, large Northern retailers, and CSOs recognized the role that various forms of co-regulation and collaboration could play in ratcheting up standards and strengthening their implementation, as well as enhancing the credibility of voluntary initiatives. These new institutions also reflect a convergence of views on state-market relations, global governance, and development strategies, which recognize that globalization and economic liberalization are here to stay but require new institutions or reforms to deal with the societal and environmental downside.

Co-regulation involves companies and CSOs and/or governmental and international agencies coming together to promote standard setting, monitoring, reporting, auditing, certification, stakeholder dialogues, and best practice learning. Several such initiatives have emerged in recent years. They include, for example, AA1000, the Ethical Trading Initiative (ETI), the Fair Labor Association, the Forest Stewardship

Council, the Global Alliance for Workers and Communities the Global Reporting Initiative, the Marine Stewardship Council, the United Nations Global Compact, global framework agreements, and certification schemes such as ISO 14001 and SA8000.

Owing to the recent origin of these initiatives it is difficult to assess their impact. By focusing attention on issues such as labor and other human rights, external monitoring, measurement of social and environmental improvements, and the responsibilities of suppliers, they have attempted to address some of the weaknesses that characterized codes of conduct and company self-regulation related to CSR. Some have also revived the notion that international labor, environmental, and human rights law applies not only to states but also to TNCs, and have opened up new opportunities and channels for exerting influence on companies. As a result, nongovernmental systems of regulation and multistakeholder initiatives are often seen as innovative institutional arrangements that go some way toward filling the regulatory deficit associated with globalization (O'Rourke 2002; UNRISD 2004a). There are, however, various concerns with both convergence and some co-regulatory institutions.

Closer relations between NGOs and big business, and the commodification of activism, imply risks associated with so-called regulatory capture, co-optation, and the dilution of radical or alternative agendas. A growing number of NGOs that form part of the new CSR industry are being drawn into both the financial circuits and the corporate culture of TNCs. The distance between this sector of civil society and the corporate world is narrowing not only in terms of its direct relationship but also in relation to perspectives on the market, development, and strategies for reform. The increasing engagement of NGOs in service delivery and best practice learning is sometimes associated with a decline in confrontational activism and advocacy for radical alternatives, as well as with analysis that shuns hard-core criticism and ignores structural issues. An influential discourse has emerged that suggests that confrontation, single-issue activism, and criticism that profiles specific problems rather than solutions is ideological or passé, and that NGO collaboration with business and engagement with the market is modern and savvy (SustainAbility 2003). The tensions associated with these trends and perceptions, in relation to both the substance of institutional reform and the forces that drive change, need to be examined carefully. It is important to avoid a situation in which the so-called modernization of activism homogenizes tactical engagement with TNCs and undermines the very forms of activism that were crucial in launching the contemporary CSR agenda in the first place.

Compared to the early experience of CSR, which centered heavily on corporate self-regulation, the new trends in convergence and co-regulation have, to some extent, raised the normative bar. Several multi-stakeholder initiatives, however, remain firmly wedded to the idea of voluntary approaches and tend to sideline the role of legalistic forms of regulation. As discussed in the following sections, some also ignore fundamental issues regarding the corporate irresponsibility and ways in which TNCs perpetuate underdevelopment through their core business practices and lobbying activities.

Some of the new multistakeholder initiatives are—or are perceived to be—excessively close to business as a result of funding ties and the degree of corporate influence exerted through governance structures. Certain initiatives have not integrated important stakeholders, such as trade unions, and have failed to engage Southern interests effectively. Important questions arise, therefore, regarding their credibility and legitimacy.

In addition to these governance and political questions, there are also more technical concerns. The early experience with the new set of nongovernmental or multistakeholder initiatives has highlighted serious questions about the possibility of scaling them up in a meaningful manner. Monitoring, reporting, auditing, and certification procedures can be extremely complex and quite costly, and the methods employed fairly superficial. Some that are more rigorous tend to involve very few companies, and those that involve more companies are often criticized for their inability to significantly improve corporate social and environmental performance (Utting 2002b).

From Corporate Responsibility to Corporate Accountability

As some sectors of civil society and business converge, we also see the rekindling of confrontational activism under the banner of "anti-" or "alternative" globalization. This, of course, is an umbrella movement—sometimes called "the movement of movements"—encompassing a disparate array of organizations, networks, and movements concerned with social, environmental, and human rights issues, which have emerged or come under the spotlight in the current era of globalization. A key concern is that globalization and contemporary patterns of economic development are primarily benefiting large corporations, in particular TNCs and finance capital, and that public policy is both serving corporate interests and being excessively influenced by them. Such concerns have spurred calls for stronger regulation of big business as well as for more profound changes to investment, trade, production, and consumption patterns. Some of these demands have been articulated by a subset of the alternative globalization movement, which has been called the "corporate accountability movement" (Broad and Cavanagh 1999; Newell 2002; Bendell 2004). Organizations and groups associated with this movement are critical of the mainstream CSR agenda for various reasons.

First, CSR allows ample scope for free-riding (whereby economic agents benefit from a particular initiative without bearing the costs) and greenwash (Greer and Bruno 1996), which is the ability of companies, through PR and minimal adjustments to policy and practice, to project an image of reform while changing little, if anything, in terms of actual corporate performance. The capacity of big business to modify its discourse is often considerably greater than its capacity to improve its social and environmental impacts. Many instances have been documented of companies saying one thing and doing another, or adopting but not effectively implementing environmental policies or codes of conduct. Hence corporate responsibility policy and practice is often characterized by piecemeal and fragmented reforms and window dressing. Furthermore, the mainstream discourse on CSR often gives the impression that the corporate sector in general is seriously engaged. The reality is very different. For example, of the world's 65,000 TNCs, an estimated 4000 companies produce reports dealing with a company's social and/or environmental performance (Holliday et al. 2002), and probably fewer have codes of conduct. Although there are nearly one million affiliates of TNCs and several million enterprises that make up TNC supply chains, only approximately 50,000 facilities had their environmental management systems certified under ISO 14001 by the end of 2002. More recently established schemes such as the Global Reporting Initiative, SA8000, and the Fair Labor Association reported 366, 1266, and 353 certified or affiliated companies, respectively, by the end of 2003 (ISO 2003; UNRISD 2004b).

Second, reforms in corporate policies often take place in a context of double standards or countertrends. These involve, for example, worsening labor standards and conditions in TNC supply chains, which are often associated with outsourcing and labor market liberalization; and increases in absolute levels of pollution, waste, and use of nonrenewable natural resources. They also involve tax avoidance and evasion, and corporate lobbying to resist social and environmental regulation or to promote macroeconomic policies that can have regressive social and environmental impacts. Reported examples of the latter include Monsanto's influence on the international debate and policy on GMOs; the tobacco industry's attempt to influence WHO and governments; the resistance of pharmaceutical companies to attempts to promote cheaper generic drugs; the ICC's lobbying against international regulation of TNCs; the efforts of the European oil industry body, Europia, to weaken EU attempts to tighten emission standards for petrol and diesel; and corporate involvement in the Global Climate Coalition's attempts to weaken international regulatory proposals to deal with global warming.

A third major criticism of CSR relates to so-called regulatory or institutional capture, that is, the increasing penetration and influence of large corporations in the public-policy process through PPPs, formal and informal consultation and dialogue, secondment, and other mechanisms. These concerns have arisen, for example, in relation to the UN summits and the recent wave of PPPs, notably those involving UN agencies and TNCs or corporate foundations (Richter 2001). Such partnerships involve a difficult balancing act, which is prone to mishap. Initiatives such as the Global Compact, for example, and various forms of corporate collaboration with UNICEF, have provoked reaction from civil society and other quarters because of the involvement of companies such as Abbott, Coca-Cola, McDonald's, Nestlé, and Nike that are associated with international concerns about nutritional health and/or labor rights. This reaction is heightened when TNCs and business organizations use their voluntary association with the UN as a tool for resisting attempts by other parts of the UN to consider other regulatory approaches. This happened recently with the attempt of the UN Sub-Commission on the Promotion and Protection of Human Rights to draft a comprehensive set of human rights norms for TNCs and related enterprises, as well as with the WHO's efforts to promote multistakeholder approaches to reduce the risks to consumer health associated with some of the products of large food and beverage corporations.

Fourth, the CSR agenda, based as it is largely on voluntary approaches and a critique of government regulation, is often perceived as an alternative to law. A series of recent proposals attempt to construct a post-voluntarist agenda in which CSR is articulated with (a) complaints procedures associated with a variety of regulatory institutions (Utting 2002b), and (b) either soft or hard law that lays down obligations, international standards, rewards, and penalties in relation to corporate transparency, accountability, and performance (Kamminga and Zia-Zarifi 2000; ICHRP 2001; Ward 2003).

The corporate accountability movement is post-voluntarist in two respects: in the sense that it goes beyond voluntary approaches by demanding a new articulation of voluntary initiatives and law; and in the sense that it recognizes that if CSR is to be meaningful it needs to be articulated with structural change and cannot rely exclusively on individual effort or agency. The CSR agenda needs to address the structural and policy determinants of underdevelopment, and the relationship of TNCs to those determinants.

A significant development has been the increasing number of concrete proposals and campaigns associated with corporate accountability, legalistic approaches, and international oversight. They include the following:

- Friends of the Earth International proposed that the World Summit on Sustainable Development consider a Corporate Accountability Convention that would establish and enforce minimum environmental and social standards, encourage effective reporting, and provide incentives for TNCs taking steps to avoid negative impacts.
- Several trade unions and NGOs in the United States have launched the International Right to Know campaign to demand legislation that would oblige U.S. companies or foreign companies traded on the U.S. stock exchanges to disclose information on the operations of their overseas affiliates and major contractors.
- The International Forum on Globalization has advocated the creation of a UN Organization for Corporate Accountability that would provide information on corporate practices as a basis for legal actions and consumer boycotts. Christian Aid has proposed the establishment of a Global Regulation Authority that would establish norms for TNC conduct, monitor compliance, and deal with breaches. Others have called for the reactivation of the defunct United Nations Centre on Transnational Corporations, some of whose activities were transferred to the United Nations Conference on Trade and Development (UNCTAD) a decade ago.
- In 1999, the European Parliament passed a resolution requesting the establishment of an EU corporate code of conduct and an implementation procedure. A large network of trade unions and NGOs that make up the Clean Clothes Campaign have been lobbying for such a mechanism, which would regulate the activities of European TNCs in developing countries.

- In 2003, the United Nations Sub-Commission on the Promotion and Protection of Human Rights adopted the Norms on the Responsibilities of Transnational Corporations and Other Business Enterprises with Regard to Human Rights, which included a provision for monitoring.
- Proposals to extend international legal obligations to TNCs in the field of human rights and to bring corporations under the jurisdiction of the International Criminal Court have been promoted by several NGOs.
- For many years trade unions and others have urged the ILO to strengthen its follow-up activities and procedures for examining disputes related to the Tripartite Declaration of Principles concerning Multinational Enterprises and Social Policy. In 2000, the OECD strengthened its Guidelines on Multinational Enterprises and national complaints procedures.
- In 2002, a coalition of CSOs and the financier George Soros launched the Publish What You Pay Campaign, which calls for a regulatory approach to ensure that extractive companies in the oil and mining industries disclose the net amount of payments made to national governments.
- In 2003, the Tax Justice Network was formed to address trends in global taxation that have negative development impacts, notably tax evasion and avoidance though transfer pricing and offshore tax havens, and tax competition between states that reduces their ability to tax the major beneficiaries of globalization.

The notion of corporate accountability, then, is quite different from CSR in various respects. Rather than placing the emphasis on moral compulsion, by saying TNCs should assume responsibility for their actions, it suggests that they have to answer to their stakeholders and be held to account through some element of punishment or sanction (Newell 2001; Bendell 2004). The rights and freedoms of companies must be balanced not just by responsibilities and voluntary initiatives but also by obligations.

Whereas standard-setting and other regulatory action associated with CSR are often undertaken by self-appointed entities whose accountability to external agents may be very limited or nonexistent, corporate accountability highlights issues of legitimacy and governance, including the question of who decides and who speaks for whom.

Rather than seeing corporate self-regulation and voluntary approaches as a superior alternative to governmental and international regulation, the corporate accountability agenda suggests a rearticulation of voluntary and legal approaches. It also focuses more attention on complaints procedures or complaints-based systems of regulation that facilitate the task of identifying, investigating, publicizing, and seeking redress for specific instances of corporate malpractice, as a complementary approach to regulatory systems that involve broad but relatively superficial systems of reporting, monitoring, auditing, and certification.

Finally, corporate accountability suggests that if CSR is to be meaningful and really work for development, then it is not enough for companies to improve selected aspects of working conditions or environmental management systems and engage in community projects and corporate giving. The corporate responsibility agenda cannot be separated from structural and macro-policy issues, such as perverse patterns of labor market flexibilization and subcontracting; corporate taxation and pricing practices that have negative developmental impacts; corporate power, size, and competitive advantage over SMEs and infant industries; and the political influence of TNCs and business lobbies.

ACKNOWLEDGMENTS

Thanks are extended to Kate Ives, Désirée Abrahams, and Anita Tombez at UNRISD for research assistance and editorial support.

NOTES

[1] The term "civil regulation" suggests a third arena of regulatory action, which is distinguished from corporate self-regulation and legalistic forms of government and international regulation (Murphy and Bendell 1999).

[2] In practice, many of the organizations mentioned as examples in this section engage simultaneously in several types of activism, combining, for example, watchdog activities with public education and advocacy, or critical research with collaborative forms of dialogue and training.

[3] This list of CSOs does not include so-called business-interest NGOs that are more directly associated with corporate interests, whether ideologically, financially, or through their governance structures. Nor does it include research and academic organizations associated with institutions of higher education, which may also engage in a range of CSR-related activities. It should also be

noted that some organizations that are often associated with NGOs or civil society are, in fact, legally constituted as companies—SustainAbility and Covalence, for example.

4 Greenpeace is legally constituted as a company.

5 Global framework agreements, negotiated between an international trade union organization and a TNC, establish a set of standards related to labor relations and working conditions that the TNC agrees to implement throughout its global structure.

6 Various reasons may account for this, including, for example, involvement in ethical trading activities, the desire to generate profits that can be used partly to support causes considered to be good, and the need to acquire legal and financial safeguards associated with limited liability.

REFERENCES

Ascoly, N., J. Oldenziel, and I. Zeldenrust. 2001. *Overview of Recent Developments on Monitoring and Verification in the Garment and Sportswear Industry in Europe*. Amsterdam: SOMO.

Bendell, J. 2004. *Barricades and Boardrooms: A Contemporary History of the Corporate Accountability Movement*. Programme Paper (TBS) No. 13. Geneva: UNRISD.

Bendell, J., and D. Murphy. 2002. "Towards Civil Regulation: NGOs and the Politics of Corporate Environmentalism." In P. Utting (ed.), *The Greening of Business in Developing Countries: Rhetoric, Reality and Prospects*. London: Zed Books.

Braithwaite, J., and P. Drahos. 2000. *Global Business Regulation*. Cambridge: Cambridge University Press.

Broad, R., and J. Cavanagh. 1999. "The Corporate Accountability Movement: Lessons and Opportunities." *Fletcher Forum of World Affairs* 23(2):151–169.

Chang, H. J. 2001. *Breaking the Mould: An Institutionalist Political Economy Alternative to Neoliberal Theory of the Market and the State*. Program Paper (SPD) No. 6. Geneva: UNRISD.

Deacon, B. 2003. *Global Governance Reform*. Globalism and Social Policy Programme (GASPP) Policy Brief No. 1. Sheffield: University of Sheffield.

Freeman, R. 1984. *Strategic Management: A Stakeholder Approach*. Boston, MA: Pitman.

Gallin, D. 2000. *Trade Unions and NGOs: A Necessary Partnership for Social Development*. Programme Paper (CSSM). Geneva: UNRISD.

Greer, J., and K. Bruno. 1996. *Greenwash: The Reality behind Corporate Environmentalism*. Penang, Malaysia: Third World Network.

Hansen, M. 2002. "Environmental Regulation of Transnational Corporations: Needs and Prospects." in P. Utting (ed.), *The Greening of Business in Developing Countries: Rhetoric, Reality and Prospects*. London: Zed Books.

Held, D. 2003. "From Executive to Cosmopolitan Multilateralism." In D. Held and D. Koenig-Archibugi (eds.), *Taming Globalization: Frontiers of Governance*. Cambridge: Polity Press.

Holliday, C., S. Schmidheiny, and P. Watts. 2002. *Walking the Talk: The Business Case for Sustainable Development*. Sheffield, UK: Greenleaf.

ICHRP. 2001. *Business Wrongs and Rights: Human Rights and the Developing Legal Obligations of Companies*. Geneva: International Council on Human Rights Policy.

ISO. 2003. *The ISO Survey of ISO 9000 and ISO 14001 Certificates. Twelfth Cycle*. Geneva: International Organization for Standardization.

Kamminga, M., and S. Zia-Zarifi (eds.). 2000. *Liability of Multinational Corporations under International Law*. The Hague: Kluwer Law International.

Levy, D. 1997. "Environmental Management as Political Sustainability. *Organization & Environment* 10(2):126–147.

Murphy, D., and J. Bendell. 1999. *Partners in Time? Business, NGOs and Sustainable Development*. Discussion Paper No. 109. Geneva: UNRISD.

Newell, P. 2001. "Managing Multinationals: The Governance of Investment for the Environment." *Journal of International Development* 13(7):907–919.

Newell, P. 2002. "From Responsibility to Citizenship: Corporate Accountability for Development." *IDS Bulletin* 33(2):91–100.

O'Rourke, D. 2002. "Outsourcing Regulation: Analyzing Non-governmental Systems of Labor Standards and Monitoring." *Policy Studies Journal* 31(1):1–29.

Polanyi, K. 1944. *The Great Transformation: The Political and Economic Origins of Our Time*. Boston, MA: Beacon Press.

Porter, M., and C. van der Linde. 1995. "Green and Competitive: Ending the Stalemate." *Harvard Business Review* (September–October):120–134.

Richter, J. 2001. *Holding Corporations Accountable: Corporate Conduct, International Codes, and Citizen Action*. London: Zed Books.

Ruggie, J. 2001. "global_governance.net: The Global Compact as a Learning Network." *Global Governance* 7(4):371–378.

Schmidheiny, S., R. Chase, and L. DeSimone. 1997. *Signals of Change: Business Progress towards Sustainable Development*. Geneva: WBCSD.

Stubbs, P. 2003. *International Non-state Actors and Social Development Policy*. Globalism and Social Policy Programme (GASPP) Policy Brief No. 4. Sheffield, UK: University of Sheffield.

SustainAbility. 2003. *The 21st Century NGO: In the Market for Change*. London: SustainAbility.

Toye, J. 1995. "The New Institutional Economics and Its Implications for Development Theory." In J. Harris, J. Hunter, and C. M. Lewis (eds.), *The New Institutional Economics and Third World Development*. London: Routledge.

UNRISD. 1995. *States of Disarray: The Social Effects of Globalization*. Geneva: UNRISD.

UNRISD. 2000. *Visible Hands: Taking Responsibility for Social Development*. Geneva: UNRISD.

UNRISD. 2004a. "Corporate Social Responsibility and Development: Towards a New Agenda?" *Conference News*, Geneva: UNRISD.

UNRISD. 2004b. *Corporate Social Responsibility and Business Regulation.* Research and Policy Brief No. 1. Geneva: UNRISD.

Utting P. 2000. *Business Responsibility for Sustainable Development.* Occasional Paper OPG2. Geneva: UNRISD.

Utting, P. (ed.). 2002a. *The Greening of Business in Developing Countries: Rhetoric, Reality and Prospects.* London: Zed Books.

Utting, P. 2002b. "Regulating Business via Multistakeholder Initiatives: A Preliminary Assessment." In NGLS/UNRISD (eds.), *Voluntary Approaches to Corporate Responsibility: Readings and Resource Guide.* Geneva: NGLS.

Ward H. 2001. *Governing Multinationals: The Role of Foreign Direct Liability.* Briefing Paper No. 18. London: Royal Institute for International Affairs.

Ward, H. 2003. *Legal Issues in Corporate Citizenship.* Stockholm and London: Swedish Partnership for Global Responsibility and IIED.

Zadek, S. 2001. *The Civil Corporation: The New Economy of Corporate Citizenship.* London: Earthscan.

FOUR

Corporate Accountability to the Poor?

Assessing the Effectiveness of Community-Based Strategies

NIAMH GARVEY AND PETER NEWELL

INTRODUCTION

This chapter seeks to identify the conditions under which community-based strategies for corporate accountability (CA) appear to be effective in engendering a greater element of accountability on the part of corporations to communities in which they invest regarding the social and environmental impacts of their investments. In this context, "effectiveness" will be taken to mean whether the mechanisms of accountability are successful in (a) improving the *responsiveness* of corporations to community demands, gauged in terms of a change in practice as opposed to rhetorical shifts; and (b) increasing the *representation* of previously marginalized groups through increasing their *accessibility* to or *inclusion* in decisions affecting their lives. This discussion contributes to debates about the role of the private sector in development and more generally to contemporary concerns with corporate social—and environmental—responsibility (CSR). We argue, however, that the mainstream CSR discourse pays insufficient attention to the politics of corporate accountability and the influence of power on how mechanisms of accountability and spaces for citizen participation in CSR initiatives work in practice.

Our study focuses on the ways in which people resist corporate misconduct as opposed to the many cases of "best practice" that are well covered in the literature on CSR and highlighted in policy initiatives such as Business Partners for Development (Long and Arnold 1995; Schmidheiny 1992; BPD 2001). It also draws on many examples that predate the contemporary Western-oriented framing of the CSR debate. What may be labeled CSR issues today are often a product of many decades of conflict over resources that constitute ongoing historical struggles for corporate and state accountability, and should be understood in this context. We analyze here cases in which communities have attempted to hold corporations accountable for the ways in which their actions impinge upon livelihood issues such as land rights, access to resources, and occupational health and environmental concerns across a range of sectors, including mining, forestry, oil extraction, and waste dumping. This discussion therefore goes beyond the popular, but narrower, framing of CSR as responsible management of environmental outputs and respect for basic labor standards at the workplace. We primarily draw on evidence from 46 case studies, but the broader argument draws upon trends observed in over 80 cases. These are predominantly from Southern settings, but also include examples from poor communities in the North, given that many of the problems faced by communities in holding corporations to account result from poverty and inequality rather than geographical location. Combining lessons from the conceptual framework with analysis of the cases, we argue that a number of state-related, company-related, and community-related factors are key to understanding the effectiveness of community-based strategies for corporate accountability.

Though the relationship between multinational companies and poorer communities in the developing world clearly has a long history, the changing relationship between states, corporations, and communities over the last decade has meant that transnational companies (TNCs) and the poor encounter one another with increasing frequency and intensity. TNCs have increased in size and reach such that approximately 60,000 TNCs and 500,000 foreign affiliates invest more than US$600 billion abroad annually and control two thirds of international trade, making them "central organizers of the emerging global economy" (Hansen 2002: 159). During the 1990s foreign direct investment (FDI) became increasingly important relative to official aid flows to developing countries (see Sumner 2005). As part of this trend, it is the transnationalization of resource extraction in particular that brings TNCs into contact with communities. As Lund-Thomsen (2003: 2) notes:

Encouraged by market- and foreign investment-led philosophies, developing countries have liberalised mining and investment laws as well as rewritten their tax codes to facilitate the participation of TNCs in their mineral economies. Combined with technological advances and favourable metal prices, new regions have been opened for mineral exploration by TNCs. This development has inevitably brought TNCs into conflict with local communities.

Parallel to this, there has been a general shift away from the command-and-control regulatory role of the state that characterized approaches to social and environmental regulation of TNCs throughout the 1970s and 1980s, toward more informal and voluntary structures and corporate self-regulation. Supportive of this move, mainstream multilateral and bilateral donors, as well as a growing number of business associations and NGOs, have increasingly sought to portray TNCs as important partners in delivering sustainable development. DFID, for example, refers to the "key role" corporations play "in making globalization work better for poor people" (DFID 2000: 59). Corporate voluntarism and strategies of partnership, which are at the heart of mainstream CSR approaches, are regarded as win-win, whereby the social and environmental performance of the firm is increased and corporations benefit from increased efficiency, productivity, and enhanced reputation.

In contrast to this laissez-faire approach to business regulation, critics have regarded the growing power of TNCs as a threat to democratic governance in situations where the global mobility and rights that companies have acquired are not matched by systems of regulation to govern their activities. While trade and investment agreements increase the entry and exit rights of TNC investors, critics argue that, in contrast, the social and environmental responsibilities of TNCs are underdeveloped. The mobility that allows companies in some sectors to relocate more easily, playing governments and workers against one another in an effort to secure the best terms, is particularly undermining of the ability of poorer communities to make accountability demands of such companies. This is in addition, of course, to broader substantive differences in power assets and capabilities between corporations and communities. Corporations secure access to decision making and privilege through their tax contribution to state resources, and to economic development more generally by providing employment, but the communities in which many TNCs invest are often far removed from the centers of political power as well as being economically marginalized.

Given the growing emphasis among official donors on the positive role of corporations in delivering sustainable development, it is important to understand the nature of accountability relations between companies and communities in settings that are more familiar to the majority of the world's people than are the situations of partnership and engagement that are emphasized in mainstream CSR literature.

FROM RESPONSIBILITY TO ACCOUNTABILITY

Various terms have emerged to express the rights and obligations of corporations. "Corporate governance" refers to policies and practices used to regulate internal relationships and fulfill responsibilities to investors and other stakeholders. "Corporate accountability" often refers, in a managerial sense, to issues of disclosure, auditing, and monitoring of business practices. "Corporate social responsibility" implies a more discretionary act on the part of companies as they consider their role and impact across a wide range of corporate activities. Lastly, "corporate citizenship" positions corporations as "citizens" with claims to the entitlements that flow from citizenship (Newell 2002). Unlike understandings of CA as management practice, we are more concerned here with the political content of accountability relationships. This more political interpretation of accountability chimes with traditional preoccupations about "how to keep power under control, . . . how to prevent its abuse, how to subject it to certain procedures and rules of conduct" (Schedler 1999: 13). Central to this definition of accountability are the concepts of answerability, an obligation to provide an account of one's actions and inactions; and enforceability, namely mechanisms for realizing that obligation and sanctioning its nonfulfillment where necessary (Schedler 1999).

Understanding accountability in these terms, it becomes possible to see that even though there has been an increase in answerability as increasing numbers of firms feel obliged to validate their actions to wide circles of stakeholders and those affected by their activities, mechanisms of meaningful answerability are often weak and underdeveloped (Newell 2003). From this perspective, mainstream CSR approaches have a number of limitations. First, many of the debates on CSR focus on initiatives such as voluntary codes of conduct and standards, and public-private partnerships (PPPs). Relatively little attention is focused on the strategies that communities themselves undertake to demand CA. The focus is on voluntarism from above rather than rights from below.

Second, although the existing literature helps to identify some of the pressures driving companies' answerability to communities, there is insufficient emphasis on how the importance of these factors may vary according to sectoral, political, and cultural contexts. For example, the vulnerability of different companies to these pressures varies according to which markets companies are producing for and, in turn, whether concerned customers in those markets have sufficient purchasing power to bring about a change in company behavior.

A third problem is that the emphasis on partnership and negotiation is apolitical, and thereby lacks a theory of power. For example, the World Bank describes how "communities take their place at the negotiating table along with regulators and factory managers" (World Bank 2000: 3), without any discussion of the range of challenges that communities may face in securing access for their place and being able to realize the advantages it confers. Power dynamics continue to be important even once a supposedly equal place at the table has been negotiated. A focus on negotiation, joint agenda setting, and partnership suggests that all agendas can be accommodated, something that assumes a position of leverage, as well as the capacity and confidence to participate effectively, on behalf of the community. It also overlooks the strategies that can be employed by the powerful to control the agenda and frame the issues in ways that deny spaces for opposition. As Peter Utting acknowledges, CSR "is not simply a technical issue of know-how, resource availability, 'win-win' situations or even greater environmental awareness on the part of key decision makers," but rather it is a political process "involving power struggles between different actors and stakeholders" (Utting 2002a: 277).

Our analysis starts from the assumption that struggles for CA are essentially contests of power between actors with competing agendas and very different capabilities, and seeks to understand the conditions under which community-based strategies are effective. To assess this, we consider the extent to which different strategies promote corporate responsiveness from above, and the extent to which changes from below facilitate greater representation of previously excluded citizens through increasing access and inclusion in decisions affecting their lives. It is therefore not just change in company behavior to accommodate citizens' demands that is significant, but changes in structures of representation that may allow for the expression of future accountability demands. We locate our analysis of the relationship between companies and communities within a broader web of accountability relationships, which also involve states, NGOs, and international institutions, often pulling in competing directions. CA to the poor may therefore be influenced by the degree to which community interests conflate or conflict with the interests of other actors within these accountability webs. The following section analyzes community-based strategies for CA drawn from 46 case studies, in order to demonstrate how factors relating to governments, companies, and communities influence the effectiveness of those strategies.

STATE-RELATED FACTORS

A number of state-related factors are key to the effectiveness of community-based strategies for CA. Government policies and legal frameworks protect and promote the relative rights and responsibilities of companies and communities. A government's willingness and ability to implement sanctions influence the extent to which these are realized in practice. Although it is acknowledged that citizen strategies aimed at changing a corporation's behavior are often a response to the ineffectiveness of the state in ensuring implementation of regulations regarding corporate activity (World Bank 2000), states also directly influence the effectiveness of community-based strategies.

Their control over resources means that states often determine the access of a corporation or community to the resources over which accountability struggles are commonly fought. Their regulatory role affords governments influence over the levels of downward accountability required of companies. In a basic sense, states can provide both incentives and disincentives to CSR actions by establishing legal requirements and investment conditions for companies that operate in their jurisdiction. Laws can require company disclosure of information on social and environmental performance to investors as well as determine levels of protection for workers and also set acceptable standards of environmental pollution.

Drawing on factors that have emerged from analysis of the case studies, we would argue that five state-related factors are key to understanding the effectiveness of community-based strategies for CA:

- The nature of the state-corporation relationship
- The nature of the state-community relationship
- State vulnerability to pressures from international groups

- The availability of information and transparency
- The legal framework and its enforcement and accessibility

These factors affect strategies in different ways, and all are essential to understanding why some strategies may be adopted by certain communities and not others, and why they may be successful in some contexts and not in others.

The relationship between states and corporations takes on different forms in different parts of the world and is subject to change in a context of globalization. On the one hand, states have the formal power to regulate corporate activities and to implement sanctions against non-compliance. Pratt and Fintel (2002) also found that government fiscal and financial policies influenced CSR in practice in Costa Rica and El Salvador. They argue that in these contexts government policies undermined CSR through subsidizing and endorsing the unsustainable use of natural resources, just as a lack of human and financial resources may also undermine the capacities of governments actively to enforce laws regarding corporate disclosure, for example (Utting 2002a: 268). Conversely, Hanks (2002) found that in South Africa the threat of punitive state actions, the political independence of relevant state authorities, and the provision of high-quality information flows promoted greater CSR. Often, however, these conditions are lacking. In order to attract FDI, governments frequently offer a range of concessions to business. These may run counter to citizens' demands for "responsible" investment. The economic crisis in Kenya, for example, led the government to side with Tiomin Inc., a Canadian mining company seeking to acquire surface rights in order to establish strip mining for titanium in Kwale in the south of the country. In order to attract investment, the Kenyan government offered substantial incentives to business, which limited the potential benefits accruing to the community (Ojiambo 2002: 8). In this way the government helped to generate opposition to the investment, which focused not on opposing the mine as such but on a campaign to "ensure responsible investment that does not lead to environmental degradation and that upholds community rights" (Ojiambo 2002: 14).

In some cases, state support of corporations depends not so much on this attempt to balance national development goals with local interests, but rather stems from the direct financial benefit accruing to government officials. The huge rents that Nigerian military governments have received over a number of decades from Shell's operations in the Niger Delta, for example, served to strengthen government resolve to silence local activists campaigning against the environmental and social impacts of oil extraction (Okonta and Douglas 2001). In Indonesia, the links between local officials and logging companies led to the granting of many illegal logging permits for companies to undertake commercial logging in the protected Biosphere reserve of Siberut Island, despite the opposition of local Mentawai communities (DTE 2001).

Once concessions have been granted, governments are often reluctant to countenance claims of negligence raised by communities in which a company invests. Particularly when a region is dependent upon a particular industry, there are added incentives not to jeopardize investment and risk the wider ramifications that doing so may have in terms of discouraging other potential investors. Ecuador's dependence on oil revenues for approximately 40–50 percent of export income led the government to oppose legal action by communities against the oil company Texaco in 1993. The government presented a diplomatic protest to the US government in an attempt to stop the legal case against Texaco being held there, fearing that it would discourage future foreign investment in Ecuador, even after the company had left (Kimmerling 1996).

Moreover, even when states are willing to use sanctions, they may be unable to implement them against more powerful TNCs. In January 1999, the US-based Delta & Pine Land Company ignored a Paraguayan court order to remove 660 tons of cottonseed that it had dumped in the rural community of Rincóni in November 1998. The seeds had been treated with toxic compounds, and adequate precautions had not been taken by the company in the handling of the materials, in the protection of the subsoil, or in the protection of community inhabitants. Medical testing found a number of cases of acute pesticide poisoning among residents. The state was unable to enforce a legal ruling against the company (Greenpeace International 2002: 60). But in July 2004, the courts ruled in favor of the Rincóni farmers and against a senior agricultural engineer held directly responsible for the dumping (Amorín and Iglesias 2004).

Relations between a state and community are key to determining the level of state protection a community can expect. Communities are more likely to be the victims of industrial pollution, for example, where they are weakly organized and discriminated against in industrial policy. Such discrimination can manifest itself in racialized planning decisions regarding the location of hazardous production sites such as toxic waste facilities and nuclear power plants (McDonald 2002). There is a large body of literature describing this trend as "environmental racism"

(Cole and Foster 2002). In the Californian towns of Kettleman City and Buttonwillow, for instance, decisions favored the siting of incinerators and toxic waste facilities in predominantly Latino areas, rather than in other predominantly white towns in Kings County and Kern County (Cole and Foster 2002). Local community members felt ill-informed about proposed developments, and believed they had been deliberately targeted for industrial development that other, wealthier, communities refused to accept. In such instances, local authorities decide upon sites where residents are least likely to oppose such developments, which a 1984 report for the California Waste Management Board suggested would be "rural communities, poor communities, communities whose residents have low educational levels . . . and whose residents were employed in resource-extractive jobs" (Cole and Foster 2002: 3).

A poor relationship between a community and a government may also manifest itself in the state's refusal to recognize a community's rights. In the case of Timika, West Papua, Indonesia, the state protected the rights of corporations over the local Amungme and Kamoro communities. The mining enterprise Freeport McMoran (major holder Rio Tinto) was granted the de facto role of government as a result of the contract it signed with the Indonesian government in 1966. The contract gave Freeport broad powers over local communities and resources, including the right to take, on a tax-free basis, land, timber, water, and other natural resources, and to resettle indigenous inhabitants with compensation required only for dwellings and permanent improvements. Compensation was not required for the loss of hunting and fishing grounds, water supplies, or damage to livelihoods (Abrash 2001). Having undermined indigenous rights vis-à-vis Freeport, the state also intervened to prevent the communities' attempts to seek justice. The state, for example, used force to prevent a lawyer meeting with local clients in 1996, prevented an indigenous activist from traveling to London to raise awareness at Rio Tinto's AGM, and engaged in the violent repression of demonstrations (Abrash 2001).

Sometimes scrutiny by an international institution of a state's conduct in the areas of human rights, environment, and other social issues can generate pressure to recognize a community's grievances. Equally, however, state dependence upon loans from institutions such as the World Bank and the IMF, whose loan conditionalities require export-led industrialization, often provides incentives to promote industrial expansion at the expense of social and environmental safeguards. Hence, while international pressure achieved some progress in gaining government recognition of traditional land rights of the U'wa people in their decade-long struggle against Occidental Petroleum Corporation (Oxy) in Colombia, these gains are potentially undermined by IMF pressure on the Colombian government to speed up oil production (Izquierdo 2001). Similarly, in Sri Lanka, IMF loan conditionalities that mandate changes in workers' rights, including the replacement of tripartite wage boards with productivity councils and the introduction of a 14-day notice of strike action, threaten to further undermine the campaign by free-trade zone (FTZ) workers to gain government and business recognition of their rights to collective bargaining (Marcus and Dent 2001).

Nevertheless, states have a range of instruments they can use to demand greater transparency and answerability from corporations, including rules regarding disclosure of information and citizens' corresponding rights to information, should the states choose to do so. The level of state commitment to making such data available and the access of poorer groups to the necessary mechanisms may be limited, however, with its concomitant implications for their effectiveness as an accountability tool. Without mechanisms making the provision of information, such as industrial chemical use, compulsory and routine, people may unknowingly "work, live, and play," to borrow a phrase from the environmental justice movement, in hazardous conditions. Without such information, people may not realize that their rights have been violated until harm has already been done. For example, the US government was actively complicit with uranium mining companies in keeping information regarding the significant health risks posed by uranium mining hidden from mine workers in Utah and Arizona from the 1940s to the 1960s. The deliberate suppression of this information prevented the workers and communities from seeking environmental justice from the mining companies that were not implementing safe ventilation procedures. Limited compensation for damages was granted only in the 1990s, after decades of campaigning by Navajo community groups (Brugge et al. 2001).

Again, mechanisms of enforceability are central to ensuring that demands for information are met. According to Greenpeace, many workers and villagers were exposed to mercury as a result of toxic vapor and effluent emissions from the Unilever subsidiary Hindustan Lever Ltd (HLL) mercury thermometer production plant at Kodaikanal in Tamil Nadu over an 18-year period. HLL disputed the claims. In October 2001, it closed down the Kodaikanal factory and transferred its operations to Gujarat. The company had previously refused to give ex-workers their health records and opposed the undertaking of an independent health or environmental survey. Such information is necessary in order for the community to consider whether it can obtain any remedy for the health and environmental damage caused by mercury pollution in the area (Greenpeace International 2002: 49–50).[1] A lack of transparency about the decision-making process, and who is responsible for what, can further undermine attempts by communities to influence decisions. In Siberut, Indonesia, the Tiop community was not given answers to its question regarding which authorities were responsible for monitoring company activities and withdrawing permits, and why logging permits had been issued at all on the UNESCO-designated "Man and Biosphere" reserve. This lack of transparency facilitated the granting of illegal permits to outside companies posing as small-scale local Mentawaian cooperatives on the island of Siberut (DTE 2001).

In this regard, legal frameworks can provide a vital political mechanism for defining rights and allocating responsibilities that are key to the practice of accountability. They can create an enabling environment for accountability in which laws governing access to key resources, determining economic entitlements, and shaping the rules of participation in public life are clarified and institutionalized. However, legal frameworks do not provide a neutral space, and may favor some to the exclusion of others. Legal frameworks can determine the level of requirements regarding corporate disclosure, the level of consultation in which corporations must engage citizens regarding proposed developments, and the level of recognition accorded to the entitlements of different groups—for example, concerning communal land rights. What remains crucial, however, is how usable and accessible such frameworks and the accompanying procedures are for poorer and marginalized groups.

Native American communities in the US state of Wisconsin successfully used legal treaties and their sovereign status in 1997 to oppose Exxon and Rio Algom's proposed development of a zinc and copper mine near their reserves. They benefited from federal government support for the development of a tribal water regulatory authority, giving them the power to regulate proposed developments affecting their environment. The existence of sovereign rights for tribal peoples provided an essential legal framework for ensuring CA in this instance. Conversely, states have been able to use colonial legislation to override more progressive legal provisions that benefit communities. The Mining Act in Kenya, for example, facilitated the compulsory appropriation of indigenous lands by the government without adequate protection of customary land ownership. The law was successfully invoked despite the existence of newer, more progressive legislation such as the Environmental Management and Co-ordination Act 1999 (EMCA), due to the government's lack of commitment to its full implementation (Ojiambo 2002: 17).

Litigation can provide a state-based channel for redress by communities afflicted by irresponsible investment. In the case of Kettleman City, despite local government support for granting the permit to the company, the fact that legal requirements had not been met allowed citizens to use litigation to prevent this going ahead, on the basis of procedural failures. However, the effectiveness of such strategies varies, and issues of cost, high legal literacy requirements, and intimidation often conspire to exclude poorer citizens from access to legal redress. In addition, the outcomes that are possible through litigation are often narrow and, in and of themselves, ill placed to uphold the rights of communities. Compensation that is reduced to a financial payout does not address livelihood alternatives that have been diminished by an industry's activities. This was the case with the Ok Tedi mining project in Papua New Guinea, for example, where it is claimed that compensation packages failed to take account of the loss of traditional livelihood options such as fishing that had been damaged by the activities of the BHP mining company (Kirsch 1996).

COMPANY-RELATED FACTORS

There are a number of company-related factors that influence the effectiveness of community-based strategies for CA. With regard to corporate-community relations, some of the traditional mechanisms of accountability and participation associated with the state are not applicable, since corporations clearly do not have the same "democratic duty" or means of dealing with conflicting rights-based claims (Newell 2002). Here, we focus on three company-related factors that are important in determining the effectiveness of community-based strategies for CA: (a) the multiple levels at which corporate power operates; (b) the vulnerability of different types of corporations to particular strategies; and (c) a corporation's approach to citizen participation.

First, the financial power of companies can be used to counter a number of sanctions that communities may take against them. Companies can invest considerable sums of money in PR campaigns to defend themselves against negative publicity, fund scientific studies countering claims made against them, and ensure that the company has the best legal advice when faced with litigation. Retaliatory legal action also serves to deter potential plaintiffs from bringing cases in the first place. In the Californian town of Buttonwillow, in Kern County, the company Laidlaw and county-level authorities sued the Buttonwillow residents for legal expenses after the community had already lost a legal challenge against the expansion of the Laidlaw toxic waste dump situated near their town (Cole and Foster 2002). Companies have also made use of SLAPPs (Strategic Lawsuits against Public Participation) to muzzle criticism of their operations. A Filipino doctor who stated in a conference that the possible carcinogenicity of a Hoechst pesticide could not be categorically ruled out was SLAPPed with a legal suit accusing him of "wilfully and falsely stating that Thiodan causes cancer" (Rowell 1996: 280). (The court dismissed the suit.)

The threat of relocation is also used as a bargaining resource by companies who pit communities' employment needs against their demands for improved levels of social and environmental protection. When campaigners in Kenya sought to engage Tiomin in a dialogue on issues including adequate compensation for people with customary land titles, and environmental protection measures, the company responded with threats to pull out of the area altogether (Ojiambo 2002: 33). Capital mobility and the possibility of relocation provides many companies with significant leverage over less mobile labor, contributing to the silencing of accountability demands in the first place or citing political mobilization as an excuse for a company to relocate its operations. For example, Mitsubishi was able to evade international demands for more responsible behavior in its Malaysian plant by shutting this plant down and reopening in China (Karliner 1997). The US-based Allied Signal Seat Belt Company used mobility to its advantage as it transferred its operations between communities in the southern US states and Mexico. According to Gaventa, the company used the threat and reality of plant closings and layoffs "as a tool for 'economic blackmail' and bargaining for labour concessions" (Gaventa 1990).

The use of expert knowledge to deny accountability claims is another tool companies use to resist communities' demands. Resorting to official scientific practices often works in favor of status quo power relations, disempowering poorer groups with lower levels of education, less access to information, and reduced ability to engage with elite terms of debate. This makes it difficult for communities to make a "scientific" case against a corporation to support claims of negligence, especially where the burden of proof rests with an under-resourced and politically marginalized community. In broader contests over the benefits and disadvantages of proposed projects, strategically useful discursive devices are also used to describe the forms of knowledge employed by oppositional groups and the livelihoods upon which they rely as "backward," "undeveloped," and "unproductive." The incentives given to large livestock-raising and timber companies in the Brazilian Amazon, for instance, were justified on the basis that latex extraction and nut harvesting by traditional populations were "backward" economic activities, and failed to use the area sufficiently (Diegus 1998: 58). Corporations construct their activities as intrinsically beneficial to local communities, the economy, and society as a whole, presenting themselves as harbingers of modernization and development. In the corporate presentation, the negative aspects of such developments are seen as unfortunate but necessary trade-offs. Such an attitude was expressed, for example, in the refusal by Golden Star Resources, the holder of 30 percent of the Omai Gold Mine in Guyana, to compensate local residents for the effects of a major cyanide spill on drinking water, livestock, and wildlife. The company claimed that such accidents "are one of the many risks of doing business" (Greenpeace International 2002: 92).

In terms of contesting these claims, it is clear that some companies are more vulnerable to citizen action than others. Whether a company is transnational or nationally based, public or private, and what sector it is based in, all appear to have a bearing on its responsiveness. For example, because of their vulnerability to international scrutiny, TNCs may be more likely than national corporations to respond to community-based strategies. National companies may be protected from sanctions to some degree if they have close ties to the national government. The government of India's commitment to the flagship company NTPC (National Thermal Power Corporation), for example, helps to explain its lack of intervention in conflicts with local communities over claims of livelihood destruction and environmental contamination (Newell 2003). The extent to which a company is an exporter and its overall position within the supply chain also determine its vulnerability to buyer-driven standards of social and environmental protection and, of course, to consumer pressure. Pratt and Fintel (2002) found that leading firms in Costa Rica that were producing for the export market were more likely to have improved some aspect of their environmental policy than those producing for the domestic market. This effect is related to pressures on firms lower down the commodity chains to adopt higher standards in order to export to international markets (Utting 2002b). This is consistent with Vogel's argument that exporters' desire to reach key markets in Europe and North America, for example, serves to drive standards up as these regions require higher levels of social and environmental performance (Vogel 1997).

Where their shareholder base is more diversified and their operations are based in countries that are home to influential NGOs active on environment and development issues, companies are more likely to find their global operations subject to scrutiny. The extent to which firms are based in countries with strong traditions of corporate governance can also be important. Zadek (2001: 30) notes that "[t]he emerging, dominant forms of global corporate citizenship are . . . deeply influenced by Anglo-American (US or UK) practice." Greenpeace claims that Shell Brazil SA responded to demands for it to buy ranches from local people whose land had been contaminated by the company, not as a result of pressure from the local authorities and community, but due to its vulnerability to negative international publicity, including the sending of a critical report about the company to the "FTSE4good" ethical investment index (Greenpeace International 2002: 41). Shareholders and financial backers may exert greater leverage over corporations than do communities themselves, something that explains why campaigners, for example, buy shares and attend AGMs, or lobby shareholders in AGMs (Marinetto 1998). Campaigns likely to be most successful are those targeted against areas of negligible value to the overall operations of the company, playing on the "hassle factor," so that the potential for reduced profits and damaged reputation in other, more important, markets makes the targeted operation a liability (Rodman 1998). Clearly, TNCs are not always vulnerable to these forms of international and consumer pressure. For instance, even though Tiomin Resources Inc. was considered a giant in Kenya, with potential to bring in much-needed FDI, the Canadian government's Mines and Geology department told campaigners against the mine that "Tiomin and titanium does not exist on our radar" (Ojiambo 2002: 26).

The distinct histories and cultures of firms also shape their perceptions of their responsibilities to the communities in which they invest, their view of the importance of community relations for long-term profitability, and their attitude toward community participation. The stance of corporations on these issues ranges from a position of non-engagement to reactive responses to communities' demands for spaces through to more explicit commitments to formal "invited" spaces for community participation. In many of the case studies companies showed little or no willingness to negotiate with the community affected by their investments. For example, PT Inco in Indonesia has shown an indifferent attitude to citizen participation. In 1994, when Inco announced the construction of two new hydro plants at Soroako, there was no public review process, no published environmental or social impact assessment, and no consultation between the company and local people. PT Inco also demonstrated that community relations were not a priority when it canceled a meeting with residents of Soro-ako who were campaigning for the company to honor agreements it had made regarding compensation for lands taken in 1973 (Moody 1999).

In other cases, companies have taken a more proactive approach to engaging communities in negotiations from the outset of a project, often a response to previous negative publicity regarding their activities. In the development of a proposed mine in Evatra, Madagascar, the UK-based mining company Rio Tinto engaged in a multipronged approach to improve its damaged reputation, conducting a thorough environmental impact assessment (EIA) and social report (involving a public consultation), setting up a biodiversity research station, and making much of the research material available in the public domain (Mulligan 1999: 53). How corporations respond to community demands is also, of course, a function of how well mobilized a community is. For instance the Innu and Innuit opponents of proposed mining at Voisey's Bay in Canada were well organized, had previous experience campaigning against low-level flying, and were also in negotiations with the government regarding the legalization of indigenous land rights. Strategies included successfully negotiating with the company that discovered the mineral resources, Diamond Field Resources (DFR), whose president met with Innu representatives (Innes 2001).

COMMUNITY-RELATED FACTORS

Although a lack of financial resources, political marginalization from decision-making processes, and dependence upon industries clearly inhibit communities' ability to hold corporations to account, communities may be able to exercise other forms of power. Beyond microstrategies of resistance, or "weapons of the weak" (Scott 1985), other work draws attention to the importance of a vocal and well-organized civil society to broader strategies of CA. It is argued here that (a) community power-lessness on a number of levels; (b) the diversity of community liveli-hood options; (c) intra-community dynamics; and (d) the nature of the relationship between communities and external actors who claim to represent them all affect both the responsiveness of companies to com-munity strategies and the representation of communities in spaces for citizen participation and in campaigns themselves.

Politically marginalized communities often lack the support of governments, which instead pander to more powerful coalitions and constituencies that may well have an interest in protecting a corpora-tion. In addition, the repeated experience of being left out of decision making, and a lack of skills, confidence, and resources with which to negotiate effectively, often prevent poorer communities from being able to take advantage of spaces for negotiation that do exist. Where corpo-rations have created spaces for participation, weaker sections of the community may be excluded or underrepresented. Barrientos and Orton (1999) show how negotiations between unions and companies over labor codes often fail to involve some of the poorest sections of the workforce that are not adequately represented by the union, such as sea-sonal workers and women. Similarly, according to Mulligan, Rio Tinto's program to engage with the local community in Madagascar did not include people who had no legal title to land (Mulligan 1999), thus excluding the most marginalized groups in the communities affected by the proposed titanium mine. Even where communities secure recognition of their rights, they often lack the power to enforce agreements made with the company. For example, in the case of PT Inco in Soroako, Indonesia, the company failed to honor agreements reached with the community in 1979 (Moody 1999). Although strategies of negotiation may provide effective mechanisms of answerability, a community's lack of power often undermines its ability to secure effective mecha-nisms of enforceability.

We previously noted how a lack of literacy and technical skills can reduce the ability of communities both to engage in meaningful dia-logue with corporations and to challenge them about the impact of their activities. Strategies of worker or barefoot epidemiology have been used to counter this exclusion (Merrifield 1993). Residents of Yellow Creek in the US state of Kentucky suspected that Middlesboro

Tanning Company was polluting a local river, thereby affecting their health. The residents carried out their own health survey, which served to draw public attention to the issue. The survey also provided the community with information it had not had before, providing a potential platform for future campaigning.

Communities often also seek to amplify their power through building alliances with other actors and movements that may be in a better position to exert leverage over a corporation. For example, in their opposition to the Ok Tedi Mine in Papua New Guinea, the Yonggom activists' role in building a network of international allies was pivotal in generating negative international publicity for Broken Hill Proprietary Company Ltd (BHP), which eventually agreed to a substantial out-of-court settlement (Kirsch 1996). It is important, however, not to overlook the extent to which community-based strategies can be effective in challenging corporate power in their own right. For example, the success of the María Elena Cuadra Women's Movement in Nicaragua in helping to secure the passage of a locally developed code of conduct as national law in 1998 was a result of local and national campaigning (Green 1998).

Communities have also sought to reduce their dependency on a corporation by constructing alternative livelihoods. In Forest County, Wisconsin, an alliance among Native American groups from three local reservations managed to generate alternative employment by becoming "one of the biggest employers" in the area. This helped to reduce demand for mining jobs from the wider community, who had originally been potential supporters of the mining development (Grossman and Gedicks 2001). Often, however, generating alternatives is not a realistic option. In Bangladesh, the lack of alternative employment for tannery workers and the competition for even such hazardous jobs meant that the workers had no bargaining position. For this reason, workers in the *Nur Bhai* tannery were initially opposed to attempts by an NGO to initiate dialogue with the company on safety and environmental issues, fearing that the company might close the operation in response to their demands (Asia Foundation, n.d.). Examples given above of companies relocating under pressure to commit resources to higher social and environmental standards suggest that these fears are often justified. To counter this, groups have developed strategies that seek to prevent companies playing workers off each other. One strategy, aimed at forging solidarity between workers in Mexico and in the Appalachian south, has been the organization of study tours so that "women who had lost their jobs in the Appalachian region could visit their counterparts who had gained similar jobs in . . . the *maquiladora* region of Mexico" (Gaventa 1999: 33). Similarly, US and Mexican participants learned about the enormous job losses in Canada that resulted from corporations moving south to the United States to avoid unions and generous social benefits. They noted that "Dialogues among US workers around NAFTA abounded with stories of how, in bargaining sessions, management would often use the threat of moving production to Mexico or elsewhere to bargain down wages and working conditions in the United States" (Cavanagh et al. 2001: 153).

The heterogeneity of communities as nonbounded groups with differing interests and imbued with relations of power has a number of implications for the effectiveness of community-based strategies. Problems relating to industrial pollution, for example, may be experienced differently by different groups within a community. The Lote-Parshuram industrial development in the Indian state of Maharashtra arguably had the most impact upon Dalits and women (Anand n.d.: 17). Lower-caste (Dalit) landless agricultural workers received no compensation for loss of livelihood, whereas landowners did. When men lost fishing and agricultural livelihood options to pollution, unlike many women they had the opportunity to work in the new industries. Conflicting attitudes within a community toward the benefits of industrial development allow corporations to focus on those people willing to cooperate, and to dismiss or ignore more confrontational views. For example, a legal case brought against Tiomin Resources Inc. in Kenya on the grounds of inadequate compensation for lands acquired by the company divided the affected community. Tiomin capitalized on this and began to work with those who were dissatisfied with the legal approach (Ojiambo 2002: 20). Who is willing, and who is able, to take advantage of "invited" spaces for participation in corporate decision making is also dependent upon relations of power within communities. For example, Village Electrical Committees (VECs) set up by the electricity company WESCO in Kerala, India, to engage stakeholders were dominated by men and members of the scheduled castes (Barney et al. 2001).

NGOs and unions can also perform representational functions in these settings, though questions about their own accountability immediately arise. In a number of cases, the involvement of NGOs has served to reduce the responsiveness of corporations to community campaigns. For example, the Western Mining Corporation (WMC) was able to use the fact that a number of external environmental groups, including the Conservation Council and Friends of the Earth, were closely involved with aboriginal opponents of the development of the Olympic Dam mine in South Australia to question the legitimacy of the campaign. The company objected to negotiating with groups on the basis that they were "cronies" of the environmental NGOs, even though the majority of the community representatives favored the NGOs' stance on the mine (Ali 2000: 88). There are also issues of how inclusive NGOs are of different elements of a local population on whose behalf they are bargaining. In Wavecrest, South Africa, opposition to a proposed heavy mineral mine came both from within the affected Xhosa tribes within the area and also from the Wildlife and Environment Society, a national NGO (Hamann 2001). The community position on the mine was divided, so in its campaign against the proposed development— to which community opposition gave credibility and legitimacy— Hamman claims that the NGO presented a misleading image of a community united against the mine (Hamann 2001). Thus, there is a balance to strike between the benefits and risks of NGO involvement in community campaigns.

CONCLUSION

This chapter has demonstrated how a number of interrelated contexts influence the effectiveness of community-based strategies for CA to the poor. These demonstrate both the numerous challenges communities face in holding to account institutions that affect their lives, and the range of innovative strategies that have been employed to confront these challenges. It has been argued that accountability—in terms of answerability and enforceability—is influenced by a number of interrelated factors concerning the state, the company, and the community in question. These factors do not have a hierarchy of relevance, but rather work in conjunction with one another. For example, where there is a lack of state support for community rights, or where the rights of corporations are protected at the expense of their responsibilities, the relationship between the community and the company takes on more importance.

These findings help to support an emerging critical agenda about the prospects and limitations of CSR in the South (Newell 2003; Lund-Thomsen 2003). They also confirm many of the lessons from the accountability literature about the importance of law, horizontal and vertical mechanisms of accountability, and combinations of formal and informal strategies for securing answerability and enforceability (Newell and Bellour 2002). Given the multidirectionality of the webs of accountability we have described, the success of community-based strategies for CA is conditional upon the right combination of contexts and strategies being adopted by other state, civil society, and corporate actors. The factors that influence the effectiveness of CA to the poor are multiple, complex, and tightly interconnected. Community-based strategies are therefore necessarily diverse, multipronged, and contingent upon the particular, context-specific balance between political, economic, and social factors.

This chapter does not, therefore, set out a neat checklist of factors of effectiveness partnered with strategies. Rather, it identifies a series of state-based, company-based, and community-based factors that help to account for the extent to which and the ways in which community-based strategies for CA appear to be effective. This brings to debates on CSR, therefore, a clearer sense of the everyday contexts in which people in a majority of settings worldwide are fighting to secure accountability from investors, with whom they are engaging on an increasing basis. Our findings, based on the "factor framework" we have developed, are merely a starting point for what we hope will be an important and timely research agenda centered on how the poor may seek to develop their own strategies and mechanisms of accountability from the corporations with and for whom they work.

ACKNOWLEDGMENTS

We are grateful to Celestine Nyamu, John Gaventa, Joanna Crichton, and Joanna Wheeler for comments on earlier drafts of this chapter.

NOTE

[1] In October 2004, invoking the "polluter pays" principle, India's Supreme Court Monitoring Committee on Hazardous Waste instructed the Tamil Nadu Pollution Control Board to collect a Rs50-crore (over €8.5 million) fine from HLL as a revolving bank guarantee to undertake clean-up operations in Kodaikanal. HLL was also asked to set up health clinics to assist local residents affected by mercury poisoning (Vackayil 2004).

REFERENCES

Abrash, A. 2001. "The Amungme, Kamoro and Freeport: How Indigenous Papuans Have Resisted the World's Largest Gold and Copper Mine." *Cultural Survival Quarterly* 25(1), available at www.culturalsurvival.org (retrieved 18 January 2005).

Ali, S. H. 2000. "Shades of Green: NGO Coalitions, Mining Companies and the Pursuit of Negotiating Power." In J. Bendell (ed.), *Terms for Endearment*. Sheffield, UK: Greenleaf.

Amorín, Carlos, and Gerardo Iglesias. 2004. "Paraguay: An Unprecedented Legal Victory for Human Rights." Information Services Latin America, 26 July, available at http://isla.igc.org/Features/Globalization/ParaguayEng.html (retrieved 22 October 2004).

Anand, V. (n.d.). "Multi-party Accountability for Environmentally Sustainable Industrial Development: The Challenge of Active Citizenship. Study conducted for PRIA and the Development Research Centre on Citizenship, Participation and Accountability, Brighton, UK: IDS, University of Sussex.

Asia Foundation. "Asia and the Environment in Seven Stories." Available at www.asiafoundation.org/Environments/stories.html (retrieved 8 June 2006).

Barney, I., A. B. Ota, B. Pandey, and R. Puranik. 2001. *Engaging Stakeholders: Lessons from Three Eastern Indian Business Case Studies*. In Focus Report 1. Swansea, UK: International Business Leaders Forum.

Barrientos, S., and L. Orton. 1999. *Gender and Codes of Conduct: A Case Study from Horticulture in South Africa*. London: Christian Aid.

Brugge, D., Benally, T., and Yazzie-Lewis, E. 2001. "Uranium Mining on Navajo Indian Land. *Cultural Survival Quarterly* 25(1), available at www.culturalsurvival.org (retrieved 18 January 2005).

Business Partners for Development (BPD). 2001. "Trisector Partnerships for Managing Social Issues in the Extractive Industries. Las Cristinas Gold Mining Project, Venezuala Health Care Partnership: A Case Study." Available at www.bpd-naturalresources.org/html/focus_las.html# (retrieved 18 January 2005).

Cavanagh, John, Sarah Anderson, and Karen Hansen-Kuhn. 2001. "Cross-Border Organizing around Alternatives to Free Trade: Lessons from the NAFTA/FTAA Experience. In Michael Edwards and John Gaventa (eds.), *Global Citizen Action*. Boulder, CO: Lynne Rienner.

Cole, L. W., and S. R. Foster. 2002. *From the Ground Up: Environmental Racism and the Rise of the Environmental Justice Movement*. New York: New York University Press.

DFID. 2000. "Eliminating World Poverty: Making Globalization Work for the Poor." White Paper. London: DFID.

Diegus, A. C. 1998. "Social Movements and the Remaking of the Commons in the Brazilian Amazon. In M. Goldman (ed.), *Privatizing Nature: Political Struggles for the Global Commons*. London: Pluto Press.

DTE. 2001. "Business as Usual in the Mentawais." *Down to Earth Newsletter* 50, available at http://dte.gn.apc.org/camp.htm (retrieved 18 January 2005).

Gaventa, J. 1990. "From the Mountains to the *Maquiladoras*: A Case Study of Capital Flight and Its Impact on Workers. In J. Gaventa, B. E. Smith, and A. Willingham (eds.), *Communities in Economic Crisis: Appalachia and the South.* Philadelphia: Temple University Press.

Gaventa, J. 1999. "Crossing the Great Divide: Building Links and Learning between NGOs and Community-Based Organisations in North and South." In D. Lewis (ed.), *International Perspectives on Voluntary Action: Reshaping the Third Sector.* London: Earthscan.

Green, D. 1998. "ETI Southern Participation Conference Report." Available at www.cleanclothes.org/codes/edu98-09.htm (retrieved 18 January 2005).

Greenpeace International. 2002. "Corporate Crimes: The Need for an International Instrument on Corporate Accountability and Liability." Available at http://archive.greenpeace.org/earthsummit/documents.html (retrieved 20 July 2004).

Grossman, Z., and A. Gedicks. 2001. "Native Resistance to Multinational Mining Corporations in Wisconsin. *Cultural Survival Quarterly* 25(1), available at www.culturalsurvival.org (retrieved 18 January 2005).

Hamann, R. 2001. "Mining in Paradise? Caught between a Rock and Heavy Minerals on the Wild Coast, South Africa." *Cultural Survival Quarterly* 25(1), available at www.culturalsurvival.org/quarterly (retrieved 18 January 2005).

Hanks, J. 2002. "Promoting Corporate Environmental Responsibility: What Role for "Self-regulatory" and "Co-regulatory" Policy Instruments in South Africa?" In P. Utting (ed.), *The Greening of Business in Developing Countries: Rhetoric, Reality and Prospects.* London: Zed Books.

Hansen, M. 2002. "Environmental Regulation of Transnational Corporations: Needs and Prospects." In P. Utting (ed.), *The Greening of Business in Developing Countries: Rhetoric, Reality and Prospects.* London: Zed Books.

Innes, L. 2001. "Staking Claims: Innu Rights and Mining Claims at Voisey's Bay." *Cultural Survival Quarterly* 25(1), available at: www.culturalsurvival.org (retrieved 18 January 2005).

Izquierdo, R. 2001. "The Thinking People: The U'wa Battle Oxy. *Cultural Survival Quarterly* 25(3), available at www.culturalsurvival.org (retrieved 18 January 2005).

Karliner, J. 1997. *The Corporate Planet: Ecology and Politics in the Age of Globalization.* San Francisco: Sierra Club Books.

Kimmerling, J. 1996. "Oil, Lawlessness and Indigenous Struggles in Ecuador's Oriente." In H. Collinson (ed.), *Green Guerrillas: Environmental Conflicts and Initiatives in Latin America and the Caribbean.* London: Latin America Bureau.

Kirsch, S. 1996. "Cleaning Up Ok Tedi: Settlement Favours Yonggom People." *Journal of the International Institute* 4(1), available at www.umich.edu/_iinet/journal/vol4no1/oktedi.html (retrieved 18 January 2005).

Long, F., and M. Arnold. 1995. *The Power of Environmental Partnerships*. Fort Worth, TX: Dryden Press.

Lund-Thomsen, P. 2003. "Towards a Theoretical Framework of CSR in the South." Paper presented at a closed workshop on CSR and Development: Critical Perspectives, Copenhagen Business School, Copenhagen, Denmark, 1 November.

Marcus, A., and K. Dent. 2001. "Campaign to Support the Free Trade Zone Workers Union of Sri Lanka." Available at www.cleanclothes.org/urgent/01-09-23.htm (retrieved 18 January 2005).

Marinetto, Michael. 1998. "The Shareholders Strike Back—Issues in the Research of Shareholder Activism. *Environmental Politics* 7(3):125–133.

McDonald, D. A. 2002. *Environmental Justice in South Africa*. Athens, OH: Ohio University Press.

Merrifield, J. 1993. "Putting Scientists in Their Place: Participatory Research in Environmental and Occupational Health." In P. Park, M. Brydon-Miller, B. Hall, and T. Jackson (eds.), *Voices of Change: Participatory Research in the United States and Canada*. Toronto, Canada: Ontario Institute for Studies in Education.

Moody, R. 1999. "Inco Update. Internationally and in Indonesia." Available at http://dte.gn.apc.org/camp.htm (retrieved 18 January 2005).

Mulligan, P. 1999. "Greenwash or Blueprint? Rio Tinto in Madagascar." *IDS Bulletin* 30(3):50–57.

Newell, P. 2002. "From Responsibility to Citizenship? Corporate Accountability for Development." *IDS Bulletin* 33(2):91–100.

Newell, P. 2003. "Corporate Accountability for Development: Two Cases from India." Draft paper for the Development Research Centre on Citizenship, Participation and Accountability. Brighton, UK: IDS, University of Sussex.

Newell, P., and S. Bellour. 2002. "Mapping Accountability: Origins, Contexts and Implications for Development." IDS Working Paper No. 168, Development Research Centre on Citizenship, Participation and Accountability. Brighton, UK: IDS, University of Sussex.

Ojiambo, E. V. 2002. "Battling for Corporate Accountability: Experiences from Titanium Mining Campaign in Kwale, Kenya." Paper presented at the Linking Rights and Participation: Advocacy Initiatives seminar, IDS, University of Sussex, Brighton, UK, 29 May.

Okonta, I., and O. Douglas. 2001. *Where Vultures Feast: Shell, Human Rights, and Oil in the Niger Delta*. San Francisco: Sierra Club Books.

Pratt, L., and E. Fintel. 2002. "Environmental Management as an Indicator of Business Responsibility in Central America." In P. Utting (ed.), *The Greening of Business in Developing Countries: Rhetoric, Reality and Prospects*. London: Zed Books.

Rodman, K. 1998. "Think Globally, Punish Locally: Non-state Actors, MNCs and Human Rights Sanctions." *Ethics and International Affairs* 12:19–48.

Rowell, A. 1996. *Green Backlash: Global Subversion of the Environmental Movement*. London: Routledge.

Schedler, A. 1999. *The Self-restraining State: Power and Accountability in New Democracies*. London: Lynne Rienner.

Schmidheiny, S. 1992. *Changing Course: A Global Business Perspective on Development and the Environment*. Cambridge, MA: MIT Press.

Scott, J. C. 1985. *Weapons of the Weak: Everyday Forms of Peasant Resistance*. New Haven, CT: Yale University Press.

Sumner, Andrew. 2005. "Is Foreign Direct Investment Good for the Poor? A Review and Stocktake." *Development in Practice* 15(30-4):269–285.

Utting, P. 2002a. "Corporate Environmentalism in the South: Assessing the Limits and Prospects." In P. Utting (ed.), *The Greening of Business in Developing Countries: Rhetoric, Reality and Prospects*. London: Zed Books.

Utting, P. (ed.). 2002b. *The Greening of Business in Developing Countries: Rhetoric, Reality and Prospects*. London: Zed Books.

Vackayil, J. 2004. "SC Panel Slaps Rs 50-Crore Fine on HLL for Pollution in Kodaikanal. *The Financial Express* (Net ed.), 8 October 2004. Available at http://www.financialexpress.com/fe_full_story.php?content_id=70819 (retrieved 18 January 2005).

Vogel, D. 1997. *Trading Up: Consumer and Environmental Regulation in the Global Economy*, 2nd ed. Cambridge, MA: Harvard University Press.

World Bank. 2000. "Greening Industry: New Roles for Communities, Markets, and Governments." *World Bank Policy Research Report*. New York: Oxford University Press.

Zadek, S. 2001. *The Civil Corporation: The New Economy of Corporate Citizenship*. London: Earthscan.

PART 2

Investing in Development?

FIVE

Public Resistance to Privatization in Water and Energy

DAVID HALL, EMANUELE LOBINA, AND ROBIN DE LA MOTTE

INTRODUCTION

Private-sector involvement in infrastructure was vigorously promoted by development agencies and international institutions in the 1990s and early 2000s. It was expected to inject both investment and efficiency into these sectors in developing countries, replacing traditional public-sector systems suffering from under-investment and inefficiency due to excessive political interference and rent-seeking behavior by vested interests including bureaucracies and labor. It was assumed that this extension of private-sector involvement would be economically successful and generally welcomed, except among those interests losing out as a result of the reform process.

In the water and energy sectors, these expectations have not been fulfilled. Private-sector investment in developing countries has been falling since its peak in the 1990s, multinational companies have failed to make sustainable returns on their investments, and the process of privatization in these sectors has proved widely unpopular and encountered strong political opposition. This resistance is now generally recognized as an important factor in the failure of private investment in these sectors, by supporters and critics of privatization alike.

This chapter examines the role of this opposition in delaying, canceling, or reversing the privatization of water and energy. It presents data on the actors, on the issues and methods of the opposition, and on the results it has achieved. We also discuss the roles of the range of (international and national) actors and interests involved, the relationship to political parties and electoral politics, the alternative policies presented, and the reaction of international institutions and companies to the opposition.

The chapter concludes, first, that civil society in developing countries can mobilize highly effective political opposition even when confronting weighty international actors such as development banks and multinational companies. Second, the opposition is based on the perceived conflicts between privatization and equity, and over the role of the state and community in these sectors. Third, the opposition has involved dynamic interactions with existing political parties and structures, including use of existing electoral and judicial mechanisms. Finally, the very success of such opposition campaigns poses challenges for the international institutions and donors, NGOs, the campaigns themselves, and the future development of national systems of electricity and water.

PUBLIC RESISTANCE TO PRIVATIZATION

Disenchantment with Privatization

There has been strong public resistance to privatization worldwide. The extent of this opposition is much greater and more widespread than is usually acknowledged, involving a general rejection of privatization across the economy that is not limited to utilities or traditional public services: a 2002 survey concluded that "privatization remains widely and increasingly unpopular, largely because of the perception that it is fundamentally unfair, both in conception and execution" (Birdsall and Nellis 2002: 1).

The collective political impact of the campaigns against privatization is remarkable. Buresch (2003: 11) suggests that, globally, "[I]t is getting harder to find political leaders that are willing to truly champion privatization for reasons other than to generate cash proceeds." The World Bank, in revising its infrastructure policy in mid-2003, stated that it was "[r]esponding to country demand by offering a broad menu of options for public and private sector infrastructure provision" (World Bank 2003a). In every instance, the campaigns were taking place against policies that were advocated by the government of the day, sometimes with the support of traditional leftist parties, and invariably—in developing countries—with the support of development banks. In many countries, the policies were reversed or significantly delayed.

Data from opinion polls in Latin America carried out in 1998 and 2000 reveal that support for privatization, which was not very strong to begin with, has decreased over time (Nellis 2003). In Sri Lanka, opinion polls show that privatization has been associated with deteriorating socioeconomic conditions (greater poverty, increased cost of living, etc.) (Nellis 2003), and in Russia two thirds of the respondents in a 2001 survey said that they had lost more than they gained from privatization, with only 5 percent saying they had gained more. Privatization has become so unpopular that governments everywhere have developed increasingly tortuous euphemisms, including "capitalization" (Bolivia), "ownership reform" (China), "disinvestment" (India), "disincorporation" (Mexico), "peopleization" (Sri Lanka), and "equitization" (Vietnam).

At the World Bank's energy week in February 2003, a speaker from the global consulting firm Deloitte noted a "growing political opposition to privatization in emerging markets due to widespread perception that it does not serve the interests of the population at large," which it attributed to a number of features of privatization: "Pressures to increase tariffs and cut off non-payers; loss of jobs of vocal union members that will be hard to retrain for the new economy; [and] the perception that only special interests are served—privatisation is seen as serving oligarchic domestic and foreign interests that profit at the expense of the country." These are not offset by any benefits from privatization because gains such as expanded coverage, improved quality, and competitive tariffs are small, dispersed, and slow, whereas the impact of price hikes and job losses "is concentrated, immediate, and falls on visible and vocal groups (e.g., labor unions)" (Buresch 2003: 9, 11, 12).

Campaigns Against Water Privatization

During the 1990s, with the encouragement of the World Bank (WB) and others, water privatization was proposed or implemented in many countries. Political resistance has been widespread, as have been economic, social, and even technical problems associated with the implementation process (Lobina and Hall 2003). The opposition to water privatization is by no means confined to developing countries. Even where privatization has gone ahead, this has often been after significant political resistance: in the UK, for example, a vigorous campaign against Margaret Thatcher's 1985 proposals for water privatization led to her abandoning the plans before the 1987 election in order to avoid electoral damage; the policy was only revived and implemented once the election had been safely won.

Three examples serve to illustrate the range of opposition to privatization schemes. In December 2001 the water contract for Nkonkobe (Fort Beaufort) in South Africa was nullified as public or municipal consent was never obtained (Mxotwa 2001). In May 2002 the city council of Poznan in Poland (with a population of 650,000) unanimously rejected a water privatization proposal: the city had already improved the efficiency of its water services and had obtained investment finance from various sources including the European Investment Bank (EIB). And in June 2002 the Paraguayan parliament voted by 32 to 7 to suspend indefinitely the privatization plans for the state-owned water company Corposana (now known as Essap) (*Business News Americas* 2002). The privatization proposal had been driven by fiscal motives, in order to comply with IMF targets. Its rejection was hailed by the trade unions as "a great victory against the IMF, the World Bank, globalisation, and neo-liberalism." The decision was upheld in August 2004 when a renewed privatization attempt was shelved as a result of pressure from protesters.

Table 5–1 shows a range of countries and cities that have rejected privatization proposals or terminated private concessions and reverted to public-sector services. The list includes cities such as Washington, DC, where a comparative evaluation of private and public options was carried out, and the latter preferred. Elsewhere, strong campaigns against water privatization have not been successful (e.g., in Chile, the Philippines, and the UK), or privatization has been abandoned by company decision and not because of popular opposition (e.g., in Mozambique, Vietnam, and Zimbabwe).

The opposition has come from a range of groups, led by different types of organizations in different countries—trade unions, consumers, water professionals, environmentalists, political groupings, and community organizations. The campaign in Brazil is an example of a broad-based long-term campaign, with the *Frente Nacional pelo Saneamento Ambiental* (FNSA) (National Front for Environmental Sanitation) bringing together 17 civil society organizations (CSOs)—unions, managers, professional associations, NGOs involved in urban reform, consumer groups, and social movements (Filho 2002).

Table 5–1. Opposition to and Rejection of Water Privatization, 1994–2003

Key to active groups: U = unions; C = consumers or citizen groups; B = (local) business; N = other NGOs; E = environmentalists; P = political parties					
Country	Place	Year of Rejection	Result	Decision Mechanism	Active Groups
Argentina	BA Province	2002	Termination of privatization	—	U, C
Argentina	Tucuman	1998	Termination of privatization	Election (state)	C, P
Bolivia	Cochabamba	2000	Termination of privatization	Government decision	U, C, B, N
Brazil	National	2002	Privatization policy abandoned	Election (national)	U, C, B, E, N, P
Brazil	Rio de Janeiro	1999	Rejection of proposals	Court ruling	U, C, B, E, N, P
Canada	Montreal	1999	Rejection of proposals	Municipal decision	E, U, P
France	Grenoble	2001	Termination of privatization	Municipal decision/election	E, C, P
Germany	Potsdam	2000	Termination of privatization	Municipal decision	C, P
Germany	Munich	1998	Rejection of proposals	Municipal decision	U, C
Ghana	Accra	Ongoing	Continuing campaign	—	N, C, E, U
Honduras	Honduras	1995	Rejection of proposals	Government decision	U, M
Hungary	Debrecen	1995	Rejection of proposals	Municipal decision	U, M
India	Delhi	Ongoing	Continuing campaign	—	E, N
Indonesia	Jakarta	Ongoing	Continuing campaign	—	U, C, E
Mauritius	National	2000	Rejection of proposals	Election (national)	C, E, U
Panama	National	1999	Rejection of proposals	Election (national)	U, C, S
Paraguay	National	2002	Rejection of proposals	Parliament decision	U
Poland	Poznan	2002	Rejection of proposals	Municipal decision	P
Poland	Łódź	1994	Rejection of proposals	Election (local)	U
Sri Lanka	National	Ongoing	Continuing campaign	—	U, C
S Africa	National	Ongoing	Continuing campaign	—	U, C, N, E
S Africa	Nkonkobe	2002	Termination of privatization	Court ruling	U

Table 5–1. Opposition to and Rejection of Water Privatization, 1994–2003 *(Continued)*

Key to active groups: U = unions; C = consumers or citizen groups; B = (local) business;
N = other NGOs; E = environmentalists; P = political parties

Country	Place	Year of Rejection	Result	Decision Mechanism	Active Groups
Sweden	Malmo	1995	Rejection of proposals	Municipal decision	U, C
Thailand	Bangkok	2002	Termination of privatization	Government decision	U
Trinidad	National	1999	Termination of privatization	Government decision	U
UK	Northern Ireland	Ongoing	Continuing campaign	—	U, C, N, P
USA	Atlanta, GA	2003	Termination of privatization	Municipal decision	U, C
USA	Birmingham, AL	2000	Termination of privatization	Municipal decision	U, C
USA	Washington, DC	1996	Rejection of proposals	Municipal decision	N

Source: PSIRU database

Campaigns Against Energy Privatization

The widespread opposition to energy privatization has also come from a broad range of civil society groups, including trade unions, community organizations, environmentalists, consumer organizations, and political parties. In some cases there have been generalized public protests, with prices—and profits—overwhelmingly the biggest single issue, followed by job losses.

Resistance to large price hikes usually entails the rejection of privatization. In Senegal, for example, the government has refused to meet the demands for price rises of three successive multinationals—Hydro-Québec, Vivendi, and AES—as a result of which even the WB abandoned the plan to privatize the electricity utility (though it is now proposing the development of private generation through independent power producers (IPPs)). Other issues include reliability, efficiency, the local impact of IPPs, environmental policy, public accountability, national control, and corruption.

Other campaigns have revolved around a broader set of interests, such as the campaign against Enron's private power plant at Dabhol, in the Indian state of Maharashtra, which was based on a long-term power purchase agreement. The campaign was supported by energy NGOs opposed to the project on social, economic, and environmental grounds, and by the local communities whose livelihoods were seriously damaged

by the plant. Demonstrations by these communities were brutally suppressed—leading to the unusual case of an Amnesty International
report on Enron (Amnesty International 1997). The campaign nevertheless achieved some success with Enron's departure from India.

The examples shown in Table 5–2 include campaigns that could be
described as successful in terms of their own objectives. In some cases
these were local issues, concerning one power station, for instance the
Cogentrix campaign in southern India, or a single city's utility, such as
the Emcali campaign in Colombia; in others they covered a whole country, such as the campaigns in Mexico, South Korea, and Thailand. They
include cases where existing systems have been successfully defended so
far, such as in South Africa and the United States (California); and others
where privatization efforts have failed to take place or been rolled back,
such as the Dominican Republic and Senegal. Not included in the list are
cases where privatization has been terminated as a result of an exit decision by the company concerned, such as in the Indian state of Orissa,
where AES abandoned an energy generation and a distribution company,
claiming excessive tariffs and an adverse business climate.

Table 5–2. Campaigns Against Energy Privatization

Key to active groups: U = unions; C = consumers or citizen groups; B = (local) business; N = other NGOs; E = environmentalists; P = political parties

Country	Location	Year of Rejection	Result	Decision Mechanism	Active Groups
Australia	NSW	1999	State utility corporatized, not privatized	Election (regional)	U, P
Brazil	National	Ongoing	Oppose privatization of utilities, generators	Elections (national and state)	U, P, N, C
Canada	Ontario	2002	Court rules against privatization of utility Ontario Hydro	Court ruling	U, C, N
Colombia	Cali; National	1997–	Oppose privatization of municipal utility Emcali	—	U, N, E
Dominican Republic	National	2003	Renationalized electricity distributors	Government decision	C, U
France	National	Ongoing	Delayed privatization of state company EdF	—	U, P

Table 5–2. Campaigns Against Energy Privatization *(Continued)*

Key to active groups: U = unions; C = consumers or citizen groups; B = (local) business;
N = other NGOs; E = environmentalists; P = political parties

Country	Location	Year of Rejection	Result	Decision Mechanism	Active Groups
India	Maharashtra	1996–	Dabhol IPP (Enron) proposed democratization, not privatization, of utility MSEB	—	N, E, U
India	Karnataka	2000	Cogentrix IPP plan rejected	Court ruling	E, N
Indonesia	National	Ongoing	Payment of corrupt PPAs withheld, electricity liberalization reversed	Utility decisions, court case	U, N
Mexico	National	Ongoing	Defer privatization of electrical utilities	Parliament, court ruling	U, P, N
Senegal	National	2002	Privatization plans collapsed	Government decision	C
South Africa	National	Ongoing	Eskom remains public utility	—	U, C, N
South Korea	National	2004	Plans to privatize and liberalize Kepco withdrawn	Government decision	U, N
Thailand	National	2004	Planned sale of shares in state electricity company withdrawn	Government decision	U
USA	California	2000	Los Angeles municipal utility avoids power crisis	—	U, C

Source: PSIRU database

DISCUSSION

Economic Issues

Opposition to privatization is based on central economic issues—prices, profits, jobs, and development. Privatization of water and energy is seen as making prices higher than they would otherwise be, and profits—and senior management pay—higher than is justified, while at the same time cutting jobs and making the remaining workers less secure. In developing countries in particular, opposition is also based on a strong sense that these sectors should be subject to local decision making, taking account of all public interests, and not left to global, commercial operators and market forces. Deloitte's analysis of opposition to energy privatization (Buresch 2003) notes all these issues, including the rejection of excessive and unjustifiable profits. The campaigns also articulate a view that the organization of sectors such as water, and to a lesser extent energy, should be determined as a matter of public policy within the country concerned, not by the operations of the market.

A significant feature of the campaigns is that they have taken place in countries at varying levels of national income, so the opposition is clearly not limited to factors that are peculiar to developing countries. As shown in the tables, countries with recent campaigns include high-income countries such as France, Germany, and the United States; transition countries such as Hungary and Poland; middle-income countries such as Mexico, South Africa, and Thailand; and low-income countries such as Ghana, Honduras, and India. As recently as 2003, the German federal parliament and many regional (*Länder*) parliaments passed motions opposing any move by the European Commission, under the GATS (General Agreement on Trade in Services) provisions of the WTO, that could lead to opening Germany's water sector to foreign private-sector competition.

It is also worth emphasizing that the opposition to privatization should not be cast as resistance to economic progress. Skepticism concerning the supposed benefits of privatization is increasingly confirmed by reviews of empirical evidence suggesting that public or private ownership makes little difference to efficiency (Willner 2001). Even an exhaustive review of the economic aspects of the mass privatizations in the UK has concluded that there was no significant efficiency gain, while there is clear evidence of a regressive effect on the distribution of income and wealth (Florio 2004). Reports from international financial institutions (IFIs) are now noticeably more cautious about the economic desirability of relying on the private sector for development in these sectors. The IMF has acknowledged the probability that curbs on public-sector investment in infrastructure have damaged economic growth, and that the evidence on the relative efficiency of the private sector is finely balanced (IMF 2004). The WB, for its part, has published a lengthy report highlighting the limitations of privatization (World Bank 2004a), acknowledging that it promoted the policy with "irrational exuberance." The opposition campaigns can legitimately feel that their positions on the economics of privatization have been vindicated by these developments in academic and official thinking.

Actors

Support for the anti-privatization campaigns is very wide, and goes far beyond the rent-seeking vested interests that the proponents of privatization regard as responsible for them. For example, a report commissioned by USAID (Padco 2002) to defend the policy of encouraging water privatization in South Africa named ten groups as highly critical of public-sector privatizations. The list includes US and South African trade unions, Public Services International (PSI), and research units (including PSIRU)—but not consumers, environmentalists, or communities—and the report chooses to ignore the growing amount of critical research being published on water privatization (Hall 2002).

There is no consistent pattern in the "leadership" of the various campaigns. Unions have played a leading role, for example, in the campaigns against water privatization in Brazil and South Africa and against energy privatization in Australia, Mexico, Senegal, and Thailand. But this is not always so: in Grenoble, for instance, unions played at most a minor role in the campaign that led to the termination of the private water concession (Lobina and Hall 2001), and in Ghana, unions did not even join the campaign against water privatization for some time.

In some cases the activity has been diffuse, with various parties actively campaigning but without forming a single alliance. In Jakarta, for example, a trade union has conducted a lengthy campaign of strike action, calling for the end of the water privatization contracts, but apparently it has not done so in coordination with protests by consumer and community groups. A similar picture emerges in Colombia, where highly active environmental groups are campaigning against energy policies that are based on privatization, alongside unions that are also campaigning against the privatization of municipal utilities, as is the case in Cali and elsewhere. In some instances, existing divisions have prevented the formation of alliances over privatization. In Thailand, for example, successful union action against the sale of shares in the state energy company did not receive active support from environmental groups, because of the lack of union support for the environmentalists' campaigns against environmentally unfriendly hydropower and coal-fired power station developments.

Without exception, these campaigns were initiated by local or national organizations: none was prompted by international agencies or originated as part of international campaigns. Many opposition campaigns have received little or no international assistance, including some of the most successful ones, such as the water campaigns in Łódź (Poland), Tucuman (Argentina), and Nkonkobe (South Africa). Even where there has been some international support, it has not been a significant element in the campaign itself. Despite the vast publicity about the "water wars" in Cochabamba, and the subsequent international solidarity visits, the entire episode of expelling the private water contractor was completed in April 2000, before most groups outside Bolivia even learned what was happening.

The international organizations active on these issues include some with an international membership of affiliated organizations, notably PSI and Consumers International (CI), as well as organizations that act globally, including a number of development NGOs. None of these organizations has a centralized structure capable of commanding local participation in a global campaign. The campaigns have not even been coordinated by international confederations, as has happened with the union campaigns against mining companies: lobbying of multinational company shareholder meetings, for example, has been almost completely absent in the water and energy sectors.

International organizations can assist in two main ways. First, they can provide material support in terms of information, liaison, and publicity: as well as local solidarity, this has a multiplier effect, whereby publicizing the issues faced in one place helps strengthen the campaigns elsewhere; some national campaigns have themselves made direct links. The availability of information through the Internet has greatly facilitated the dissemination of such information. Second, international organizations have also been active at the global level, principally in interacting with multilateral bodies, such as the WB, especially at events such as the World Water Forums in The Hague and Kyoto. Specific global demands have included ending conditionalities tied to privatization. The impact achieved at these events has been significant, but mostly because of the known existence and success of the national campaigns.

Political Parties and Processes

The campaigns have exhibited a range of connections with political parties and processes. In some cases, they have in effect been supported by, and supportive of, specific political parties. The campaign against energy privatization in the Australian state of New South Wales was constructed explicitly around an alternative policy of the then opposition Labor Party. But there have also been cases when campaigns have been unable to work with the party from which support would naturally have been expected, because that party was in government and promoting privatization. In Berlin, for example, the Social Democratic Party (SDP) headed the city government that proposed and implemented the water privatization. In South Africa, the government of the African National Congress (ANC) has been introducing water privatization. In both cases, individual rebel councilors were effective actors in the campaign, but became isolated from their parties.

Most campaigns seek broad-based political support. In Brazil, for example, proposals on water privatization were rejected at parliamentary level on at least three occasions before the election of Lula's center-left PT government in 2002. In Mexico, energy privatization proposals were rejected by a parliament whose political composition did not favor the campaign. Other campaigns have enjoyed similar political success, but were overruled by final decisions. In Chile, for instance, water privatization was authorized in 1999 by the lame duck presidency of Eduardo Frei, who was not standing for reelection, despite opposition from all political parties, including the Christian Democrats (*Financial Times* 1999).

The opposition campaigns have on occasion gained significance within wider political movements that eventually have reshaped political positions and organizations. The best known is the Bolivian example of Cochabamba, where the resistance to water privatization was coordinated by the *Coordinadora de defensa de agua y de la vida* (the coordinating group to defend water and life), which had an extremely broad-based agenda and membership, including local businesses, labor, community groups, water vendors, and local farmers. In Panama, too, opposition to the water privatization plans became part of a wider movement including student protests about education fees, ultimately leading to the election of a new president committed to opposing privatization. This contribution to the reshaping of national politics has also been seen in other sectors. For example, the campaign against healthcare privatization in El Salvador was a significant factor in the emergence of a new left-leaning leadership in one party.

The energy campaigns also relate to political parties in a variety of ways. In Australia, a campaign organized mainly by trade unions succeeded in influencing the results of elections in New South Wales.

The voters rejected the Conservative Party, which was proposing privatization of electricity, in favor of a Labor Party that promoted the public-sector, corporatized Energy Companies, which now have a long future. This followed similar election results in Tasmania, where Labor defeated a Conservative Party that was proposing electricity privatization, a policy that has also been rejected in South Australia and Queensland, leaving Victoria as the only state that has privatized power. South Korean unions, by contrast, have waged a long campaign against the privatization of electricity, gas, and other utilities, without relying on the support of any one party. The campaign has included parliamentary pressure, general strikes, and research, and more recently collaboration with environmental groups and others. At the time of writing (early 2004), the electricity utility had still not been privatized.

Courts, Elections, and Referenda

Where campaigns have been successful, it has almost always been through existing democratic institutions. This has sometimes involved pursuing cases through the courts to rule privatization policies illegal on constitutional or other grounds. There are examples of successful court actions in both high- and low-income countries, including Brazil (court ruling that the proposed water privatization of Rio de Janeiro was unlawful), Canada (reversal of proposed electricity privatization in Ontario), France (where the courts ruled both that illegal corruption had taken place in Grenoble, and that customer bills had been wrongly calculated), India (ruling against the legality of a proposed power station on environmental grounds), and South Africa (where a contract was ruled invalid for lack of public consultation). The tactic has sometimes been successfully nullified by attacks on the courts by supporters of privatization: when campaigners brought court cases against the water privatization in Manila, for instance, six chambers of commerce— including the United States, Japanese, EU, and Australian–New Zealand bodies—criticized what they termed "excessive challenges to public biddings" (*Financial Times* 1997) and there were dire warnings of "terrorists in robes" threatening future foreign investment (*Philippine Daily Inquirer* 2003).

The campaigns have sometimes significantly affected the outcome of elections. In Łódź, the 1994 campaign focused on the municipal elections, with unions undertaking door-to-door leafleting of every household in the city. The result was a defeat of the party advocating water privatization: the outgoing mayor thought that the effect of the water campaign was so significant that he brought a court case challenging the result on the grounds that the unions had acted illegally in engaging in electoral politics (he lost the case). Privatization policies were significant electoral issues in Argentina (Tucuman, water), Australia (New South Wales, electricity), and Panama (water). In some cases development banks have imposed conditionalities preventing the implementation of such election results. For example, in Cartagena, Colombia, elections were won by politicians opposing privatization, but the winner was prevented from acting on the election result because of WB loan conditionalities: the victorious mayor was forced to allow the privatization to continue.

The prospect of referenda has also been used to some effect. In the US city of New Orleans it was decided that any future proposals to privatize water would have to be put to a referendum: the prospect alone led Suez to announce that it would not seek a concession that would be subject to such a vote. Campaigners in Germany, for example, in Hamburg, are also using the referendum as a tactic to oppose water privatization.

Alternative Positions

The opposition campaigns have not always articulated a specific alternative policy. The information costs of doing so are very high, and most campaigns do not aspire to detailed restructuring and management of utilities. Some campaigns are effectively defending the status quo, without necessarily ruling out other changes. This is most often the case in water, where there is an existing public utility in place, however poorly functioning. The public sector water operator is the alternative—the technical and financial measures needed to deal with service problems such as extensions or continuity of service or collection of bills can be expected to be dealt with within this framework.

In other cases, there may be an obvious need for changes on social, financial, environmental, or technical grounds, and the campaign then implicitly demands the seeking of a solution other than privatization. Examples of situations where the need for change is widely accepted would be water in South Africa, where restructuring and extension are necessary for social and developmental reasons; water in Brazil (Recife), where the municipality acknowledged the need for restructuring but refused to accept WB attempts to impose privatization as a loan condition; and electricity in India, for example, Maharashtra, where the need to restructure and improve the performance of the state electricity board is widely accepted, but privatization is not (Hall and de la Motte 2004).

It is unlikely that generalized alternatives would ever be developed because local conditions and demands vary so greatly. Procedural positions can, however, be pursued in a way that supports the democratizing aspect of any campaign, without requiring commitment to one particular type of system. The World Resources Institute offered a version of this approach in 2002, with a review of recent energy reforms in Argentina, Bulgaria, Ghana, India, Indonesia, and South Africa (Dubash 2002). It identified major problems with the goals and processes of electricity reform in nearly all these countries:

> By focusing on financial health, reforms in the electricity sector have excluded a range of broader concerns also relevant to the public interest. In this study, we have examined the social and environmental concerns at stake in these reforms. We have found that not only are they inadequately addressed, but that socially and environmentally undesirable trajectories can be locked-in through technological, institutional, and financial decisions that constrain future choices. (Dubash 2002: 171)

This report puts forward four clear recommendations for what it calls "a progressive politics of electricity sector reform":

1. Frame reforms around the goals to be achieved in the sector. A narrow focus on institutional restructuring driven by financial concerns is too restrictive to accommodate a public benefits agenda. . . .
2. Structure finance around reform goals, rather than reform goals around finance. . . .
3. Support reform processes with a system of sound governance. An open-ended framing of reforms will reflect public concerns only if it is supported by a robust process of debate and discussion.
4. Build political strategies to support attention to a public benefits agenda. (Dubash 2002: 168–171)

Locally, too, procedural issues have become central to alternative reform proposals, as can be seen from the following two examples.

The Indian energy group Prayas (www.prayaspune.org) advocates the application of three principles: transparency, accountability, and participation (TAP). Its website states:

> [A]ll the governance functions and governance agencies are made amenable, on mandatory basis, to full transparency to the public, direct accountability to the public, and meaningful participation of the public. . . . The three major governance agencies—the state, the utilities, and the regulatory commissions—could be TAPed in a variety of ways. However, the space and capabilities of civil society institutions will be the important determinants of successful TAPing of these agencies. (Prayas Energy Group 2001)

Prayas agrees that there is a crisis in the power sector in India, but also recognizes the achievements of the existing model, based on state ownership, self-sufficiency, and cross-subsidy to agriculture and households: in 50 years, capacity has increased 55 fold, with 78 million customers, and 500,000 villages connected. That being said, half the population is still unconnected, and there are power shortages, weak accounting and metering, and huge financial losses (Wagle 2000).

In South Africa, the public-sector union SAMWU not only organized a campaign of action to oppose privatization of public services including water and energy but also ran a series of workshops for its members to address the issue of developing alternatives, looking at both international dimensions and local issues. The workshops analyzed cases of successful public sector restructuring: the participatory local government budgeting process in Porto Alegre, Brazil; a union-led internal restructuring of local government departments in Malung, Sweden; and the public-public partnership (PPP) for water services in Odi, in South Africa (Pape 2001).

IFI, DONOR, AND MULTINATIONAL COMPANY REACTIONS

The political resistance to privatization has been acknowledged by the WB as a significant factor in its lack of success in both water and energy. In February 2003, the WB director for these sectors, Jamal Saghir (2003), identified the problems in the energy sector as including "decreasing faith in markets." In July 2003 the *Wall Street Journal* quoted senior WB officials on their reappraisal of privatization policies in these sectors:

> "There's certainly a lot of soul-searching going on" says Michael Klein, the World Bank's vice president for private-sector development. . . . World Bank officials have now decided it doesn't matter so much whether infrastructure is in public or private hands . . . the World Bank itself must pay far greater attention to the fiery politics of privatization and especially to the effect of rising prices on the poor and disaffected. (*Wall Street Journal* 2003)

At the same time, a new infrastructure policy paper was approved by the WB board, which did not refer to the "fiery politics" spelled out by the *Wall Street Journal*, and continued to concentrate on measures to support the private sector's involvement (Hall et al. 2003).

Multinational companies (MNCs) have reacted more sharply, in both energy and water, with a series of withdrawals from developing countries. Suez announced in January 2003 that it was reducing its investments in developing countries by one third, insisting on higher and more certain profitability. A series of US energy multinationals, including AEP, Enterdy, NRG, Reliant, Southern/Mirant, and TXU (as well as Enron), have withdrawn from overseas investments; others, such as PPL, would withdraw if they could find any buyers. The largest US international electricity company, AES, has also made sudden exits, abandoning major investments in Orissa (India) and Yorkshire (UK), and the controversial Bujugali dam project in Uganda.

The water multinationals have started developing initiatives to reduce the political risk of private water ventures, especially in developing countries. RWE-Thames Water has gone the furthest, associating itself with some of the key criticisms raised by the opponents of water privatization. The company has used conferences to announce that it does not want to be associated with private ventures resulting from conditionalities imposed on communities by donors or lenders, as well as to dissociate itself from the European Commission's initiative in the GATS negotiations. The UK Department of Trade and Industry is similarly dissociating itself from the water initiative in GATS, an equally surprising move that may be connected with the RWE-Thames position. RWE-Thames is also seeking to build advance acceptance from potentially critical international NGOs, or simply build influence with key politicians. There is no sign of any such initiatives from energy companies.

CONCLUSIONS

Donor Responses

The experience of opposition poses a number of challenges to donors. In terms of development policy, the IFIs and other multilateral and donor agencies need to address the question of whether privatization and liberalization in sectors such as water and energy can possibly deliver economic sustainability in the absence of political legitimacy. Insofar as the agencies seek to promote the extension of these services, they should encourage the development of national and local policies through democratic processes that are recognized as legitimate, and then provide financing for the resulting policies. In 2003, the WB made encouraging statements to the effect that its position on privatization in water and energy was being completely reviewed, but no new approach has yet emerged that would enable the Bank to support public-sector developments with the same vigor (World Bank 2004a). Given the increasing global harmonization of aid, the position of the WB on this issue is of even greater importance than ever before.

The same donor organizations may also feel that they face the question of how to maximize the size of the market open to international companies in these sectors in the face of such widespread resistance. There are clear signs that the WB is addressing this issue, for example through the Guarantco mechanisms, which protect companies from political risks and so make markets more attractive; and through financing pro-privatization information through the public-private infrastructure advisory facility (PPIAF), thereby actively promoting privatization in local political discourse (World Bank 2003a, b; 2004a, b). The MNCs also have to reappraise the nature of their business in this sector, especially in developing countries. The retreat by many companies in 2003 was a widespread response: the exploration by RWE Thames Water of a role based on consensus with NGOs exemplifies a longer-term approach. It remains to be seen what long-term sustainable role there may be for MNCs in these sectors.

Global Politics

The opposition to privatization in water and energy (and other public services) represents a series of relatively successful engagements by national or local organizations with global politics. Initiatives from

IFIs or MNCs have met with national and local opposition and in many cases have been withdrawn. Civil society in developing countries can mobilize highly effective political activity even when confronting significant international actors such as development banks and MNCs. However, this has not happened as part of an internationally coordinated initiative, which means that the organization of the opposition does not mirror the structure of the global policy makers it is engaging, as Herod (2001) has observed in relation to union solidarity campaigns. It is thus different in kind from campaigns such as those for the abolition of child labor, or campaigns launched by an international organization against the activities of mining or forestry multinationals.

Political Structures and Processes

The opposition has operated through existing political structures in a wide variety of ways, and with some degree of success—except where there is dictatorship or a lack of democratic institutions. Opposition to privatization has affected the policies and leadership of political parties. The impact on elections at all levels indicates that campaigns on privatization have a consistent effect of priming the election by making it an issue that affects voting patterns, an effect that has also been observed in relation to referenda (de Vreese 2004; Krosnick and Kinder 1990). The widespread recourse to the law also indicates a surprising readiness of courts to rule against proposed or existing privatizations on public interest grounds.

In a few countries, most notably Brazil, the resistance to privatization and the development of coherent democratic alternatives have been closely integrated with political parties and the broader political system. Elsewhere, however, this link has been absent, which may be an indicator of a political vacuum, in terms of parties that stand for the development of public infrastructure and public services.

Public Interest

The opposition to privatization is based on widespread perceptions of the damaging effect on equity (Birdsall and Nellis 2002). The broad base of social support for opposition also suggests that there is extensive disagreement with the orthodox view of the IFIs, the EU, and the

OECD on the appropriate boundary between political decisions and the market in relation to the structure and operation of public services. The attempt to impose a single model of the role of the state is as weak in policy terms as it is theoretically, and the attempt to introduce privatization as a global policy emphasizes that markets themselves are contentious political constructs that are subject to specific local conflicts (Chang 2003; Harriss-White 2003). The inadequacy of the neoliberal paradigm for the state is increasingly recognized, and analysts are emphasizing the importance of building strong state institutions, based on local culture and conditions (Fukuyama 2004). The politics of the water and energy campaigns should thus be seen as linking to the future rather than to the past.

REFERENCES

Amnesty International. 1997. "The 'Enron Project' in Maharashtra—Protests Suppressed in the Name of Development." Available at http://web.amnesty.org/library/pdf/ASA200311997ENGLISH/$File/ASA2003197.pdf (retrieved 19 October 2004).

Birdsall, N., and J. Nellis. 2002. "Winners and Losers: Assessing the Distributional Impact of Privatization." Center for Global Development Working Paper No. 6. Washington, DC: Center for Global Development.

Buresch, M. 2003. "The Declining Role of Foreign Private Investment." Paper presented at World Bank Energy Forum, Washington, DC, 24–27 February, available at http://www.worldbank.org/energy/week2003/Presentations/EnergyForum1/BureschWBForumpresentation.pdf (retrieved 20 October 2004).

Business News Americas—English. 2002. "Senate Blocks Corposana Sale Process." 6 June.

Chang, H. J. (ed.). 2003. *Globalisation, Economic Development and the Role of the State*. London: Zed Books.

Dubash, N. (ed.). 2002. *Power Politics: Equity and Environment in Electricity Reform*. Washington, DC: World Resources Institute.

Filho, A. de O. 2002. *Brazil: Struggle against the Privatization of Water*. Report to PSI InterAmerican Water Conference, San José, 8–10 July 2002, available at http://www.psiru.org/Others/BrasilLuta-port.doc [Portuguese], http://www.psiru.org/Others/BrasilLuta-es.doc [Spanish], and http://www.psiru.org/Others/BrasilLutaing.doc [English] (retrieved 19 January 2005).

Financial Times. 1997. "Manila Contract Challenges Criticised." 6 February.

Financial Times. 1999. "Emos Sell Off Leaves Frei in Fresh Disarray." 15 June.

Florio, M. 2004. *The Great Divestiture—Evaluating the Welfare Impact of the British Privatizations 1979–1997*, Cambridge, MA: MIT Press.

Fukuyama, F. 2004. *State Building: Governance and World Order in the Twenty-first Century.* London: Profile Books.

Hall, David. 2002. *Secret Reports and Public Concerns—A Reply to the USAID Paper on Water Privatisation "Skeptics."* London: PSIRU.

Hall, D., E. Lobina, and R. de la Motte. 2003. "Public Solutions for Private Problems? Responding to the Shortfall in Water Infrastructure Investment." London: PSIRU, available at http://www.psiru.org/reports/2003-09-W-strats. doc (retrieved 19 January 2005).

Hall, D., and R. de la Motte. 2004. *Dogmatic Development: Privatisation and Conditionalities in Six Countries.* PSIRU report for War on Want. London: PSIRU, available at http://www.psiru.org/reports/2004-02-U-condits.pdf (retrieved 19 January 2005).

Harriss-White, B. 2003. "On Understanding Markets as Social and Political Institutions in Developing Economies." In H. J. Chang (ed.), *Globalisation, Economic Development and the Role of the State.* London: Zed Books.

Herod, A. 2001. "Labor Internationalism and the Contradictions of Globalization: Or, Why the Local Is Sometimes Still Important in a Global Economy." *Antipode* 33(3):407–426.

IMF. 2004. "International Monetary Fund: Public Investment and Fiscal Policy." Washington, DC: IMF, available at http://www.imf.org/external/np/fad/2004/pifp/eng/PIFP.pdf (retrieved 19 January 2005).

Krosnick, J. A., and D. R. Kinder. 1990. "Altering the Foundations of Support for the President through Priming." *American Political Science Review* 84(3):497–512.

Lobina, E., and D. Hall. 2001. "Private to Public: International Lessons of Water Remunicipalisation in Grenoble, France." London: PSIRU, available at http://www.psiru.org/reports/2001-08-W-Grenoble.doc (retrieved 19 January 2005).

Lobina, E., and D. Hall. 2003. "Problems with Private Water Concessions: A Review of Experience." London: PSIRU, available at http://www.psiru.org/reports/2003-06-W-over.doc (retrieved 19 January 2005).

Mxotwa, M. 2001. "Nkonkobe Water Contract Nullified by High Court." *Dispatch Online* 15 December, at http://www.dispatch.co.2a/2001/12/15/easterncape/CNULL.htm (retrieved 19 January 2005).

Nellis, J. 2003. "Effects of Privatization on Income and Wealth Distribution." Presentation to World Bank Energy Week 2003, Washington, DC, 24–27 February.

Padco. 2002. "A Review of Reports by Private-Sector-Participation Skeptics." Presentation prepared for the Municipal Infrastructure Investment Unit (MIIU), South Africa and USAID, available at http://www.psiru.org/others/PadcoSkeptics.doc (retrieved 19 January 2005).

Pape, J. 2001. "A Public Sector Alternative: SAMWU's Efforts." *South African Labour Bulletin* 25(4):45–50.

Philippine Daily Inquirer. 2003. "Terrorists in Robes?" 28 May, at http://www.inq7.net/nat/2003/may/28/nat_12-1.htm (retrieved 12 April 2006).

Prayas Energy Group. 2001. "Lessons of the Enron Disaster: Democratization through TAPing of Governance as the Remedy." Available at http://www.prayaspune.org/energy/24_INFRA_Rep_01.pdf (retrieved 19 October 2004).

Saghir, J. 2003. "Opening Session Presentation to World Bank Energy Week 2003." Washington, DC, 24–27 February.

Vreese, C. H. de. 2004. "Primed by the Euro: The Impact of a Referendum Campaign on Public Opinion and Evaluations of Government and Political Leaders." *Scandinavian Political Studies* 27(1):45–64.

Wagle, S. 2000. "Reforms in the Indian Electricity Sector: Resisting the World Bank Model." Pune, India: Prayas Energy Group, available at http://www.prayaspune.org/energy/20_WB_model_presentation.zip (retrieved 19 January 2005).

Wall Street Journal. 2003. "The World Bank as Privatization Agnostic." 21 July, p. 2

Willner, J. 2001. "Ownership, Efficiency, and Political Interference." *European Journal of Political Economy* 17(4):723–748.

World Bank. 2003a. "Infrastructure Action Plan." Available at http://www.worldbank.org/infrastructure/files/InfrastructureActionPlan.pdf (retrieved 19 October 2004).

World Bank. 2003b. "Implementing the World Bank Group Infrastructure Action Plan." Available at http://siteresources.worldbank.org/DEVCOMMINT/Resources/Fall-2003/DC2003-0015(E)-Infrastructure.pdf (retrieved 19 October 2004).

World Bank. 2004a. *Reforming Infrastructure Privatization, Regulation, and Competition*. New York: World Bank/OUP.

World Bank. 2004b. "Credible Regulation Vital for Infrastructure Reform to Reduce Poverty." Press release, 14 June. Available at http://www.cefe.net/forum/CredibleRegulation.pdf (retrieved 19 October 2004).

SIX

Public Service Privatization and Crisis in Argentina

LEOPOLDO RODRÍGUEZ-BOETSCH

INTRODUCTION

In the 1990s, during the administration of Carlos S. Menem, Argentina implemented sweeping economic reforms aimed at the complete revamping of the country's productive and administrative structure. The aim was to overcome macroeconomic instability and sluggish growth through the introduction of market incentives and the retrenchment of state activity in the economy. Meticulously applying many of the policies of what came to be known as the Washington Consensus, the Menem administration was lauded in the international press, as well as by G7 governments and international financial institutions (IFIs), as a champion of effective government to be emulated by developing countries worldwide. Indeed, the policies initially appeared to work extremely well. A program of macroeconomic stabilization known as the Convertibility Plan, the brainchild of Minister of the Economy and Harvard graduate Domingo Cavallo, rapidly brought down inflation to levels common in developed industrial economies, and did so without sinking the country into a deep or prolonged recession. Deeper structural reforms supplemented the macroeconomic stabilization package. Privatization, deregulation, and trade liberalization proved effective in attracting new capital flows, which promoted the rapid modernization of the economy. Argentina was living proof that the swift implementation of market-oriented reforms could rapidly erase decades of misguided state intervention and lead to sustained growth.

The mirage did not last long. In 1995, as a result of the Mexican peso crisis, GDP in Argentina declined by 3 percent and unemployment reached 16 percent. The so-called "Tequila effect" should have served as a warning of the vulnerability of the Argentine economy to external shocks. Although the period 1996–1998 saw the restoration of vigorous growth rates, a series of external shocks led to a prolonged recession matched only by the Great Depression of the 1930s. The severe crisis suffered by Argentina holds important lessons for the academic and policy-making communities. Given the dramatic collapse of a developing economy that had been widely advertised as a model to be emulated, the reforms enshrined as dogma during the 1990s should be carefully examined. Such a task necessitates methical research on the role that market-oriented policies played in the turn of events in Argentina.

This chapter discusses the role of privatization in the economic reforms and the subsequent economic crisis afflicting Argentina. We start with an analysis of the function that privatization played in the macroeconomic stabilization and overall reorganization of the Argentine economy, followed by a description of the macroeconomic context of the Convertibility Plan. Finally, we explore the relation between the pricing of privatized public services and the macroeconomic crisis that Argentina faces. We conclude that the macroeconomic and regulatory context within which privatization took place played a critical role in undermining the ability of the Argentine government to respond to external shocks. This resulted in a prolonged recession and balance-of-payments (BOP) crisis. Significant productivity gains in many privatized state-owned enterprises (SOEs) indicate that a microeconomic rationale existed for the privatization of several sectors. However, the failure to pass these gains to the public in general can be attributed to a lack of political will and/or political inability to prevent an excessive concentration of economic power in the hands of a very few. Given that politics is an inherent part of the privatization process, other countries should pay special attention to the impact of privatization on the balance of economic and political power between diverse groups (including foreign investors) and the national government.

THE THEORY AND PRACTICE OF
PRIVATIZATION IN ARGENTINA

Privatization in Theory

For economic theory, the main attraction of privatization is the promise of greater microeconomic efficiency when an enterprise is transferred from bureaucratic administrators to private control. The improvement in efficiency is said to come from the difference between the incentives faced by political appointees and those faced by business managers. The former must make decisions based on a variety of goals, such as the financial soundness of the enterprise. They are not free of political considerations regarding the number of employees, investment decisions, setting of service rates, and so on. By contrast, business managers can be far more single minded about the operations of the enterprise, focusing on cost cutting and revenue expansion as strategies to maximize shareholders' returns. The expected outcome of privatization is a better-run enterprise, and it is able to generate profits while also improving the quality of services and reducing prices. However, there is no guarantee that these results will materialize. The market structure and regulatory environment within which the newly privatized firm will operate is extremely important in determining outcomes. If such a firm has to operate within a tightly regulated environment where it enjoys very little ability to make decisions, the conditions of production may see practically no change. On the other hand, if a firm is privatized into a monopolistic market, and is free from government interference, then the focus on profit maximization is likely to result in important cost-saving measures and significant price increases for consumers. In other words, it is not a foregone conclusion that privatization will result in greater economic efficiency.

Many advocates of market-oriented reforms claim that privatization also promises to improve the macroeconomic outlook (Williamson 1990). In cases where SOEs have contributed significantly to government deficits, privatization seems like a natural solution to their reduction. The proceeds from selling off SOEs would not only directly contribute to government revenue, but they also would eliminate future budgetary needs such as operating costs and capital investment. Politicians find the theoretical link between deficit reduction and privatization useful as a signal of their commitment to economic reforms. Empirical evidence for this claim is, however, less than scant. In a study of privatization in Latin America, Pinheiro and Schneider (1995:769) found that "it is not reasonable to expect significant short-term fiscal gains from privatization." In their view, privatization cannot be considered a serious tool for deficit reduction, and they warn that a privatization process focused on such a goal can have a detrimental effect on economic efficiency.

Privatization has also been advocated as a solution to government corruption, because SOEs present abundant opportunities for corrupt officials to line their pockets through rigged contract bidding processes, over-invoicing of costs, preferential provision of services, and so on. Clearly, these practices can also take place under private control, but it is commonly assumed that shareholders have a stronger incentive and greater capacity to demand transparency from business managers than citizens have over appointed bureaucrats. We should recognize, however, that privatization also presents ample opportunities for graft. The transparency of the bidding process, the nature of the regulatory framework, and the pricing mechanism for public services have an enormous impact on the potential profitability of a privatized firm. Prospective investors and new owners alike have large incentives to seek advantages for their firms through many kinds of illegal practices. Once international capital is involved, the magnitude of the problem may potentially reach dimensions beyond all imagination in SOEs with much smaller budgets. Unfortunately, privatization theorists and advocates have generally chosen to overlook these dangers and their potential repercussions. For example, Krueger (1990) points out the advantages of private economic activity over government intervention, emphasizing the potential for rent seeking present in SOEs, but he fails to mention even once the potential for corruption under private ownership. Repeatedly expressed by prominent economic theorists and policy makers (Krueger was pivotal at the World Bank (WB) during the 1980s and currently works for the IMF), such views carried significant weight among IFIs and governments seeking effective economic reforms (Domínguez 1997).

Since the 1980s, IFIs such as the WB, the IMF, and the Inter-American Development Bank (IDB) have been unconditional supporters of privatization in developing countries. Not only have they advocated privatization as an essential component of structural adjustment programs, but on several occasions they have also made privatization a condition of renewed lending. In many cases, loans have been extended to support the administrative overhaul, severance payments, and early retirements associated with privatization. During the early 1990s, the

Standard WB prescription regarding privatization was that it had to take place as rapidly as possible in order to prevent the organization of pressure groups that may be effective in opposing it. Unfortunately the rush to privatize not only undermines the possibility of popular participation in the process, but it is also likely to result in terms that are unfavorable to the state and a weak regulatory environment. Greater attention to questions of reform sequencing has exposed some of the flaws in IFI policy prescriptions.

Economic Reforms and Privatization in Argentina

During the military regime of 1976–1983, relatively cheap and easily available external credit was used liberally to finance large fiscal deficits. Although some of the funds went to finance infrastructure and the expansion of SOEs' physical capital, much was used to support a failed monetary scheme and to cover undisclosed military expenditures (including the violent repression of political dissent that resulted in the disappearance of 9,000–30,000 people).

Throughout the 1980s, the Argentine economy suffered bulging government budget deficits. Often financed with credit from the Central Bank, these deficits had severe inflationary consequences. Facing bloated foreign-debt payments, largely the result of excessive government spending under the military regime and the nationalization of private debt, the administration of Raúl Alfonsín was unable to reduce government expenditure. In an effort to calm inflationary pressures, Alfonsín capped the prices charged by SOEs in key sectors of the economy such as energy and public utilities. SOEs were also suffering from the excessive borrowing that had taken place during the easy credit period of the 1970s. To make matters worse, many of these enterprises had the additional political mandate of absorbing labor that had become redundant in other sectors of the economy in order to keep unemployment rates low.

The use of SOEs as tools of macroeconomic policy, also a common practice in prior administrations, severely weakened their ability to undertake necessary capital investment and sustain an adequate quality of services. As the practice continued, their ability to provide services deteriorated, on some occasions resulting in substantial losses to the state and widespread discontent among users. With service rates below average costs of production, SOE deficits represented up to 4 percent of GDP in the 1980s (Galiani and Petrecolla 2000:82).

In 1989, the economy experienced repeated hyperinflationary episodes, forcing an early transition to the presidency of Carlos S. Menem. The critical macroeconomic conditions faced by the Menem administration required swift action. Fiscal deficits and hyperinflationary expectations had to be addressed immediately. Privatization rapidly emerged as a cornerstone of policies aimed at stabilization and deep structural reform. First, privatization was promoted as a deficit-reduction measure. SOEs had contributed to the fiscal deficits for several years, and the proceeds from privatization could help shore up government revenue and/or reduce debt interest payments. Second, privatization provided a strong political signal of Menem's commitment to market-oriented reforms. He had won the presidency as the candidate of the *Partido Justicialista*, the Peronist party traditionally associated with populism and state intervention. In order to ease domestic and foreign investors and gain IFI approval, Menem sought to establish his credentials as a staunch reformer. Finally, privatization could be used to attract new foreign direct investment (FDI) and thereby help reestablish growth. At a time of crisis, the drawbacks of such policies seemed minimal. Although labor unions objected to privatization, the most powerful unions acceded because of their close links to the Peronist Party. In any case, macroeconomic conditions were so adverse that emergency measures were widely accepted as necessary, while the large deficits and decline in quality of SOE services during the 1980s had created an atmosphere favorable to privatization among the general public.

These were far from optimal conditions in which to carry out an orderly privatization. Under IFI pressure and needing to establish its reform credentials, the Menem administration rushed the process. Budget strains encouraged the use of short-term revenue-improving criteria at the expense of long-term efficiency-enhancing outcomes. The process was broad and swift. Based on the Law of State Reform passed soon after the accession of Menem to office in 1989, the vast majority of SOEs were sold to private investors or dismantled between 1990 and 1994. In just five years, the National Telecommunications Enterprise (ENTEL), the airline company (*Aerolíneas*), the state oil enterprise (*Yacimientos Petrolíferos Fiscales*), most state electricity generation and distribution enterprises, state petrochemical firms, steel mills, radio and television channels, the state natural gas company, shipyards, and many others, were privatized. In the years to follow, the few public services that remained under government control were also targeted, including the postal service, the regulation of airwaves, and the issuance of passports.

The result was a privatization experience noted for its shortcomings regarding competition and regulation. A common observation is the prevalence of monopolistic markets in privatized sectors, even when more competitive structures could have been created. Another observation is the delay in the establishment of a regulatory framework and independent regulatory agencies to constrain the monopolistic power of privatized enterprises (Gerchunoff and Cánovas 1996). Monopoly power was essentially traded for higher bids in an effort to boost short-term revenue and establish Menem's credentials as a reformer.

Efforts at ownership dispersal were also absent. Entry to the bidding process was limited to a few conglomerates that could prove enormous financial resources and administrative capabilities. Those winning the bids were invariably composed of powerful local business groups associated with multinational enterprises and with foreign financial institutions holding Argentine debt. Practically no effort was made to sell shares to the general public, reserving at best no more than 10 percent for unions and employees. Galiani and Petrecolla (2000:86) describe the process as "a form of take-over of state enterprises by a powerful coalition of national holding companies, international financial investors, and some foreign operators of public services." Basualdo et al. (2002) point out that the privatization process brought together local business groups and international creditors whose interests had been opposed during the 1980s. The result was an unprecedented concentration of economic and political power outside the grasp of the state.

In order to make SOEs even more attractive and to boost bids, service fees were often increased prior to privatization. In the ten months prior to the privatization of ENTEL, the U.S. dollar price of a telephone pulse was raised by 711 percent. Between 1992 and 1993, the average price of a cubic meter of natural gas increased by 23 percent in real terms; the service was privatized in January 1993 (Aspiazu 2002:12). The higher fees were intended to guarantee a comfortable level of revenue to the new owners, but labor costs were also slashed. In 1990, at the beginning of the privatization process, seven SOEs in the telephone, mail, air transportation, water, sewage, electricity, railway, and natural gas sectors employed 222,800 workers. By 1994 only one SOE remained and 32 privatized firms had emerged from the other six, employing a total of 99,000 workers, representing a drop of 55.6 percent. By 1998, when all SOEs in the initial group had been privatized into 33 enterprises, employment among these firms stood at only 75,800. Over the period 1985–1998, there was a 68.9 percent drop in the number of jobs among the same group of firms (Duarte 2002:73). The drastic staff cuts in SOEs prior to privatization were achieved through the extensive use of voluntary retirement and severance pay. Considering the delicate fiscal position of the government during the early 1990s, such outlays would have been impossible had the WB not stepped in with generous loans. A total of 86,274 employees "voluntarily" retired from public service SOEs, at a total cost of US$1.3 billion in 1992–1993, or about US$20,000 per retired worker during that period (Duarte 2002:81).

The shedding of labor by SOEs was to have a significant impact on overall unemployment levels. Prior to the prolonged recession that hit the country from 1998 to 2002, Argentina's unemployment rate showed a clear upward trend coinciding with privatization and the rapid and unilateral liberalization of trade. According to IMF figures, unemployment stood at 6 percent in 1991, climbed to 12 percent by 1994, and jumped to 16.6 percent by 1996. Official government figures show an even more dramatic increase in unemployment during the same period. Duarte (2002) estimates that at least 2 percent of the unemployment rate recorded in the late 1990s can be directly linked to SOE layoffs. Privatization also resulted in lower demand for domestically produced inputs. As subsidiaries of foreign-based corporations, many privatized firms switched suppliers from local firms to the parent company, resulting in the reduction of manufacturing employment in Argentina.

Evaluating Privatization in Argentina

There can be little doubt that privatization served as an excellent instrument to signal Menem's commitment to market-oriented reforms. Large capital inflows during the early 1990s are evidence of its success in this arena. However, the privatization process in Argentina failed to accomplish the three primary economic benefits attributed to it. Perhaps, as Pinheiro and Schneider (1995) would argue, this failure is a result of the high costs of using privatization as a political signal.

Improved efficiency—the central goal of privatization from an economic perspective—was not attained in the economy overall. The drastic drop of labor among privatized firms had a strong positive impact on productivity in all the enterprises in question. Fewer workers, the intensification of the labor process, and new physical capital resulted in an average increase in labor productivity of 16.9 percent per year between 1993 and 1998. However, the benefits derived from higher productivity were not transferred to the workers in the form of wage increases, nor were they passed on to consumers as lower prices. Instead, as we shall later see, the firms captured these gains in the form of extraordinary rates of return (monopoly rents). Although the privatized firms significantly improved cost efficiency in public services, society at large hardly saw any benefits (Geldstein 1997).

A second goal of privatization, the long-term improvement of fiscal accounts, also failed to materialize. Efforts to enhance short-term government revenue from privatization resulted in a net increase in debt. Between 1990 and 1994, the privatization process generated US$10.4 billion in cash receipts and US$15.1 billion in debt reduction at nominal value (the market value of the debt was substantially lower). Debt-for-equity swaps represented a little over US$13.5 billion in debt reduction. The additional US$1.6 billion was debt transferred to the newly created private enterprises operating in the gas and electricity sectors. In the same time period, the Argentine state absorbed an estimated US$20 billion of outstanding SOE debt, delivering debt-free enterprises to the private sector. This represents a net increase in the debt held by the state of US$6.5 billion (Basualdo et al. 2002). In other words, current revenue was increased temporarily, thus reducing budget deficits during the early 1990s, but future budgets were compromised by the increased indebtedness.

Finally, privatization and the consequent reduction of state intervention in the economy did not result in a reduction of rent-seeking activities as predicted by economic theorists and IFI policy makers. On the contrary, the privatization process opened up unprecedented opportunities for rent-seeking activities by local and foreign business groups, particularly in the context of a rushed process that lacked an adequate regulatory framework. The privatization process in Argentina created monopoly rents that dwarf by magnitudes of thousands those that might previously have been obtained from import licensing, the original target and source of inspiration of rent-seeking theory (Krueger 1974). Allegations of widespread corruption involving hundreds of millions of dollars, and the enormous concentration of power among a reduced group of business conglomerates, indicate a rise in the prevalence of rent-seeking activities during and after the privatization process.

THE MACROECONOMIC CONTEXT OF
CONVERTIBILITY AND ITS CRISIS

Cavallo became Minister of the Economy in 1991 and rapidly implemented a radical anti-inflationary program. Pegging the Argentine peso
to the U.S. dollar at 1:1 and linking the supply of pesos to the amount of
dollars held in Central Bank reserves, Cavallo intended to reestablish
confidence in the ability of the national currency to function as a store
of value. In theory, the Central Bank no longer had discretionary power
over monetary policy. The money supply was to be determined by a single rule: one dollar in reserves, one peso in circulation. If reserves were
to increase by one U.S. dollar, peso supply would increase by one peso
times the money multiplier (determined by the required reserve ratio),
but if dollar reserves were to decline, then the peso supply would have
to experience an equivalent decline. The Central Bank was mandated to
convert pesos into U.S. dollars at the ratio of one to one. The Convertibility Plan proved extremely successful, causing inflationary expectations to plummet and leading to a rapid decline in the inflation rate
between 1991 and 1994 (Cavallo 1997).

A key complement to the Convertibility Plan was the rapid and
broad liberalization of trade. The unilateral elimination of import
licensing and the sharp reduction of other trade barriers allowed foreign
goods to enter Argentina practically unimpeded. This facilitated the
function of the fixed exchange rate as a price anchor. If the prices of
domestically produced goods were to rise faster than the U.S. dollar
prices of the same goods produced abroad, the influx of imported goods
would place a check on these prices—or even pull them back down.
However, not all goods and services are traded across international borders. Trade liberalization is effective on tradable goods and services,
but may have little or no deflationary impact on the prices of nontradables, such as public services.

The early 1990s were certainly an auspicious time to implement pro-
market reforms. The effervescent mood of international financial markets
in the face of the break-up of the Soviet Union, and extremely low interest rates in industrial nations, generated an atmosphere propitious for significant capital flows to developing nations and transition economies.
With inflation under control and a massive program of privatization and
liberalization in place, Cavallo and Menem received international praise.
Argentina became an exemplary case of successful market reform to
be emulated by other nations. Financial capital readily flowed into

Argentina, seeking a slice of the much-lauded "emerging market." The inflow of funds facilitated an impressive economic expansion in the period 1991–1994, providing the Central Bank with adequate reserves to expand the money supply and accommodate economic growth.

The Mexican peso crisis of 1994–1995 was the first warning sign that Argentina was becoming excessively dependent on often fickle international capital flows. Although the key economic indicators in Argentina did not show signs of distress prior to the crisis, international investors withdrew funds from Argentina on the heels of the devaluation of the Mexican peso. The resulting BOP difficulties threw the Argentine economy into a significant recession in 1995. By 1996, robust growth had been reestablished and any cautionary lesson from that crisis was thrown to the wind by both the Argentine authorities and the international financial community.

Reliance on external financial flows cannot be considered a significant offense, particularly in the case of developing countries that are experiencing rapid growth. However, a dangerous and sinister process was well in motion by 1995, and continued after that year's crisis. With the nominal exchange rate fixed, the Argentine peso had become overvalued in real terms. Between 1991 and 1994, Argentina's rate of inflation was significantly higher than the U.S. rate, making Argentine goods and services relatively expensive. This naturally translated into growing current account deficits (primarily the result of rapidly growing imports and sluggish exports), which required substantial capital-account inflows to maintain the BOP. The period of economic recovery that followed the 1995 recession carried indications of this real exchange overvaluation. Although rapid GDP growth was reestablished between 1996 and 1998, unemployment did not drop below 12 percent. A significant jump in the current-account deficit from US$6.8 billion in 1996 to US$14.5 billion in 1998 indicates that the recovery relied heavily on capital inflows. A shock to the capital account would require either a significant devaluation in order to reduce the deficit, or the reduction of domestic prices in order to restore the price competitiveness of Argentine exports.

In the fourth quarter of 1998, the Argentine economy entered a four-year recession. GDP declined by 3.5 percent in 1999, by 0.5 percent in 2000, by 5.5 percent in 2001, and by a record 12.5 percent in 2002. Growth was reestablished in 2003, but only after a sharp devaluation and the largest default on external obligations in history (Basualdo et al. 2002). What turned a buoyant economy, the pride and glory of advocates for market reform during the 1990s, into a severely depressed basket case? Much of the blame lies with the vulnerability to a BOP crisis created by market-friendly policies adopted throughout the 1990s, to which a flawed privatization process was no stranger.

Starting in 1998, Argentina faced a series of severe external shocks. The 1997 SE Asian crisis sent shockwaves through international financial markets, drying up capital flows to so-called emerging markets. Aware of the Argentine economy's vulnerability to contagion from distant financial crises—a lesson learned in 1995—the government sought to inspire confidence through the establishment of an IMF Extended Fund Facility of US$2.8 billion. Nevertheless, contagion from the Russian and Brazilian crises resulted in reduced capital inflows and rising domestic interest rates. The economy inevitably shrank as consumption and investment declined. With privatization having run its course, the Argentine state no longer had assets at its disposal to attract foreign capital. In any case, the mood in international financial markets did not favor further investment in Argentina.

The slowdown of capital inflows was not the only external shock. In the same period, the effective real exchange rate of the Argentine peso rose. Several events contributed to the reduced price competitiveness of Argentine products among its main trading partners. The sharp devaluation of the Brazilian real in early 1999 made Brazilian goods extremely inexpensive in Argentina, while Argentine goods became prohibitively expensive in Brazil. Inevitably, the trade balance with Brazil turned sharply into a deficit. Shortly thereafter, the U.S. dollar started to appreciate against the newly launched Euro. Europe was Argentina's second largest trading partner after Brazil, so the subsequent appreciation of the Argentine peso against the Euro further deteriorated Argentina's trade accounts. To make matters worse, rising interest rates drove up payments on large public and private debts accumulated in the early and mid-1990s, and the repatriation of profits and royalties by foreign subsidiaries—among them many privatized public services—caused a further deterioration of the current account.

Facing dual shocks to the capital and current accounts, Argentina was hard pressed to find solutions to the growing BOP disequilibrium. Having no control over capital inflows, interest rates on U.S. dollar loans, or the repatriation of company profits, Argentina was forced to increase exports of goods and services and reduce imports. Meanwhile, IMF assistance became indispensable to meet external obligations, and IMF-style adjustments were rapidly implemented. The solution devised was standard IMF fare minus the devaluation. The trade surplus would be generated by austerity measures such as reduced government expenditure and rising taxation. Reduced consumption would in turn reduce imports and free up resources for the export sector. Normally, a dramatic cut in consumption would be accompanied by currency devaluation. However, in the Argentine case this was practically impossible. First, the Law of Convertibility required an act of Congress to lift parity to the U.S. dollar. Congressional debate on the issue would immediately result in massive capital outflows and the virtual collapse of the financial system, exacerbating the crisis rather than solving it. Second, the Argentine economy was highly dollarized, with significant contractual obligations denominated in U.S. dollars. Devaluation would have endangered the financial soundness of the entire productive apparatus as well as large segments of the middle- and upper-income groups. Finally, convertibility was associated in the minds of most Argentines with the defeat of hyperinflation and constituted the inviolable promise of a stable currency. Changing the peso parity to the U.S. dollar would have amounted to political suicide.

The impossibility of devaluation meant that the entire burden of reducing imports and expanding exports had to fall on reducing consumption. As previously discussed, the overvaluation of the Brazilian Real exchange rate during the early 1990s and the revaluation of the effective exchange rate in the late 1990s reduced the price competitiveness of Argentine products. The contraction of consumption would have to be severe enough to drive domestic prices down and restore the price competitiveness of Argentine goods and services—effectively depreciating the Brazilian real exchange rate. The adjustment sought a reduction in wages, forcing prices to drop and restoring international price competitiveness. In other words, the policy response to external shocks was to be deflation.

The severe recession of 1999 enabled a reduction of wages and domestic prices, starting a slow process of deflation. The recession contributed to a reduction of the trade deficit in goods and services from US$7.5 billion in 1998 to US$5 billion in 1999 (Basualdo et al. 2002). However, the current-account deficit remained large at US$12 billion and the government deficit practically doubled. In 2000, Fernando de la Rúa became president and opted to continue abiding by IMF demands, which by then was adamant about a large reduction of the government deficit. De la Rúa's administration raised taxes to perilous levels and enacted an across-the board cut in government salaries and pension payments of 13 percent. As a result, an incipient recovery in 2000 was choked off. Urged by the IMF, de la Rúa also pushed a labor market flexibilization law through the legislature amid allegations of kickbacks from the executive to members of Congress. The subsequent economic contraction reduced the balance of trade in goods and services to a deficit of US$2 billion. Nevertheless, the Argentine current account still registered a deficit of US$9 billion. In 2001, as the external accounts continued to improve slowly, domestic conditions rapidly worsened. In an effort to cut government expenditures, de la Rúa drastically reduced social assistance programs. The consequent decline in consumption drove the balance of trade in goods and services into a small surplus. However, unemployment climbed to a record 18 percent as the government's austerity program was disenfranchising people. Three years of deflationary efforts were slowly having an impact on external accounts, but their social and political cost had reached boiling point.

In September 2001, the IMF, unsatisfied with progress in the reduction of government deficits, suspended financial assistance to Argentina. What capital inflows may have remained came to a halt and an imminent devaluation became possible. Cavallo, the original architect of Convertibility, had been resurrected to the Ministry of Economy after a five-year hiatus. In an effort to stem capital flight and prevent the collapse of the banking system, Cavallo froze all bank deposits, infuriating a middle class that was already suffering lower wages and high unemployment. After more than three years of recession and rising unemployment, many among the poor and the unemployed were going hungry. By December, food riots broke out in the outskirts of Buenos Aires, as mobs sacked grocery stores. The government attempted to restore order through police repression. On this occasion, the middle class, traditionally indifferent to the plight of low-income sectors, poured into the central streets of Buenos Aires and other major cities to demand Cavallo's resignation. When de la Rúa responded with further police repression, the population demanded his resignation as well. In the ensuing weeks, debt payments were suspended and the peso was floated against the U.S. dollar.

THE ROLE OF PRIVATIZED PUBLIC SERVICES IN THE ECONOMIC CRISIS

Privatized Public Service Enterprises (PPSEs) were not innocent bystanders in the prolonged process of economic, political, and social deterioration that afflicted Argentina. Deflation is never an easy task. Not only does it place severe strains on the financial system and depress investment, but it also heightens political tensions as unemployment and social distress escalate. The monopolistic power and special contractual arrangements retained by PPSEs made matters worse. Just as austerity measures were implemented to drive prices down and recover international price competitiveness, the fees charged by many public services were rising. This in turn meant that the contraction in the consumption of other items had to be more severe, exacerbating the difficult conditions faced by the vast majority of Argentine households (Geldstein 1997). Electricity rates, water and sewage fees, natural gas prices, and transport costs increased as incomes shrank and unemployment exploded. While the economy sank, PPSEs' profits grew. We must explore the pricing of public services post-privatization in order to understand this seeming paradox.

The combination of trade liberalization and privatization had a profound impact on relative prices in the economy. The rapid and unilateral reduction of trade barriers kept the prices of goods and services traded across international borders down. Industrial and manufacturing firms originally established behind high levels of protection hardly had any time to adapt to the new competitive conditions. Although the firms were dedicated to the production of tradable goods, many floundered in their struggle to survive, resulting in the significant increase in unemployment noted above. On the other hand, the prices of nontradables were largely unaffected by international competition and continued to increase in the midst of trade liberalization. Public services represent an important proportion of nontradables. Many of these, such as electricity, roads, and telecommunications, are critical to the production of tradable goods and comprise a significant proportion of essential household expenditures.

The lack of competition often inherent in the provision of public services is a result of economies of scale and their nontradable nature. Regulatory authorities are generally established to determine reasonable prices for public services. A common pricing mechanism used by regulatory authorities is the price-cap system, determining a maximum rate that can be charged for a public service. The maximum rate is periodically adjusted to accommodate changes in input costs and factor productivity. The regulatory agency would dictate lower service fees if significant productivity increases were obtained, or they would input prices declined in order to guarantee that gains from such increases are shared with the population at large. In the case of an increase in input prices, the regulatory agency would increase the maximum rate in order to protect the earning of the public service provider. In principle the price-cap mechanism would guide the regulation of public service fees in Argentina. In practice virtually no downward adjustments of service fees took place to distribute the benefits of large increases in productivity. Instead, the price-cap mechanism was used to obtain automatic rises in service rates through adjustments to the U.S. rate of inflation.

During the 1980s, prices and wages had been periodically and automatically adjusted for inflation, transmitting past inflation into the future. The Convertibility Plan declared all automatic adjustments of prices and wages null and void to eliminate this source of cost-push inflation and reduce inflationary expectations. The ban on price indexation included all PPSEs. However, since public services were subject to regulated maximum rates, and these would no longer be adjusted, this measure did not sit well with PPSEs and potential investors in firms up for privatization. In 1992, the contracts for telephone services were renegotiated to allow the two service providers biannual adjustments of service fees according to the U.S. consumer price index (CPI). The firms argued that inputs to the industry were imported and service rates should be adjusted to a foreign price index. Given the anchoring of the peso to the U.S. dollar, they claimed that such indexation could do no damage. The authorization to adjust service fees in relation to U.S. inflation clearly contravened the Law of Convertibility passed by the Argentine Congress. Illegal or not, the Menem administration ceded to the firms' request, allowing indexation to the U.S. CPI. The privatization process was only in its early stages and Menem intended to give a clear signal that his administration was bent on protecting the interests on foreign investors. Public services that had already been privatized renegotiated their contracts to incorporate a clause allowing fee adjustments to the U.S. CPI. Indexation of service fees to the U.S. CPI became a standard feature of subsequent privatizations.

The special treatment granted to privatized firms, albeit illegal, proved to be a boon to foreign investors. Between January 1995 and June 2001, the Argentine CPI declined by 1.1 percent, and the Argentine producer price index (PPI) increased by 1.6 percent. During the same period, the U.S. CPI increased by 18.4 percent and its PPI by 9.8 percent. While the Argentine economy was experiencing severe deflation, PPSEs were allowed to increase service rates, causing further imbalance of tradable to nontradable prices and slowing down any gains in the price competitiveness of Argentine products.

In addition to the periodic indexation of service rates, some PPSEs were able to negotiate additional rate increases and reduce their contractual commitments. For example, Aguas Argentinas negotiated a fee increase of 13.5 percent in July 1994, even though the regulatory framework stipulated no fee increases for ten years. By the end of 1997, a new renegotiation of its contract postponed or eliminated various investment projects agreed to in the original privatization contract. In 1998, the enterprise obtained an additional service-rate increase of 5.1 percent. Renegotiations of the contract in 1998 introduced the periodic indexation of fees to the U.S. CPI. Negotiations during de la Rúa's administration resulted in a 9.1 percent increase in service fees in 2001. Consequently, residential rates for water and sewage services increased by 88.2 percent between May 1993 and January 2002, whereas the Argentine CPI increased by only 7.3 percent (Aspiazu and Forcinito 2003:1–2). The repeated renegotiation of fees and the cancellation of investment commitments by a significant number of PPSEs indicate that, contrary to the arguments of market-reform advocates, opportunities for rent seeking and corruption expanded as a result of privatization.

With a captive market, the provision of public services under monopolistic conditions entails only a modicum of entrepreneurial risk. Low risk in turn implies that rates of return, if fees are properly regulated, should be small relative to high-risk sectors. However, the lack of an appropriate regulatory framework and proper regulatory agencies guaranteed a higher than normal rate of return to PPSEs. In effect, profit margins for public service providers in Argentina were significantly higher than profit rates in other industries in the country, as well as those obtained by public service providers in Europe or the United States. Between 1993 and 1999, the largest 200 firms operating in Argentina generated nearly US$26 billion in profits. Of these, 54 percent went to 26 PPSEs, resulting in average profits of US$2 billion per year. In the same period, the rate of profit among the top 200 firms was 10.8 percent for PPSEs and 6.4 percent for firms with ownership links to PPSEs. Firms in the same group but with no ownership links to PPSEs registered an average rate of profit of only 1.6 percent (Basualdo et al. 2002:37).

Other measures of profitability do not alter the picture significantly. Between 1994 and 1999, the average rate of profit relative to the firm's net assets was 15.4 percent for PPSEs, with road concessions and water and sewage services averaging over 20 percent. The only sector below 10 percent was electricity with 5.6 percent. The average rate of profit to sales for PPSEs was 12.3 percent for the same period with less variation between sectors. In comparison, in 1999, the largest 100 firms excluding PPSEs had an average rate of profit to net assets of 3.4 percent, and an average rate of profit to sales of 1.2 percent (Basualdo et al. 2002:38). Clearly, during the period under observation, investment in public services and associated nontradable industries was extremely profitable, whereas investment in manufacturing and other tradable sectors held little to no appeal. It should therefore come as no surprise that Argentina faced a very serious struggle in trying to reduce its current-account deficit between 1999 and 2001.

Comparison with rates elsewhere helps to place the exceptionally high rate of profits attained by PPSEs in Argentina within a global context. For example, in the United States, the United Kingdom, and France, a normal rate of profit on net assets for water and sewage service providers is considered to be between 6 percent and 7 percent. As a result of repeated renegotiations, the indexation of fees to the U.S. CPI, a weak regulatory framework, and co-opted regulatory agencies, Aguas Argentinas received an average rate of profit on net assets of 23.3 percent between 1994 and 1999. In the case of telephone services, Telecom Argentina generated an average rate of profit three times larger than its parent companies France Telecom and Telecom Italia, while Telefónica Argentina was twice as profitable as Telefónica de España (Abeles et al. 2001). Another telling example comes from the two companies in charge of natural gas transportation whose average rate of return was 40 percent; a reasonable rate of return for this sector is considered to be between 10 percent and 20 percent (Basualdo et al. 2002:39–40). The exorbitant profit rates obtained by PPSEs can only be interpreted as evidence of unchecked monopolistic power and the exertion of strong influence over regulatory agencies and government alike.

The evidence reviewed above indicates that PPSEs contributed to the prolonged depression of 1999–2002 and the collapse of convertibility in a variety of ways. PPSEs' rising fees contributed to the overvaluation of the Argentine peso, diminishing the price competitiveness of Argentine products abroad. The PPSEs also borrowed heavily in international markets, requiring foreign exchange to repay debts; and they repatriated their profits when growth prospects declined, placing an undue burden on the current account. We analyze each of these below.

First, the special treatment regarding the adjustment of fees granted to PPSEs undermined efforts to reestablish the international price competitiveness of Argentine products between 1999 and 2001. Wheras the entire economy was submerged in a deflationary process for three consecutive years, the prices of most public services continued to increase at the U.S. rate of inflation, or even above in the case of some contracts renegotiated during that period. This not only slowed down internal price adjustments, rendering Argentine goods less competitive, but it also generated significant hardship among low- and middle-income households already suffering from declining wages and growing unemployment. Second, PPSEs borrowed extensively overseas during the early 1990s. Most SOEs had been transferred to private hands debt-free, but PPSEs used their extensive assets as collateral in acquiring large debts. Interest and principal payments on these debts eventually required significant foreign exchange, with the subsequent pressure on the current account and the exchange rate. Given that PPSEs produce nontradable services, the foreign exchange needed to meet their debt payments had to be generated in the tradables sector. Finally, the somber growth outlook between 1998 and 2001 led to the repatriation of profits to parent companies abroad, precisely at a time of severe BOP difficulties. Like payments on PPSEs' foreign debts, this contributed to recurrent deficits in the current account and placed pressure on the exchange rate.

CONCLUSION

The fall of de la Rúa was followed by a couple of weeks of political wrangling in Congress from which Eduardo Duhalde emerged as the new interim president. Duhalde added the abrogation of the Law of Convertibility, effectively letting the peso float against the dollar, to a payments moratorium declared shortly after de la Rúa's fall. The ensuing devaluation required that all contracts, prices, and fees previously established in U.S. dollars be converted into pesos, including deposits in the banking system and domestic debts. Furthermore, the special indexation privilege thus far available to PPSEs was summarily abolished. These emergency measures resulted in a severe dislocation of the economy, as the financial system teetered on the verge of collapse and enterprises with foreign debts struggled to stave off bankruptcy.

Analysis of events since January 2002 is beyond the scope of this chapter. Suffice it to say that the Argentine government has kept most public service fees frozen. Only in mid-2004 were some energy-sector fees raised in an effort to curb fast-growing demand for natural gas and electricity. Between 2002 and 2004, PPSEs have put pressure on the Argentine government to raise public service fees. From lawsuits at the United Nations international court for dispute resolution, to lobbying of G7 nations with influence in the IMF, and even veiled threats and actual interruptions of services, PPSEs have sought to reestablish the golden days by any means at their disposal. After much wrangling, the administration of Néstor Kirchner has apparently reached agreements with PPSEs in various sectors regarding the renegotiation of contracts.

A rushed and flawed privatization process that did not establish an adequate regulatory framework and the corresponding independent regulatory agencies is responsible for much of the disappointment surrounding PPSEs in Argentina. A privatization process that concentrated wealth and power resulted in few or no benefits to society at large. Significant productivity gains in all PPSEs ought to have brought large benefits to consumers of public services, but for the most part these gains were seized by PPSEs exercising monopolistic power. Contrary to what happened in Argentina, privatization should not represent the complete forfeit of state authority over public services. Governments of developing nations should pursue privatization with extreme caution. A regulatory and legal framework that limits the activities of PPSEs and grants the state broad powers of intervention ought to be established prior to the transfer of state assets to the private sector. As the case of Argentina shows, swift privatization for the sake of short-term expediency can carry enormous long-run costs.

REFERENCES

Abeles, Martín, Karina Forcinito, and Martín Schorr. 2001. *El Oligopolio Telefónico Argentino Frente a la Liberalización de Mercado*. Buenos Aires: Universidad Nacional de Quilmes.

Aspiazu, Daniel. 2002. "Privatizaciones en la Argentina: La Captura Institucional del Estado," *Realidad Económica* 189:8–16.

Aspiazu, Daniel, and Karina Forcinito. 2003. "Privatización del Sistema de Agua y Saneamiento en Buenos Aires: Historia de un Fracaso." Paper presented at the III World Forum on Water, Kyoto, 16–23 March.

Basualdo, Eduardo, Daniel Aspiazu et al. 2002. *El Proceso de Privatización en Argentina*. Buenos Aires: Universidad Nacional de Quilmes.

Cavallo, Domingo. 1997. "Lessons from Argentina's Privatization Experience." *Journal of International Affairs* 50(2):459–474.

Domínguez, Jorge I. (ed.). 1997. *Technopols: Freeing Politics and Markets in Latin America in the 1990s*. University Park, PA: Pennsylvania State University Press.

Duarte, Marisa. 2002. "Los Impactos de las Privatizaciones en el Mercado de Trabajo: Desocupación y Creciente Precarización Laboral." In Daniel Aspiazu (ed.), *Privatizaciones y Poder Económico*. Buenos Aires: Universidad Nacional de Quilmes.

Galiani, Sebastián, and Diego Petrecolla. 2000. "The Argentine Privatization Process and Its Aftermath: Some Preliminary Conclusions." In Melissa H. Birch and Jarry Haar (eds.), *The Impact of Privatization in the Americas*. Coral Gables, FL: North-South Center Press.

Geldstein, Rosa. 1997. "Gender Bias and Family Distress: The Privatization Experience in Argentina." *Journal of International Affairs* 50(2):545–571.

Gerchunoff, Pablo, and Guillermo Cánovas. 1996. "Privatization: The Argentine Experience." In William Glade with Rossana Corona (eds.), *Bigger Economies, Smaller Governments: Privatization in Latin America*. Boulder, CO: Westview Press.

Krueger, Anne. 1974. "The Political Economy of the Rent-Seeking Society." *American Economic Review* 64(3):291–303.

Krueger, Anne. 1990. "Government Failures in Development." *Journal of Economic Perspectives* 4(3):9–23.

Pinheiro, Armando Castelar, and Ben Ross Schneider. 1995. "The Fiscal Impact of Privatisation in Latin America." *Journal of Development Studies* 31(5):751–776.

Williamson, John (ed.). 1990. *Latin American Adjustment: How Much Has Happened?* Washington, DC: Institute for International Economics.

SEVEN

Size Matters:

*The Need for Human-Scale Economic
Institutions for Development*

JULIAN ORAM AND DEBORAH DOANE

INTRODUCTION

In March 2004, a UK think tank and a global oil company hosted a breakfast meeting entitled "Big Can Be Beautiful" to explore the ways of encouraging innovation and entrepreneurship in large organizations. Their general thesis was that larger organizations (from multinational corporations to public bureaucracies) could innovate, deliver development resources, and support people more effectively by achieving economies of scale and by connecting people across continents.

This chapter sets out to challenge this assumption, which reflects a prevailing belief within mainstream economic thinking that large-scale companies, markets, and institutions are the most effective means of delivering "development." We argue that, by designing economic institutions (including business models, market frameworks, and legal systems) to meet different needs at different scales, we are more likely to achieve long-term sustainable development outcomes. Through an analysis of "new economics" thinking, we look specifically at how the concept of subsidiarity could be applied to development thinking at the community and business levels, and we draw on some examples of where the concept is already manifest in practice.

The ideas presented here are not intended to be a blueprint vision for a utopian future. Rather, they are an initial attempt to connect the thousands of disparate small-scale economic initiatives that have been quietly growing within the undercarriage of the global economy with a common theoretical thread arising from the considerable body of literature devoted to the ideas of "new economics." In doing so, this discussion seeks to identify the missing pieces of the puzzle, and specifically to describe the kinds of decentralized development and business models that could enable people and communities in the global South to meet their development needs at the scale that yields the greatest social, environmental, and economic value.

WHY LARGE-SCALE DEVELOPMENT HAS FAILED

Size matters. Although attempts have been made to redress the large-scale bias within development thinking and practice,[1] the favored approach of macroeconomic intervention is still rarely held up to sufficient critique. Our political and economic institutions continue to favor the "large" when it comes to project and policy interventions—often to the detriment of local communities and ecosystems. From energy projects to agriculture, the small rarely survives in a world where narrowly defined measures of economic efficiency are the only determinants of success.

Indeed, ever since the word "development" first became manifested as an aspirational goal within national and international political institutions, the approaches to achieving it have been conceived and implemented primarily from a macroscale perspective. From the Keynesian welfare state model of the 1930s to the state-planning systems of the former Eastern bloc countries to the Washington Consensus that gained prominence in the 1990s, our ability to come up with new forms of macroeconomic management seems endless.

Arising from the perceived failure of state-led aid, a massive shift in emphasis toward private-sector-led growth within development policy through a combination of foreign direct investment (FDI) and export-led growth has occurred over the past 15 years (Easterly 2001: 8). The Finance for Development conference held in March 2002 in Monterrey, for example, called for increases in private capital flows to developing countries as one of the primary ways of helping to achieve the Millennium Development Goals, arguing that public sources of funds are no longer adequate to overcome the seemingly insurmountable problems of poverty, disease, and environmental degradation. And this cry is not just the domain of the Bretton Woods Institutions; 2002 also marked the launch of the Trade Justice campaign by influential NGOs, calling for increased access to Northern markets by Southern producers to make trade fair and equitable.

Whereas most would agree that FDI is not a panacea (especially for the least developed countries, which capture just 1.4 percent of all FDI inflows into developing countries), it has nonetheless come to occupy an increasingly prominent position within national economic development strategies. According to UNCTAD (2004: 1), "the emphasis on trade liberalization and export orientation in the past decade has led to phenomenal growth in world merchandise trade, which has consistently grown faster than output." In 2001, FDI to developing countries reached a staggering US$205 billion, with grants and loans at only US$56 billion in comparison. Just a decade before, in 1990, grants were a full 16 percent higher than FDI flows (Doane and Greenhill 2002: 13).

Those in favor of foreign investment argue that such trends will spell more jobs, higher reserves of much-needed foreign exchange, and transfer of new technologies and production processes to poor countries. This, so the theory goes, will lead to higher incomes among the middle classes, enabling them to buy more goods and services and thus spurring greater levels of employment and eventually income growth in other parts of the economy. So, FDI should bring about reduced poverty, economic success, and wealth creation.

Unfortunately, the focus on aggregate statistics at the macro level means that there has been little consideration given to the way in which this foreign investment has been delivered, or to the resulting microeconomic and human development impacts. While international institutions hasten to provide "sound investment climates" (including the legal protection of property and the ability for capital to flow in and out at will), factors that have an impact on communities—such as displacement effects on local small and medium-sized enterprises (SMEs), the generation of environmental externalities, or the impacts of capital flight—are largely ignored. Take the case of India. As in many countries, FDI has been touted as the magic wand that will transform "underdeveloped" India into an advanced nation. In his 1999 inaugural address, Mr. Vajpayee spoke about the priority his government would give to promoting FDI. The unqualified underlying assumption was that everyone would benefit from increased levels of foreign investment.

But a quick look at the facts reveals that, although GDP has grown at an average of around 6 percent per year over the past decade, this growth has failed to make an impact on the estimated 350–400 million living below the poverty line, 75 percent of whom live in rural areas. As inward investment, export earnings and foreign exchange reserves sky-rocketed between the early 1990s and 2000, the rate of new-job growth registered at barely 1 percent, as job growth focused on the hi-tech ICT or pharmaceutical sector, representing just 0.1 percent of the population, according to investment bank Goldman Sachs. Reflecting on the government's lack of progress in tackling poverty during the 1990s, the long-serving former BBC South Asia correspondent Mark Tully noted in 2001 that economic reforms enacted by the government in the early 1990s "have improved life for the middle classes but done little or nothing for the poor," and concluded that India's strategy of market liberalization had "done exactly what the noisy and sometimes violent opponents of capitalism say it always does, increased the divide between the rich and the poor" (Tully 2001).

The tendency to consider development synonymous with the construction of big infrastructure projects, accumulation of FDI, and export growth has led countries across the South to aim towards an ever-shifting set of goalposts. As agricultural exports expand, so international commodity prices (and hence export revenue) drop. As power and transport infrastructure develops, the energy bills of oil- and gas-importing countries skyrocket. As financial markets liberalize and foreign portfolio investment grows, national balance-of payments accounts slide towards the red and national currencies grow vulnerable to speculative attacks. Four key failures, or unintended consequences of large-scale growth strategies, are discussed below.

The Employment Gap

It is generally assumed that economic growth through the introduction of larger multinationals into an economy is more likely to spawn employment than other forms of enterprise. But data on both the quality and quantity of this type of employment are questionable; and the benefits of such employment are potentially outweighed by the increases in global inequality that this produces. Between 1983 and 1999, 200 of the world's largest corporations provided a 14 percent increase in global employment—but increased their profit by 362 percent over the same period. Often, the type of employment provided is low paying and based on casual labor. FDI also tends to bypass the informal economy, meaning that the jobs created by corporate investment often fall outside the reach of the majority of poor people within developing countries (Potts 2001: 40).

Monopolies and Cartels

Trade at the global scale currently creates a bias in favor of larger companies, and seems ultimately to bring about less competition, rather than more. Global brand names draw their power within international markets largely from their ability to exercise a high level of control over their supply chains. A recent UNCTAD report notes that "[r]eal profits come from those who control critical points along the chain, own established brand names, or have access to shelf space in supermarkets" (UNCTAD 2004: 27).

The companies' control has led to near monopolies over certain supply chains and virtually no power for small producers. Large garment manufacturers can sign and cancel contracts at will, in the name of competition, leaving smaller suppliers consistently vulnerable without a safety net. In places like Sri Lanka, small garment manufacturers are facing increased competition from China. They are demanding their own government to change laws that would ultimately drive labor standards down in order to enable them to compete (Doane 2003).

In agriculture, most producers have no choice but to enter into arrangements with larger multinationals if they want to gain access to international markets. Just three companies control 90 percent of world coffee exports—each of which has a turnover rate larger than most African economies—and four agribusiness firms control 40 percent of cocoa grinding (FAO 2003). Companies such as ConAgra, Cargill, and ADM, meanwhile, are huge players in global soy and livestock markets, and also control the bulk of the feedstuffs market along the entire chain from South America to Europe. At the retail end, producers and SMEs face a global supermarket sector where the top 30 companies account for around a third of grocery sales. Supermarket chains are also rapidly penetrating middle- and lower-income countries, exerting ever-greater influence over prices and production methods in these locations (Jacobsen et al. 2003).

The Commodity Conundrum

Related to the issue of monopolies and cartels is the commodity conundrum. Ricardo's original theory of "comparative advantage" has naively dominated current development thinking to the detriment of many farmers and workers in poor countries. By specializing in the production of certain key commodities geared to international markets, developing countries have been assured that they will generate sufficient foreign exchange to import other goods and services and invest in public services. For many countries, however, this strategy has simply created a dangerous level of dependence on volatile commodity markets, while placing considerable pressure on local ecosystems through monocrop farming and extractive industries. Agricultural commodities in particular have been subject to continuous declining prices due to oversupply and high levels of corporate concentration within international agricultural commodity markets.

But the problem extends beyond foodstuffs. In the extractive industries, the benefits of the commodity, even at high prices, rarely accrue to the local communities. According to the think tank SustainAbility, Nigeria received US$8 billion of oil revenue in 2001, but US$7 billion of that was returned to beneficiaries outside the country; including corporate shareholders, creditors, and others. UNDP has pointed out that it is often the countries that are the most highly integrated into the global economy which are becoming even more marginal. Exports from sub-Saharan Africa have reached nearly 30 percent of GDP (compared to 19 percent in OECD countries), but the number of people living in poverty continues to grow (Doane and Greenhill 2002; UNDP 2003).

Social and Environmental Costs

Reports about millions of dollars going directly from the oil majors into the hands of dictators are, unfortunately, all too frequent. This is in part the result of high levels of corruption in some oil-rich nations, but the burden of responsibility falls equally on the shoulders of the large extraction companies, who, seeking ever-more sources of oil, are willing to make the deal at whatever cost.

The "efficiencies" achieved through economies of scale also lead to perverse environmental outcomes. Andrew Simms (2000) has argued that growth in international trade has occurred in tandem with increased carbon-dioxide emissions and consumption patterns that have fed into global climate change. Some of the largest manufacturers have attempted to put numbers on this. The Ford automobile company estimates that its products contribute to 2.5 percent of the greenhouse gas emissions responsible for global warming. Meanwhile, growth in the global airline industry (including the increase in air freight) is projected to contribute to 5 percent of climate-change emissions over the next decade (Mann 2004).

Another example is that of palm oil, found in roughly one in three products on supermarket shelves, from lipstick, to soap, to biscuits. The versatility and growing use of palm oil in consumer goods have led to a massive growth in oil-palm plantations in Indonesia. But this growth has come at a huge price, causing the disappearance of tropical rainforests at a rate of more than 2 million hectares a year, wiping out wildlife, forcing local communities from their land, and destroying their livelihoods (FoE 2004). These sorts of externalities are, of course, rarely factored into conventional price-setting mechanisms, meaning that neither the buyers nor consumers of palm oil are forced to pay for the costs of widespread habitat and livelihood disruptions.

This quest for growth is thus fraught with a series of perils that have proved to be major stumbling blocks to progress. After more than 50 years of large-scale development planning and policies, many countries are therefore still no closer to achieving the status of "developed economies." The feeble rate of progress over the past few years towards meeting the challenges set out in the UN's Millennium Declaration is merely the latest testimony to this failure.[2]

FROM REDUCTIONIST ECONOMICS TO NEW ECONOMICS

As the legitimacy of multilateral economic institutions and corporate-led globalization has been challenged by a growing number of development activists, new spaces have opened up within the global economy that are rapidly being filled by a plethora of local self-help initiatives. Over the past decade, there has been an explosion of community-based strategies designed to increase local self-reliance. Some of these have been crafted by communities primarily as a response to the failure of national development policies and foreign corporate investment to fulfill local development needs.

The remainder of this chapter is dedicated to better understanding how these local actions fit within a broader context of "new economics" thinking, centered on an analysis of scale that could challenge neoliberal ideology and drive the creation of new institutional, market, and business models to facilitate local development.

Theoretical Foundations

Thinking around the idea of "scale" in development is not exactly new. Its roots lie in the rich (if often overlooked) tradition of "humanist economics," which can be traced back to Jean Sismondi's work, *The New Principles of Political Economy*, published in 1815. Sismondi challenged the pursuit of economics as a reductionist science and called for the discipline to focus on a political economy approach that explicitly acknowledges the values that inform decisions about how resources are best used to improve social welfare. Sismondi questioned the use of an economic paradigm that calculated human progress simply by "the production of useful and elegant things" or the "rapidity with which inanimate machines execute human work." Instead, he argued that what really counts is "how an economy serves the happiness of the people," and whether an economy provides people with things such as an abundant, varied, and wholesome diet, sufficient clothing, decent accommodation, and "the certainty that the future will not be inferior to the present" (Lutz 1992: 91).

Sismondi's influence at the time was small, but his ideas influenced subsequent generations of "new economics" thinkers, including John Ruskin, John Hobson, Richard Tawney, Mohandas Ghandi, and E. F. Schumacher. In *Small is Beautiful*, Schumacher built on these theoretical foundations by adding his analysis of environmental degradation with a focus on small-scale units of production and consumption. As in the case of his predecessors, the focus of Schumacher's economics was not on the production of goods, but rather on people, who, he believed, "can be themselves only in small comprehensible groups." In terms of development, Schumacher challenged economists to "learn to think in terms of an articulated structure that can cope with a multiplicity of small scale units" (cited in Lutz 1992: 101).

Another key contributor to new economics thinking, Manfred Max-Neef (1991), has called for "human-scale development," which he describes as "focused and based on the satisfaction of human needs, on the generation of growing levels of self-reliance, and on the construction of organic articulations of people with nature and technology, of global processes with local activity, and of civil society with the state" (Max-Neef 1991: 8). To achieve human-scale development, Max-Neef proposes greater economic and political decentralization, as well as the strengthening of democratic institutions and the increased autonomy of groups of people through social movements. The sociologist Severyn

Bruyn has advocated a similar approach in relation to business, wherein power of economic decision making is devolved to smaller-scale units. Bruyn (1978: 379) argues that "[t]o develop the legal innovations needed for free enterprise to promote a system of social justice and provide the economic foundations for a genuine community . . . calls for a system of social regulation which is decentralized and socially accountable at the local level."

The core principles behind new economics can thus be summarized as follows: an explicitly normative approach that rejects reductionist thinking; a central concern with human welfare; the *a priori* assumption of equality; and the need to reembed economic relationships within social and environmental systems. These principles—combined with Schumacher's scale analysis as well as Max-Neef's and Bruyn's focus on decentralized political, market, and business structures—provide the foundation for a profoundly different paradigm that could guide economic policy making and market development in rich and poor countries alike.

The Pursuit of Subsidiarity

There have been surprisingly few attempts to link the principles of new economics with the groundswell of community-led development initiatives celebrated by the critics of globalization. One notable exception is the Filipino economist Walden Bello, who has laid out a set of key principles to achieve what he terms "deglobalization" (Bello 2002). This process, he insists, is *not* about withdrawing from the international economy, but merely about reclaiming the role of democratic process in key economic decision-making activities—what Karl Polanyi described as "re-embedding the economy in society, rather than having society driven by the economy." For Bello, deglobalization involves the following:

- Financing development from domestic sources rather than through FDI and financial markets
- De-emphasizing growth and maximizing equity, through measures to redistribute land and income to create vibrant domestic markets, among other things
- Subjecting strategic economic decisions to democratic processes, rather than leaving these to the market
- Creating a new production and exchange complex that includes community cooperatives and private and state enterprises, and excludes TNCs

- Enshrining the principle of subsidiarity by encouraging the production of goods at the community and national level if it can be done at reasonable cost

This principle of subsidiarity, expounded by Schumacher, essentially proposes that work should be done at the smallest social unit possible, and that the larger units exist to serve the smaller ones (Simms 2003). The basic rule is that production and consumption take place at the smallest appropriate scale such that, wherever possible, goods and services are produced and consumed locally. Where such resources (whether natural, human, labor, or capital) are insufficient or inadequate to meet local needs, a market structure at the next scale up is accessed. When this, in turn, is insufficient, the next highest order of market scale is used, and so on. Thus, there is a high level of interconnectivity between firms at the local level, which declines as one moves gradually outwards to progressively larger market scales.

RETURN TO SCALE: CASE STUDIES AND IMPLICATIONS FOR DEVELOPMENT

Energy

Microrenewable energy sources are already yielding huge development benefits. For example, the village of El Paraíso, located in a remote part of the Amazon region in northeastern Peru, is well off the country's national energy grid system, and is unlikely to be connected in the foreseeable future. With the help of the Intermediate Technology Development Group (ITDG), the community has developed a turbine to use the power of the river current to provide it with energy. Now, El Paraíso and two neighboring communities have improved basic health services, with a vaccine refrigerator, lighting for the community, health centers, schools, and other community facilities benefiting about 800 people. As a result of its success, other neighboring villages have already requested support to do the same, and intercommunity workshops have also been set up to transfer technology more widely.

The example of El Paraíso shows that, in many cases, local microrenewable technology supplies represent a much more viable option for meeting local energy needs than do investments in large-scale grid systems. Providing electricity through a large-scale centralized grid system linked to fossil-fuel-burning power plants is a highly inefficient and uneconomical way of reaching poor and remote energy users in developing countries. This message was reinforced by the head of UNEP, Klaus Topfer, who in an October 2003 speech to a group of bankers in Tokyo argued that, for poor countries in particular, "the reliance on fossil fuels and centralized infrastructure will not serve the vast majority of people in rural areas where the economic benefits of a modern energy system are elusive" (UNEP 2003).

For the three billion people who remain unconnected to large-scale centralized systems, small-scale renewable technologies therefore represent the only cost-effective option to fill this energy gap. In fact, people such as Indian solar-energy pioneer Bunker Roy suggest that the problems inherent in national grids mean that their days are numbered as the primary focus of energy policy. The work of Roy's Barefoot College in Rajasthan has helped spread solar power to over 130 remote villages in the Himalayas, improving the lives of 15,000 people. Winters in this part of the world can last six months, with temperatures dropping to as low as –40°C. Before the installation of solar power and lighting, families—who often shared buildings with animals—relied upon dim kerosene lamps and candles for the duration of winter.

By training "barefoot solar engineers," the college helps oversee ambitious domestic electrification schemes that bring light and power to cash-poor households. To get one month's supply of kerosene used to mean a two-day walk with a 20-liter jerrican. Solar energy brings both cleaner air in the house and less eye strain. The technology helps generate local employment both directly in terms of installing and maintaining the clean technology, and sometimes in quite literal spin-offs that create new opportunities. Two hundred women gained work due to new solar-powered spinning wheels, and solar water-heaters have been used to dry vegetables (UNEP 2003).[3]

Microrenewable energy supplies also reduce the vulnerability of communities to external shocks such as oil price hikes or disruptions to the energy supply chain. Finally, small-scale energy technologies based on resources such as sun, wind, and water create minimal environmental impacts, meaning that the use of energy by one community does not threaten to compromise development in another location (i.e., by local air or water pollution or greenhouse gas emissions that contribute to climate change).

Commodities

Another example of subsidiarity in practice comes from the "Just Change" trade model pioneered between Indian tea producers and local consumer cooperatives in Germany and the United Kingdom. The Just Change model saw its origins in the mobilization of a large group of Adivasis (tribal peoples who fall outside the Hindu caste system) in the Nilgiri Hills in south India, who organized a huge, and ultimately successful, campaign to reclaim their tribal land.

Once the Adivasis recovered the land, they decided to plant tea—a crop which, up to that point, was planted only by huge landowners and multinational companies. Whereas this represented an important economic and political step for the Adivasis, it soon became clear that they had potentially moved from one form of dependency to another. Stan Thekaekara, coordinator of the Just Change movement, explains:

> We were very successful with this tea-planting project. It had changed the economy as well as social and political relationships. But one of our colleagues challenged this and said—you have moved these people from a local wage economy into a global market economy. And in this process have made them more vulnerable than they ever were. Because when they were local wage earners—if a landlord did not pay them a proper wage, we could mobilise a few hundred tribal people to go and grab hold of the employer's collar and demand a fair wage. But when tea prices crash, as they have done in the last few years, whose collar do you grab? (Thekaekara 2003)

In response to this dilemma, the Adivasis decided to try to link up with the Fair Trade movement. They contacted a fair trade organization in Germany called Gepa, which started buying the tea for a higher price. However, the Adivasis soon decided that it was wrong that the people in countries like Germany and the United Kingdom, who made a special effort to buy their tea, should have to pay a higher price. They wished to introduce a new element into the concept of fair trade, whereby it would be possible to determine prices not just on market forces but also on other values centered on human relationships.

This was the basis upon which Just Change was established. The project is an attempt to link producers, consumers, and investors in a cooperative chain where they can trade directly with each other. The Indian growers located a buyer in Chesterfield, who agreed for his facility to be part of a cooperative to bag the loose tea. These bags then go directly to five community groups in three UK cities, who repackage it and then sell it to their members and to other people.

Thekaekara argues that in the present market economy, including in Fair Trade, the moment tea is put into the market chain, the first point of contact would determine the price. But, in the Just Change model, the real value of tea is a negotiated one:

> Negotiation that depends on the power of the person who is paying and the vulnerability of the person who is selling. The real value of tea is what a person drinking it, is willing to pay for it. . . . As a cooperative, or as a collective, we as producers along with the people of Manchester, the people of Orissa, the people of Gloucester, who as consumers buy our tea, would jointly own the surplus that had been generated. And it would be up to us to decide how to distribute the surplus (Thakaekara 2003).

The Just Change model represents a powerful example of how exchanges across national and cultural boundaries can still take place at a human scale. Rather than relying on international markets and anonymous commodity buyers to broker exchange relationships, Just Change suggests that international trade can be successfully conducted on a trans-local basis, where human relationships remain central to the nomination of value and generation of wealth.

The examples of microrenewable energy and agricultural trade via the Just Change model demonstrate that a shift in scale (whether in technology or markets) can be the deciding factor in determining whether development is successful in meeting local needs. But development along these lines will require that appropriate enterprise and market models be devised to support, complement, and engage with such local initiatives.

Considering Scale within Business Models

A business model describes what a firm will do to build and capture wealth for its stakeholders. The limited liability company (LLC), the legal foundation on which most large global corporations are built, is one such model. The LLC concept was derived in the mid-1800s as a mechanism to raise capital for risky, large-scale infrastructure projects in the United States. This model—in tandem with the joint-stock company or publicly listed company (PLC)—has been replicated in almost every country around the world, and has created a business landscape where companies exercise the rights of individuals without taking on the corresponding responsibilities. This has contributed to the problems of jobless growth, monopolies, bad governance, declining commodity prices, and failure to account for social and environment externalities referred to earlier.

There are, however, many more potential models upon which enterprises can be established and run, each of which has different implications for how wealth is generated and distributed among their stakeholders, while providing for more of the conditions necessary to achieve sustainability. According to Shann Turnbull (2003), one of the key requirements for business to be sustainable is that organizations be kept to a reasonable "human scale." This means that they must be governed democratically, and, in order to achieve an alternative version of economies of scale, be networked.

Turnbull examines several alternative structures in which new forms of wealth can be generated, including Employee Share Ownership Plans, Ownership Transfer Corporations, Land Banks, and Producer/Consumer Cooperatives. These four systems share a number of features that aim to correct problems within shareholder-owned multinationals:

- New methods are established for the ownership of and entitlements to tenure over land, technology, and enterprises.
- New ways for transferring wealth become possible.
- The structures are self-financing, so that people do not need to reduce their personal cash flow in order to acquire entitlements to assets.
- The methods are compatible with existing structures.
- Individual property rights are replaced with collective ownership, associated with voting entitlements for management of resources.
- Property rights are limited in time duration: by the life of an individual in the case of the land bank, or by the owner-transfer period in the case of a corporation.

Because of the different imperatives of stakeholders as opposed to shareholders, stakeholder governance is likely to place less emphasis on company growth than on long-term stability, and even distribution of benefits. As smaller companies with a closer proximity to their consumers and communities, these types of firms are also less likely to contribute to the negative consequences of scale discussed earlier in this chapter. Organizations developed with these characteristics at their heart are also more likely to use different measures and indicators of success. In addition to looking at turnover and profit, key performance indicators for such companies may also include quality of employment, contribution to social cohesion, or levels of trust among their consumers.

The Mondragon cooperatives in Spain are often cited as an example of the adoption of such models in practice. These are employee-owned businesses that do not have the imperative for growth caused by shareholder-driven incentives. As a result, once they reach a certain size (between 100 and 500 people), the Mondragon cooperatives break off into distinct entities. A World Bank study has found that, even in narrow economic terms, these firms are often more efficient than investor-owned firms. Like mutual enterprises, the stakeholder firms do not require equity investors to bring them into existence or to make them efficient. Over 80 percent of investor-owned firms typically fail in their first five years compared with less than 1 percent of the Mondragon firms (Turnbull 2003).

Although such models may seem unrealistic in the context of a developing country, Bruyn (1978: 375) observes that "surprisingly, the business system has already begun to yield such solutions." Thus, as local firms have, under the market economy, tended to become "national" and have developed under corporative command systems, new firms have also been developing to democratize and localize control over land, labor, and capital. According to Bruyn, these new "democratic firms . . . show promise of eliminating the oppressive conditions of the market and even suggest that social justice may combine with the free-enterprise system, and tell us that it is possible to introduce what might be called 'structures of accountability' in this period" (Bruyn 1978: 375).

Only a failure of imagination will stop us from realizing that such business models are more likely to avoid some of the pitfalls of large corporations. Having said this, in an integrated global society, it is very likely that enterprises that reach a given size—or that stay small in their organizational structure but work in sectors such as IT (which defy local or national boundaries)—will "cross over" different scales of economic activity. Thus, in the same way that large companies now adapt flexible operational relationships to fit different locational contexts, so the growth of smaller-scale, stakeholder-owned, and other forms of enterprise in developing countries (or those whose products and services naturally imply trans-local markets) will require that the overall business model of the company is flexible enough to handle functional, ethical, and value differences across different contexts.

In some cases, this might require that organizations split as soon as a certain degree of scale is achieved; in others, it might require that new forms of governance are adopted to reflect the transition to a new unit of scale. Better understanding where these transition points lie, and the institutional questions they raise in relation to markets, national legal structures, and global governance will, in our opinion, represent the critical challenges to new economics pioneers and development practitioners alike over the next 50 years.

CONCLUSION

While still in their fledgling stages, what we are witnessing now through the many thousands of disparate local development initiatives is the beginning of a parallel economic system based (wittingly or otherwise) on the principles of subsidiarity and new economics. It is not that small doesn't fail, but that the impact that large has when it does fail can be overwhelming. If a small firm goes out of business, the impact isn't likely to send shocks through an entire economy, as did the range of recent corporate scandals, from Enron to Parmalat. In the poorest of developing countries, when the big guys go bust or move out, it can devastate entire communities.

However, although multinational corporations would, under subsidiarity, play a less central role in the livelihood prospects of individual communities in developing countries, it is our contention that they would still have a role to fulfill. This would be to provide the necessary capital and human resources to develop new technologies, processes, and products to help drive sustainability. Research into hydrogen-fuel-cell technologies, for example, might most ably be conducted by large energy companies with the investment budgets and client networks to produce and distribute hydrogen-powered automobiles across many different countries. Similarly, governments in developing countries may need to access capital from global commercial banks to finance investment in the dissemination of microrenewable technologies.

This is what subsidiarity means: that finance, food, energy, construction materials, bicycles, computer equipment, and so on are provided *at the appropriate scale*. The U.S. author Michael Schuman (1998: 49) made the following observation:

It's easy to dismiss the principle of self-reliance by pointing to many complex products that communities cannot manufacture on their own. The goal of a self-reliant community, however, is not to create a Robinson Crusoe economy in which no resources, people, or goods enter or leave. *A self-reliant community simply should seek to increase control over its own economy as far as is practicable.* It should try to encourage local investment in community corporations, and local consumption of goods made or services delivered by them. (Emphasis in the original.)

Viewed in this way, subsidiarity could hold major attraction points not only for local communities and governments but also for TNCs. Large companies would still be expected to operate to globally accepted principles of social and environmental responsibility, but they would be freed of the burden of having to meet human development needs at all levels. HSBC wouldn't be condemned as a bad company because it didn't lend to a lone entrepreneur in Accra who was trying to expand her convenience shop run from her living room to a larger storefront venture. It would simply be acknowledged that it is the wrong scale company to fulfill this role.

Essentially, the sooner economic policy makers, corporations, and development NGOs let go of the idea that large corporations, institutions, or central governments should provide for human development needs at all levels, the sooner communities, small-scale enterprises, local institutions, and government agencies can set about the urgent business of devising the right mixture of business models, market systems, infrastructure, and public services for different layers of the economy.

NOTES

[1] The most notable attempts have been within the areas of microfinance and growing support for decentralization of government functions to state and local levels.

[2] This was confirmed in February 2004, when Britain's Chancellor of the Exchequer, Gordon Brown, and the President of the World Bank, James Wolfensohn, jointly penned an article in the *Guardian* that described how the international community has been drifting away from meeting the targets rather than closing in on them. In particular, they showed that sub-Saharan Africa was more than a century off-target to meet its goals of expanding primary education, cutting child mortality, and halving poverty.

164   *Julian Oram and Deborah Doane*

The examples of El Paraíso and the Barefoot College have been submitted to the Ashden Trust renewable energy awards, and are documented in a report published by the New Economics Foundation (nef) in June 2004 on renewable energy entitled "The Price of Power."

REFERENCES

Bello, Walden. 2002. *Deglobalization: Ideas for a New World Economy.* London: Zed Books.

Bruyn, Severyn T. 1978. *The Social Economy.* New York: Wiley.

Doane, Deborah. 2003. "Commentary and Analysis: Corporate Social Responsibility." *International Journal of Corporate Sustainability* 10(2):4–7.

Doane, D., and R. Greenhill. 2002. *Chasing Shadows: Re-imagining Finance for Development.* London: New Economics Foundation.

Easterly, William. 2001. *The Elusive Quest for Growth.* Cambridge, MA: MIT Press.

FAO. 2003. *Trade Reforms and Food Security: Conceptualizing the Linkages.* Rome: FAO.

Friends of the Earth (FoE). 2004. *Greasy Palms—Palm Oil, the Environment and Big Business.* London: FoE.

Jacobsen, M., A. Werth, and B. Vorley. 2003. *International Agricultural Reform and Power Balance in Agrifood Chains.* London: IIED.

Lutz, Mark. 1992. "Humanistic Economics: History and Basic Principles." In Paul Ekins and Manfred Max-Neef (eds.), *Real-Life Economics: Understanding Wealth Creation.* London: Routledge.

Mann, Daniel. 2004. "Calls to Control Low-Cost Flights." [24 April]. Available at http://news.bbc.co.uk/1/hi/sci/tech/3625931.stm (retrieved 30 April 2004).

Max-Neef, Manfred. 1991. *Human Scale Development: Conception, Applications and Further Developments.* London: Apex Press.

Potts, Ruth. 2001. *Where We Stand: A Reference Compendium on the State of the Planet and Its People.* Cambridge: HRH The Prince of Wales' Business and the Environment Programme, University of Cambridge.

Schuman, Michael. 1998. *Going Local: Creating Self-reliant Communities in a Global Age.* New York: Free Press.

Simms, Andrew. 2000. *Trade and Climate Change: Free Trade's Free Ride on the Global Economy.* London: New Economics Foundation.

Simms, Andrew. 2003. *Return to Scale: Alternatives to Globalisation.* London: New Economics Foundation.

Thekaekara, S. 2003. *Beating the System: Local Solutions to the Globalisation Crisis.* The nef Alternative Mansion House Speech, London's living room, City Hall, 12 June.

Tully, Mark. 2001. "How Global Reform Failed India's Poor." CNN.com/ World. Available at http:// edition.cnn.com/2001/WORLD/asiapcf/south/07/ 28/tully.column/ (retrieved 26 July 2004).

Turnbull, S. 2003. *A New Way to Govern: Organisations and Society after Enron*. London: New Economics Foundation.

UNDP. 2003. *Human Development Report 2003*. New York: Oxford University Press.

UNEP. 2003. "UN Environment Chief Challenges World's Financiers." Press release, 20 October. Geneva: UNEP.

United Nations Conference on Trade and Development (UNCTAD). 2004. *Economic Development in Africa: Trade Performance and Commodity Dependence*. Geneva: UNCTAD.

EIGHT

Java Furniture Makers:

Globalization Winners or Losers?

LIENDA LOEBIS AND HUBERT SCHMITZ

INTRODUCTION

Who gains and who loses from globalization is one of the big questions of our time. The people of East and SE Asia were thought to be among the winners until a financial crisis hit the region in 1997. Indonesia, it seemed, was particularly affected, with millions of people sinking into poverty. However, it became clear soon afterwards that some parts of Indonesia had actually benefited from the crisis. The sudden and large depreciation of the rupiah raised the export competitiveness of local enterprises overnight. Agro-processing was one of the sectors that benefited most because it used local materials and, as a result, required low levels of foreign currency. The furniture industry of central Java is another good example, growing rapidly in the wake of the crisis.

Can we therefore conclude that the furniture enterprises and their workers are among the winners of globalization? This is the first question addressed in this chapter. The second question is whether the observed growth is sustainable. We address these questions with information collected in Semarang, Jepara, and Klaten in May and June 2003, and with data from secondary sources.

In seeking answers, this discussion feeds into a debate that is important for both researchers and policy makers. Does participation in the global economy lead to sustainable income growth? Some contributors to this debate are skeptical; they emphasize the danger that producing for global markets means entering a race to the bottom (Kaplinsky 2000; Kaplinsky et al. 2002). The furniture industry of central Java is a good test case, as underlined by the spate of recent papers on this industry (Sandee et al. 2000; Sandee 2002; Sulandjari and Rupidara 2002; Muhtaman 2003; Posthuma 2003). This chapter contributes to this debate in three ways.

First, it records the gains that have been made in the furniture industry in central Java. The growth in the number of enterprises and in the number of jobs is undeniable: the number of firms increased from 2,439 to 3,700 from 1997 to 2002, and the number of workers grew from 38,264 to 58,210 in the same time period (data provided by the District Office of Industry, Trade and Cooperatives). This chapter further suggests that workers' earnings have increased substantially.

Second, it questions the industry's prospects for further growth. On the input side, the industry is suffering from the increasing scarcity and cost of raw material. On the output side, it is suffering from intensifying competition from Vietnam and China, among others. In spite of this undeniable squeeze, the producers themselves are surprisingly optimistic. How can one explain this?

Third, this chapter connects findings from this case study to the debate on small and medium sized enterprise (SME) promotion. Does support for SMEs only drive them deeper into the race to the bottom? Averting this danger, we conclude, requires a coalition of actors along the local-global axis. The policy issues are, however, merely laid out and not discussed in detail.

THE LOW AND HIGH ROADS
TO COMPETITIVENESS

There are two ways in which local enterprises can compete in the global economy. Taking the *low road* means competing by paying the lowest possible wages, disregarding environmental standards, and avoiding taxes. Taking the *high road* means competing by upgrading processes and products. In the furniture industry of Central Java, one finds examples of both.

It is no secret that many enterprises have taken the low road. The majority of enterprises, especially the small ones, are not registered. By implication, their workers are not registered either. According to recent estimates, 83 percent of central Java furniture enterprises and 67 percent of workers are "informal" (Sulandjari and Rupidara 2002). Taxes and social security payments are thus avoided on a large scale. Although this practice is widespread, there is no consensus on whether registration should be enforced. Some argue that the informal sector is a source of future growth, but others argue that the informality traps the small producers in low-productivity, low-profit activities.

No such disagreement exists on another dimension of low-road competition, the use of illegal raw materials. This practice is increasingly common in the furniture industry. Muhtaman (2003:1) concludes that "the overuse of forests and inadequate management practices have in many cases depleted the resource base for the industry and as a consequence undermined the sustainability of the wood based industry." It is estimated that the rate of forest loss in Indonesia has accelerated from 1 million hectares per year in the 1980s to 2 million hectares per year since 1996 (IIED/ICTSD 2003).

The management of forests and the sale of timber is entrusted to the state enterprise, Perhutani. It continues to be the main source of wood, especially teak, but an increasing share of the wood comes from thieves. The thriving illegal trade is particularly damaging because many of the trees are underage (Muhtaman 2003). There is a consensus that illegal logging damages both short- and long-term prospects of the industry. It undermines those competing enterprises that use legally acquired wood. It also accelerates deforestation and thus threatens the industry's long-term viability (Posthuma 2003).

LOCAL UPGRADING IN GLOBAL CHAINS

One way forward is to upgrade products and processes. How can local enterprises achieve this? Local cluster theory emphasizes that the knowledge needed for upgrading comes from within the cluster. Global value-chain theory emphasizes that the know-how comes from outside the cluster, in particular from global buyers (Humphrey and Schmitz 2002; Humphrey 2003; Schmitz 2003). Some furniture enterprises in Central Java have been able to grow and upgrade rapidly by inserting themselves in global value chains, as we were able to confirm in the course of our factory visits and interviews. Take the company Duta Jepara, for example. It has 850 workers and produces garden furniture made from teak wood. The entire output is exported, more than half going to three Scandinavian buyers. Duta Jepara has longstanding relationships with these customers, who exert pressure and provide support for upgrading products and processes. Or take the company Suwastama, located near Solo, which has 650 workers and produces rattan and other furniture mainly for the Swedish company IKEA. Suwastama, in turn, has 350 suppliers who have further subcontractors. It is a buyer-driven value chain that provides more than 7,000 jobs and constitutes one of the big Java success stories. Key to this success is Suwastama's program of enabling its suppliers to improve quality and timely delivery. This fostering role vis-à-vis its suppliers could only develop in the context of a relationship with a foreign customer providing innovative designs and regular large orders.

The Role of Buyers

This is not to suggest that these large Indonesian manufacturers have a cushy relationship with their foreign customers. On the contrary, the manufacturers find themselves in captive relationships with their Scandinavian buyers. In itself, this is not necessarily a problem because there is a mutual commitment between producer and buyer to solve difficulties jointly rather than terminate the relationship. The problem lies in the fact that these same global buyers have also begun to buy furniture in Vietnam and China. Seeking goods from other countries leads to intensifying competition and shrinking profit margins for the Indonesian manufacturers. They informed us that margins have decreased by 20 percent or more since 2000. However, in spite of the squeeze on profits, we can conclude that the local suppliers have benefited from the close, albeit captive, relationship with their big customers.

SMEs also produce for global markets, but the relationships with their buyers tends to be different; in most cases they are purely market based. Like the large enterprises, SMEs are demand-driven, but they rarely enjoy information-rich relationships with their buyers. Neither producers nor buyers invest in their relationships. We visited a number of such enterprises. Take the example of Aulia Ariffin (a real case, but the name has been modified in order to protect his identity) in Jepara. His enterprise is informal, employs 17 workers, and makes many different types of furniture. He has many customers, but these customers do not help to improve products and processes. Ariffin's initial stock of knowledge was "inherited"; it came from working with his father. Now he relies entirely on learning by doing and copying from other enterprises in Jepara. Since Jepara is a cluster with more than 3,000 furniture producers, it attracts many traders that connect the many small enterprises to distant markets in Indonesia and abroad. Being located in this cluster offers small enterprises easy access to buyers, but the relationships with these buyers rarely contain the combination of challenge and support that leads to upgrading. In fact, the product quality tends to be inconsistent, and the wastage of raw material high.

The Optimism of Entrepreneurs

It would be wrong to give the impression that all large enterprises are progressive and all small enterprises are backward. Such stereotypes are unhelpful and often wrong. There are a number of small enterprises that have made enormous progress and many large enterprises that adopt dubious practices. Above all, there is a dynamic middle segment of enterprises that are registered, have specialized in particular niche markets, and have developed their own designs. They showed us with much pride their new products and displayed a refreshing optimism about their future.

Remarkably, such optimism also prevailed among the small entrepreneurs who were competing on the low road. We found this optimism surprising because there are so many of them. According to the Provincial Office of Industry, Trade, and Cooperatives, there are about 3,500 enterprises in Jepara, the vast majority of which are of micro or small size. Even though they are not registered, they are easy to find. One sees them by just driving or walking around Jepara and its nearby villages. It is impressive how much hard work goes into these small businesses. But their operations are clearly precarious and the competition is intense. So, what explains the optimism that we found among the owners we spoke to? The answer they gave was that the customers kept coming.

We cannot, however, generalize from Jepara to other clusters. This became particularly clear when we visited Serenan, a younger and less well-known furniture cluster near Klaten. Enterprises in this cluster had also benefited from the export boom of the 1990s, but by mid-2003, they were struggling to find customers. The contrast between Serenan and Jepara was striking. Being located in the more developed and famous cluster gives its producers easier access to customers; this seems one reason for the optimism of Jepara's producers. However, being located in a cluster does not to suggest that the views and experiences within a given cluster are uniform. Sandee et al. (2002), for example, give a more pessimistic view of Jepara's prospects.

THE DILEMMA OF SUPPORT INSTITUTIONS

Although the experiences and prospects of furniture makers in central Java vary, there is a common factor that has a huge influence on the ability to compete, and that the producers do not like to talk about: they cut corners in order to reduce costs and remain competitive. Using illegal wood is an enormous cost saver. Raw material accounts for about 60 percent of the cost of most teak furniture, so acquiring cheaper (illegal) wood makes a huge difference to price and profit.

Such low-road practices pose a dilemma for the Indonesian organizations and foreign donors concerned with small enterprise development. On the one hand, assisting small enterprises can result in support of the illegal wood trade. On the other hand, small enterprises provide a lot of employment and generate income. For the time being, the support for small enterprises continues. For example, the Ministry of Industry and Trade has established the Department for Small and Medium Enterprises, a very active department that specifically targets SMEs and works closely with business associations such as ASMINDO (the Association of the Furniture Industry). The work of these public and private organizations is sometimes complemented by donor projects, some of which we have followed closely (through direct visits or evaluations). For example, JICA (the Japan International Cooperation Agency) has an interesting pilot project that involves strengthening the clusters of Sidoarjo (metalwork), Kebumen (tiles), and Serenan (furniture). Similarly, GTZ (the German agency for technical cooperation), ADB (the Asian Development Bank), the ILO, and UNIDO (United Nations Industrial Development Organization) have projects to support small enterprises in specific regions and sectors of the Indonesian economy. They are all concerned with enhancing the competitiveness of small entrepreneurs, and they are doing good work in the localities in which they operate. The problem is that the opportunities and dangers often come from outside the locality.

Our visits to Semarang, Jepara, and Klaten, and our discussions with business people in other locations, made it clear that we need a wider perspective if we want to understand the prospects of SMEs. We need to understand the global value chain in which these SMEs operate: the furniture chains are buyer driven and, as we previously stressed, the upgrading prospects depend very much on the types of relationships that producers have with their buyers.

Understanding what goes on at the other end of the chain is equally important. Much of the furniture industry of central Java depends on a continuing supply of teak, but this supply is in danger. The big buyers and their customers, the people who buy the furniture in European stores, are aware of the depletion of the teak supply. Their awareness of this issue is why they insist on certification that the wood has come from well-managed forests. Perhutani, the state company responsible for these forests, used to provide such certificates, but has now suspended certification, partly because it has lost control of the timber trade. As a result, even the responsible furniture manufacturers are unable to provide certificates about the origin of the wood. Although their buyers have accepted this, any optimism that pressure from them would help to stop the abuse of the forests has evaporated. It is clear to all involved that current practices are not sustainable.

The need to examine the problems of SMEs in the context of the value chains in which they operate is beginning to be recognized by policy makers. For example, the Ministry of Industry and Trade and the ILO held a joint workshop titled "Value Chain Analysis for Policy Makers" in Jakarta at the end of April, 2003. The workshop raised several important issues: What drives the chain? Where are the key bottlenecks? Which actors need to be brought together to work out a solution? These questions need answers and the global value-chain approach provides a fresh way of understanding the problems and forging alliances for change. Policy makers, business leaders, and researchers present at the workshop agreed that it is time to experiment with new approaches that bring together progressive organizations along a local-global axis.

The furniture industry of central Java is a good test case. The industry has been very successful in recent years but its sustainability is in doubt. Can the enterprises upgrade sufficiently and escape the relentless low-price competition from China and Vietnam? Can more effective regulation of the forests and the timber trade be put in place? We do not know the answers to these questions, but we do know that the expectations are high. The entrepreneurs we spoke to, including, for example, Akhmad Fauzi, the leader of the Jepara furniture association, are optimistic about their upgrading initiatives.

EMPLOYMENT, INCOME, AND MOTORCYCLES

Such optimism also seems to prevail among the workers in this industry. They expect the upward trend of the past few years to continue. The increase in employment opportunities is clear from the statistics. As noted in the introduction, in Jepara, employment in the furniture industry increased from 38,264 in 1997 to 58,210 in 2002. Although such precise statistics do not exist for wages, Herry Purwanto, Head of the District Office for Industry, Trade, and Cooperatives, estimates that wages have risen by 10–15 percent (in real terms) per year over the period 1997–2002. Increases in real wages in domestic currency overstate the international purchasing power of these wages due to devaluation, but there is no denying that workers are better off. A proxy for the general improvement of workers' earnings is reflected in the statistics on registered motorcycles. In Jepara, the total increased by 53.6 percent over the period from 1998 to 2001 (data provided by the District Office of Industry, Trade, and Cooperatives). Motorcycles have become the workers' favorite form of transport. Direct observation provides clear examples. As one drives into the grounds of the Duta Jepara factory, what catches the eye is the parking bay with hundreds of motorcycles. There is hardly a bicycle to be seen. When the shift ends, the young workers show off their shiny acquisitions—keen to be seen on their motorized two-wheelers. The motorcycle has become a status symbol among the workers. And it is not just the men who use motorcycles; they are also popular among women.

Putting together available statistics and casual observation, it seems that export-oriented Jepara is better off than other small towns. It can also be noted that prosperity in Jepara has increased over recent years. Can we therefore conclude that the Jepara furniture manufacturers and their workers have been among the winners of globalization? Our answer is yes, but we must also stress our doubts over whether the gains are sustainable.

WHAT CAN GOVERNMENT DO?

The clearest policy implication is that exclusive reliance on the market would be a disaster. Participating in the global market has brought many benefits to the furniture industry, but competitive pressures are now dragging the industry into a race to the bottom. What can be done to nudge the industry from the low road to the high road? This is a big question to which this short discussion can only begin to give answers.

The positive policy implications are clear in principle, but they are complicated in practice. The immediate priority lies in halting the plundering of the forests. Stronger state intervention is urgently needed, but it is not forthcoming because the Indonesian state is decentralizing. In principle, devolving powers to the provincial and district levels could help the local government to regain control over the forests, but the process of devolution is slow and painful. At best, it will lead to uneven progress; at worst, it will lead to a protracted power vacuum in which theft and corruption continue to thrive.

Given the difficulty of solving the problem at the supply end of the chain, initiatives are under way to curb demand for illegal wood. The Indonesian government is preparing a memorandum of understanding with the EU and Japan that would ban the entry of illegal logs into their respective countries. Enforcing such bans, however, remains difficult, and other parallel measures will need to be adopted. Many schemes are being discussed in national and international forums. Here is just one example: allocate a designated share of existing forests to a consortium of furniture producers and buyers; then let this consortium manage this part of the forest so that the sustainability of the participating enterprises is ensured. In some market segments, certified ecological responsibility is critical. Because competition in these segments is less price driven, there would be less of a conflict between short-term profitability and social responsibility.

Encouraging private production is another important strategy. In fact, the state enterprise Perhutani is already doing so. Perhaps this deserves more emphasis. Similarly, community forests also deserve more attention. International experience suggests that local communities are an undervalued force in responsible forest management.

Ensuring a sustainable supply of raw material is the first policy priority. The second priority is to help the industry upgrade its products and processes. As stressed above, global buyers can provide a fast track for such upgrading, but few small producers are allowed access. They rely on business development services, notably for training, testing, supply-chain management, and certification. It is widely recognized that such services are best provided in conjunction with business associations or other private actors.

The problem is that disadvantaged producers often do not recognize their need to upgrade and are reluctant to follow the advice of consultants. Producers are more likely to listen to their customers. Therefore, support programs should confront small producers with the customers' perceptions of their shortcomings. There are now simple but effective techniques for doing this.

The most difficult areas in which to lend effective support are design and marketing. There is no agreement on "best practices" for such support, so the only way forward is experimentation. There is, however, no doubt about the importance of fostering design and marketing capabilities. Without such capabilities, it will be difficult to achieve better prices and higher incomes.

CONCLUSION

This chapter has investigated whether the furniture makers of central Java are among the winners or losers of globalization. More specifically, it addresses two questions. First, have enterprises and workers gained from producing for the global economy? Second, are the gains sustainable? Our answer to the first question is yes; our answer to the second is no, not under current circumstances.

Given the pessimism that has beset much of the globalization debate, it is important to record that gains in terms of employment and income growth have been substantial. Most of this growth was generated by SMEs, who were able to benefit from the financial crisis of late 1997 and to increase their exports.

The viability of these exports has, however, become dependent on the use of a resource that risks depletion. An increasing part of the raw material, especially teak, comes from illegal sources. Illegally felled timber tends to be younger, thus threatening the sustainability of the forests. Halting this process is difficult because intensifying price competition in the international market makes enterprises prefer the cheaper illegal wood. No single actor or single measure can reverse this process. Stricter state control of the timber supply is essential, but top-down directives are not sufficient. Local communities play an important role in promoting and undertaking a socially responsible use of the forest. Helping furniture enterprises to redirect their competitive strategy also plays a part. Relying on cheap raw material for competing in global markets is not a viable strategy. The future lies in competing on the basis of quality, design, and image. Using wood from a certified source is an important part of changing the image. Helping enterprises to make this switch is not easy. However, understanding the relevant global value chain(s) is an important first step in making this switch.

REFERENCES

Humphrey, J. 2003. "Opportunities for SMEs in Developing Countries to Upgrade in the Global Economy." International Labour Organization SEED Working Paper 43, Geneva: ILO.

Humphrey, J., and H. Schmitz. 2002. "How Does Insertion in Global Value Chains Affect Upgrading in Industrial Clusters?" *Regional Studies* 36(9):1017–1027.

IIED/ICTSD. 2003. "Trade and Forests: Why Forest Issues Require Attention in Trade Negotiations." In *Policy Views on Trade and Natural Resource Management*. London and Geneva: International Institute for Environment and Development and International Centre for Trade and Sustainable Development.

Kaplinsky, R. 2000. "Globalisation and Unequalisation: What Can Be Learned from Value Chain Analysis?" *Journal of Development Studies* 37(2):117–146.

Kaplinsky, R., M. Morris, and J. Readman. 2002. "The Globalization of Product Markets and Immiserizing Growth: Lessons from the South African Furniture Industry." *World Development* 30(7):1159–1178.

Muhtaman, D. R. 2003. *Raw Material Supply for the MSME Furniture Industry in Central Java*. Bogor: SmartWood.

Posthuma, A. C. 2003. *Taking a Seat in the Global Market Place: Opportunities for "High Road" Upgrading in the Indonesian Wood Furniture Sector?* [Mimeo.] Geneva: InFocus Programme on Boosting Employment through Small Enterprise Development, ILO.

Sandee, H. 2002. "The Impact of the Crisis on Small-Scale Enterprises in Java: Findings from Selected Case Studies." In M. P. van Dijk and H. Sandee (eds.), *Innovation and Small Enterprises in the Third World*. Cheltenham: Edward Elgar.

Sandee, H., R. K. Andadari, and S. Sulandjari. 2000. "Small Firm Development during Good Times and Bad: The Jepara Furniture Industry." In C. Manning and P. van Diermen (eds.), *Indonesia in Transition*. Singapore: Institute of Southeast Asian Studies.

Sandee, H., B. Isdijoso, and S. Sulandjari. 2002. *SME Clusters in Indonesia: An Analysis of Growth Dynamics and Employment Conditions*. Jakarta: ILO.

Schmitz, H. (ed.). 2003. *Local Enterprises in the Global Economy: Issues of Governance and Upgrading*. Cheltenham: Edward Elgar.

Sulandjari, S., and N. S. Rupidara. 2002. "Value Chain Analysis of Wood Furniture Clusters in Central Java." [Draft report.] Salatiga: Centre for Micro and Small Enterprise Dynamics.

NINE

The World Bank's Land of Kiosks:

Community-Driven Development in Timor-Leste

BEN MOXHAM

A LAND OF KIOSKS

It's hard to avoid kiosks and their sad stories in Timor-Leste. In one quiet, dusty clearing in the village of Meligo, in Bobonaro district, five groups of widows had set up five of these small shops next to each other. Here, the customers most likely to purchase some of their imported, packaged goods were the scabby, salt-resistant bushes littering the clearing. The women had each obtained a microcredit loan as part of the World Bank's Community Empowerment and Local Governance Project (CEP), and saw only one business option in the wretched economic environment of the newly independent nation (World Bank 2000; 2002).

Fifty-four percent of CEP microcredit loans have gone to kiosks, and the resulting "oversupply" has led to predictable complaints by kiosk owners of few customers and too much competition. These difficulties are exacerbated by the skyrocketing price of wholesale goods due to the inflationary pressures of the international reconstruction circus with its well-paid consultants and US-dollar economy.

The widows from Meligo don't know the exact financial health of their businesses because they are illiterate. However, a World Bank researcher who does monitor these businesses' financial data concluded that in 70 percent of cases, widows who received microcredit under this program wouldn't make enough money to pay back the original loan. If the CEP actually enforced loan repayment, most of the recipients would have plunged further into poverty. Welcome to independence.

THIS NEW BUSINESS OF
COMMUNITY-DRIVEN DEVELOPMENT

As the dust cleared in the aftermath of the chaos orchestrated by the Indonesian military following the 30 August 1999 vote for independence in East Timor, the World Bank arrived. With key Timorese elites, it led a "Joint Assessment Mission" that drew up a policy blueprint for the new nation and created the Trust Fund for East Timor (TFET), which the Bank would administer to channel donor funds. While the UN focused on elections, law and order, and the creation of an interim national government, the World Bank, the IMF, and the Asian Development Bank (ADB) set about reshaping the country's economy.

The widows of Meligo are a tragic example of what happens when the World Bank's agenda of hastily building a market economy (the leitmotif of all the Bank's projects in Timor-Leste) is imposed on a deeply scarred subsistence economy. The CEP was the microeconomic flagship of this agenda, and much more. It was meant to kick-start the rural economy and to "build democracy" by decentralizing government through block grants given to locally elected CEP councils to spend on small projects they felt best met their community's development priorities.

Commencing in early 2000, the US$18 million project covered the entire country, using all of the new vocabulary of development: a decentralized system of village development councils would (a) exercise good governance through the transparent and accountable use of three cycles of project funding in order (b) to empower communities to participate in their own poverty alleviation. At the project's conclusion nearly three years later, more than 400 CEP councils have helped cover the country with a range of community projects such as repaired roads, water sanitation projects, and microcredit-funded kiosks.

The CEP is part of the Bank's foray into what it labels community-driven development, or CDD. Many developing countries now have some variant of this program. In all, US$5.6 billion was spent on CDD in fiscal years 2000, 2001, and 2002, and the figure rises to US$9.7 billion if expenditures to lay the groundwork for these programs are included (Kumar 2003: iii).

The move into CDD and "good governance" also mirrors the Bank's move into the financially riskier area of post-conflict reconstruction. As Anne Carlin from the Bank Information Center points out in a report on international financial institution (IFI) activity in Afghanistan, IFIs such as the World Bank have moved into nation-building as a "new line of business" to offset the reduced demand of large borrowers such as India and China (Carlin 2003: 1). Timor-Leste's Bank-managed trust fund system has been replicated in Afghanistan and was recently proposed for Iraq. All of these developments strengthen the claim that the World Bank and other IFIs are the de facto managers of the so-called developing world.

"DRIVE-BY" NATION-BUILDING

The Bank's CEP in Timor-Leste epitomizes the contradictions inherent in the new trend of nation-building on the quick. It tried both to deliver speedy material assistance and to leave behind robust institutions of local governance that would empower communities to tackle their own development. The Bank prioritized the former, keen to show project results in a competitive reconstruction environment accountable primarily to donors.

After pressure for the quick disbursement of project funds, training timetables were cut short, forcing the more participatory training topics to be scrapped. As one project trainer reflected, "The CEP had a pile of rules to limit corruption but a participatory development model needs time to develop and this was wiped out through program speed." Detailed project rules and novel council structures need explanation, and community confusion was consequently rife. "The irony here," remarked one district CEP worker, "is that they'd ask us to finish in two months but the community would not understand the project and this would create conflict. As a result, it would end up taking four months."

The Bank states that participation is the keystone of the CEP: "projects will be produced *by communities* for community activities" (emphasis in original) (World Bank 2000: 2). However, this idea of empowerment was usually limited to deciding in what order the community would build either a water project or a bridge. But there are so many more exciting possibilities of what empowerment can mean. From Porto Alegre in Brazil to Kerala in India, the decentralization of state power into local hands has been a positive response to a state burdened by debt, corruption, or IFI-enforced austerity programs. Participatory budgeting in Porto Alegre, for example, attempts to allow the grassroots actors to challenge state power by setting and acting on their own budget priorities. In the process, linkages that were severed by budget cuts or policy stagnation have been revitalized.

The communities under the CEP, on the other hand, got very limited autonomy and had to settle instead for a technocratic World Bank task manager sitting atop a massive project infrastructure of project manuals, procurement guidelines, organograms, supervision missions, and key performance indicators. According to one project trainer, the councils "began to resemble little more than an aid disbursement mechanism."

Even the scope of the communities' choice of projects seems to have been restricted by the Bank's preference for infrastructure geared at nurturing the market. As the first Bank project appraisal document states, only "economic infrastructure" would be built under the CEP (World Bank 2000: 9). Although this language was changed in subsequent documents, such biases appeared already to have seeped into the project-approval processes. For example, despite education and health being identified as the top priorities during broad community consultations for a national development plan, schools and health clinics were barely funded under the CEP.[1] Yet a nation where nearly one in every 100 women dies during childbirth (RDTL 2003: 75) is in dire need of rural health facilities. Educational facilities are also required, given an average of 52 students for every one teacher (ETTA 2001: 39). Can kiosks double as birthing clinics?

This brand of participation did little to engender enthusiasm among community members. As a result, "participation" was identified by many CEP staff and council members as the biggest problem facing the project. Without people to monitor and contribute to council processes, the system was placed under an incredible strain that no amount of curt Bank memos to project staff could fix. The CEP is an unfortunate example of the depoliticization and bureaucratization of radical and participatory experiments in popular democracy that have been attempted elsewhere (Harriss 2002: Chapter 6).

Bringing Democracy to the Countryside

Project designers were initially enthusiastic that the CEP councils were to be the key institution of local governance. The councils were introduced on the contradictory premises that they would not only fill a governance void at the local level, but that they would also provide clarity to the complex structures already in place. It was a deliberate attempt to alienate both the political power of a pervasive and legendary clandestine resistance network and the more traditional structures of local leadership. This idea was marketed as part of a "civilizing" mission: a way to bring a one-size-fits-all model of democracy to the countryside. But these preexisting authorities enjoyed the kind of genuine local legitimacy that the CEP councils never acquired.

In contrast, the CEP councils struggled to establish a purpose beyond being the transmission line to Bank-controlled dollars. They were frequently identified by community members as "Banco Mundial" councils or part of "the company." Their fragile political status and financial muscle often led to a variety of problems, as preexisting authorities tried to usurp them, or they caused community loyalties to splinter in the early confused and usually unaccountable scramble for council funds. Consequently, other providers of external assistance such as international NGOs were deterred from consulting with the tarnished councils and usually relied on more traditional structures of power (East Timor Community Development Working Group 2001). Despite these crises, many communities had their own successful and diverse ways of emerging through this to make good use of project resources.

Stunting Government

The CEP played a role in the Bank plan of entrenching a small government in Timor-Leste by providing for the outsourcing and self-management of many service-delivery arms of government, as well as local-level governance structures. As a justification for its neoliberal prescriptions, the Bank warned Timorese elites of the need to avoid reawakening the bureaucratic ghosts of Suharto. They recommended not replicating a bloated and corrupt government, "disconnected from the needs and wants of the people" (World Bank 2000: 9).

But this fear oversimplifies the Indonesian administration. Although military actions in Timor-Leste are a strong contender for one of the worst acts of genocide of the twentieth century, the administration, as remembered by one Timorese, "opened a lot of schools, created work for unemployed people, built up the infrastructure, shops, markets and other facilities" (Hohe and Ospina 2001: 55). Now, the free market has ushered in mass unemployment and expensive basic commodities, causing the conversations drifting along the streets of Dili to cast a positive light on these positive aspects of the old regime.

The CEP treated Timor-Leste as a blank slate, bypassing any institutional knowledge in the former administration. Instead, the project used technical assistance from the fledgling private sector that lacked the skills and ability to plan or coordinate with other projects. Two years later, with technical failure common and many projects proving unsustainable, one World Bank report concluded that perhaps it would have been better if projects had coordinated with line ministries "who have the technical capacity to advise on appropriate design guidelines" (World Bank 2002: 39).

It is a common story across Bank-run CDD projects. In his review of its 2004 World Development Report, Tim Kessler noted that the Bank "typically [bypasses] local government" and that "a significant sample of CDD (Social Fund) water operations revealed a likely sustainability of 24 per cent of operations" (Kessler 2004).

At a heated meeting in the Manatuto District, local government staff were angry about a decentralization model that failed where they believed they could have succeeded. For them, technical failure, corruption, and community confusion and conflict were the common symptoms of an uncoordinated and poorly designed system of governance. After the meeting, the agitated District Development Officer led the research team across miles of sweeping rice paddies to what he thought summed up the failures of CEP: an irrigation project that had lost its tussle with some basic laws of physics. The consequences of cost cutting and poor technical skills would be expensive to fix. "This thing just floods," he sighed.

The CEP frustrated a national government that felt it was being treated like the *bombeiros*, firefighters called upon only to douse the flames of project failures. Although the CEP was nominally under a government department, this department was left out of the day-to-day running of the project. In practice, CEP staff were more accountable to the Bank. Fueling this division between the parties was the Bank's attempt to create CEP staff in its own image. Superior salaries and resources for project staff caused tensions with government, especially as the director of the government department handling the CEP was meant to supervise a project manager earning four times his own salary.

This is a theme now transcending national boundaries: a well-paid, managerial elite overseeing the outsourcing and impoverishment of social services, while communities are forced to pick up the slack in an act of what establishment social scientists have excitedly misdiagnosed as "community empowerment" or the "rebuilding of social capital" (Fine 2002). One disgruntled community member interviewed didn't need as many words to describe this: "We are just doing the work government used to do but being paid less for it."

The project did achieve some successes. Water projects in particular vastly improved communities' access to better quality water, especially helping women who do the bulk of cooking, washing, and cleaning. But its failures overshadow these achievements, especially as 58 cents of every dollar was spent on overheads (World Bank 2003: 25), largely to prevent the problem-ridden project from derailing. In addition, although much of this money went into capacity building and institutional development, these skills will be scattered to the wind when a frustrated, newly elected government winds up the project.

RETURNING TO THE LAND OF KIOSKS

The most enduring legacy of the CEP will be its problems with microcredit. Microcredit can usually do little wrong in the eyes of the development establishment. Donors and NGOs alike are excited by what is a rare breed of development project—one that is friendly to neoliberal prescriptions and manages (sometimes) to alleviate poverty. However, the correlation is always a fragile one. Simply assuming that handing out some capital and a few basic accounting skills is all that is needed for the poor to blossom into savvy microentrepreneurs ignores the deeply rooted causes of people's poverty.

Instead, in the case of Timor-Leste, credit often placed recipients in a precarious position, as many spent the money on urgent needs or to run what, for them and everyone else, was the only option—a kiosk. Overall, poor business health, combined with a lack of education about the scheme and a dysfunctional system of incentives to repay, has meant that only 30–40 percent of credit will eventually be repaid.

But focusing on repayment rates is a distraction from the main question: are microenterprises alleviating poverty? Surveying the burgeoning informal economies in the cities of Africa, Rogerson distinguishes between survivalist and growth enterprises, where the former are generally "run by women, usually fall short of even a minimum living standard and involve little capital investment, virtually no skills training and only constrained opportunities for expansion into a viable business" (Rogerson 1997: 347–351). Timor-Leste's predominantly survivalist economy, nurtured by CEP-style programs, needs the support of a formal economy to provide important, wage-driven linkages to assist such microenterprises in evolving out of their overcrowded and unprofitable trading niches.

Like the path trodden by every developed country, this would take the interventions of a strong, yet donor-unpalatable, developmentalist state. Instead, the Bank tried to correct these structural deficiencies in the CEP by arguing for more training for credit recipients and better and more accessible information on market activities. But there are stark limits to what training and information can remedy. One credit recipient living on the lonely and barren coastline of the Bazartete sub-district cynically observed that she was thankful for the one day of training in business tactics she'd received from the project two years ago. It helped confirm her long-held conclusions that her kiosk was miserable, as were any other possible business options.

One ardent supporter of microcredit in Timor-Leste defends the proliferation of kiosks, arguing that, having seen foreign goods on sale, farmers have an incentive to increase their production. Apparently, it takes the lure of kiosks selling instant noodles to motivate farmers to increase local food production, something seasonal hunger—experienced by 78 percent of Timorese—hasn't managed to do (ETTA 2001: 59). Instead, kiosks are often undermining local production by selling cheaper imported cooking oil, rice, and coffee. With almost half the population living on less than 55 cents per day—the UN's absolute poverty line—Timor-Leste is the last country in Asia that can afford these free-market experiments. Instead, development should promote local industries and agriculture and move beyond Timor-Leste's noncompetitive advantage in selling other people's goods.

WHO'S DRIVING COMMUNITY-DRIVEN DEVELOPMENT?

The Bank's entry into community development and local governance has been met with mixed responses from affected communities, aid workers, and activists. Perhaps the Bank should bear in mind the following.

First, the CEP shows that the Bank has borrowed concepts such as "community empowerment" and the "rebuilding of social capital," and used them like pieces of theoretical putty to cover up the gap between its rhetoric and the manifest failures of the past 20 years of structural adjustment. In the process, these concepts are being emptied of their meaning and used as a smokescreen for extending the Bank's ambit of operations.[2] For these reasons, this model should be resisted and the Bank's license for using terms like "empowerment" and "participation" should be revoked.

Second, if the Bank's Transitional Support Strategy was meant to place the Timorese government "in the driver's seat"—the Bank's current phrase of choice—then in the case of the CEP, the government was the taxi driver, taking instructions and money from its World Bank passenger. And where was that car driving? Through a maze of contradictions inherent in trying to build a nation on the quick, and across flimsy theoretical foundations that masked the inappropriate imposition of free-market economics on the grassroots. Perhaps it's time for the Timorese to regain control of the car, and kick out the freeloading passengers.

ACKNOWLEDGMENTS

The author assisted a joint Timorese government–civil society research team to study the CEP. They deserve strong thanks and include Bonifacio Belo, Tomas Freitas, Julino Ximenes da Costa, and Mateus Goncalves, as well as Emilia Pires from the National Directorate of Planning. All quotes in this article are from the report produced by the team (Rolling Think Tank Initiative 2004) unless otherwise indicated. I am also grateful for the suggestions and comments offered by Shalmali Guttal, Joy Chavez, Nicola Bullard, and Dan Nicholson.

NOTES

[1] A nationwide consultation for Timor-Leste's National Development Plan organized more than 1,000 forums covering more than 38,000 Timorese citizens. They produced a 20-year national vision for the country, identifying education, health, and employment as the top priorities.

[2] Ben Fine argues forcefully that such concepts have been used by the Bretton Woods institutions to enable their brand of economics to "colonise the social sciences" (Fine 2002: 18–33; see also Harriss 2002).

REFERENCES

Carlin, Anne. 2003. "Rush to Reengagement in Afghanistan: The IFIs' Post-conflict Agenda with a Special Focus on the National Solidarity Program." Bank Information Center. Available at http://www.bicusa.org/bicusa/issues/Afghanistan_Report_Trip1.pdf (retrieved 12 January 2005).

Democratic Republic of Timor-Leste (RDTL). 2003. *Timor-Leste: Poverty in a New Nation: Analysis for Action*. Dili, Timor-Leste: RDTL, UNDP, World Bank, JICA, UNICEF, UNMISET, and ADB.

East Timor Community Development Working Group. 2001. "East Timor Community Development Review Report." Unpublished report. Dili: East Timor Community Development Working Group.

East Timor Transitional Administration (ETTA), Asia Development Bank, World Bank, and UNDP. 2001. *The 2001 Survey of Sucos: Initial Analysis and Implications for Poverty Reduction*, Dili: ETTA, ADB, World Bank, and UNDP.

Fine, Ben. 2002. "It Ain't Social, It Ain't Capital and It Ain't Africa." *Studia Africa* 13:18–33.

Harriss, John. 2002. *Depoliticizing Development: The World Bank and Social Capital*. New Delhi: Left Word.

Hohe, Tanya, and Sofi Ospina. 2001. "Traditional Power Structures and the Community Empowerment and Local Governance Project: Final Report." Unpublished report. Dili, Timor-Leste.

Kessler, Tim. 2004. "Review of World Development Report 2004, 'Making Services Work for the Poor.'" Available at http://www.networkideas.org (retrieved 15 January 2004).

Kumar, Nalini. 2003. "Community Driven Development: Lessons from the Sahel, an Analytical Review." Working Paper, World Bank Operations Evaluation Department. Washington, DC: World Bank.

Rogerson, Christian. 1997. "Globalization or Informalization? African Urban Economies in the 1990s." In Carole Rakodi (ed.), *The Urban Challenge in Africa: Growth and Management of Its Large Cities*. Tokyo: Tokyo University Press.

Rolling Think Tank Initiative. 2004. "Lessons Learned: The Community Empowerment and Local Governance Project (CEP)." Dili, Timor-Leste: National Directorate of Planning and External Assistance Coordination, Ministry of Planning and Finance, Democratic Republic of Timor-Leste.

World Bank. 2000. "Community Empowerment and Local Governance Project: Report No. 20312 TP, Project Appraisal Document." Washington, DC: World Bank.

World Bank. 2002. "Third Community Empowerment and Local Governance Project: Report No. 24119 TP, Project Appraisal Document." Washington, DC: World Bank.

World Bank. 2003. "Background Paper to the Timor-Leste and Development Partners' Meeting 3–5 December: Annex 3: Key Issues in Expenditure Policy and Management." Washington, DC: World Bank.

PART 3

Pressure for Change: Fair Trade and Ethical Codes of Conduct

TEN

Managing Ethical Standards:

When Rhetoric Meets Reality

SUMI DHANARAJAN

INTRODUCTION

In March 2004, the UK Department for Trade and Industry (DTI) issued a Draft International Strategic Framework on Corporate Social Responsibility (CSR) for consultation (available at www.dti.gov.uk). The draft prompted a 16-strong coalition of British human rights and development NGOs to write an open letter to the secretary of state outlining major concerns with the substance of the document and the approach taken. Four points were made to support the contention that the proposed strategy was an inadequate tool for securing responsible corporate behavior with regard to social and environmental impacts:

- The majority of companies are not integrating their social and environmental commitments and responsibilities into their business models.
- Existing CSR initiatives are not delivering results to the scale required to effectively meet the key challenges.
- The market's failure to reflect social and environmental costs can only be overcome with public policy intervention.
- Corporate governance needs to be addressed in this context.

To be fair, the current draft does reflect the most common approach taken by companies toward CSR: the voluntary undertaking of ethical (social and environmental) commitments to address externalities to the extent that these pose a sufficient risk to the company. But this is an approach that is failing to deliver. Drawing on research undertaken by Oxfam International (OI), this chapter shows that when the rhetoric of ethical commitments meets reality—the impact of the business model—the limitations of the current CSR model for change are exposed. As one commentator suggests, "at its best it is a creative approach to address poverty and inequality within the parameters of existing markets; . . . at its worst, however, it appears to be a convenient smokescreen to distract attention from the uncomfortable reality of some business impacts" (Tickell 2004: 1).

The chapter is divided into three sections: the first recaps why CSR has been placed on the agenda; the second illustrates—using the retail sector as an example—why there is a pressing need to rethink current approaches toward managing ethical standards; and the third concludes by suggesting what can be done unilaterally by companies and explaining why public-policy interventions are necessary to counter the failure of the market to respond to social and environmental impacts.

WHY THE DEMAND FOR CORPORATE RESPONSIBILITY?

The call for companies to behave responsibly is not a new one. What is expected of companies, however, has mutated as the nature of the corporation and its interaction with people and governments has evolved. In the last two decades, we have experienced immense changes in the structure and function of global markets, with the transnational corporation (TNC) emerging as a dominant player in the political economy in both the industrialized and the developing world. This growth in power and influence in itself has attracted demands for greater responsibility and greater accountability. Alongside this, a number of other factors have placed the TNC within the frame:

- *The massive disparity between huge profits reaped by TNCs and incidences of dire poverty in countries where they operate.*
- *Global trade rules that expand the privileges and rights of TNCs while seemingly contracting those of poor people.* The 1994 Uruguay Round of GATT talks that established the WTO brought this to the forefront with the Trade Related Intellectual Property

Rights Agreement (TRIPS) and the General Agreement on Trade in Services (GATS), which were effectively written and pushed through by a heavily influential corporate lobby. Developing countries—in the course of the horse-trading that took place during this Round—had to accept these agreements despite certain anti-developmental characteristics.

- *Economic liberalization and the consequential growth in international competitiveness.* This has led to TNCs looking for ways to strip out costs, often from the production end of the supply chain, leaving those with the least bargaining power to bear the biggest risk. In the retail sector, for example, the ultimate brunt in the form of unhealthy, unsafe, and undignified working conditions is borne by those working on farms, in factories, and, in some cases, in the home.
- *Privatization of basic services.* Whether it is water, electricity, health, or education, companies are increasingly becoming the main providers of basic services as governments, either through their own volition or through conditionalities, delegate their role to the private sector. Although privatization is not bad per se, in a number of instances the failure by companies to deliver services equitably to poor people has become a problem.
- *The strength of TNCs' political influence* over local, national, and international institutions, especially when it is used to promote anti-poverty policies and measures.
- *Evidence of direct liability for or complicity with human rights abuses, including environmental rights.*

TNCs have the capacity to bring substantial benefits to societies in the developing world through job creation, revenues, technology transfer, and the delivery of goods and services, although there are questions about the quality of these benefits or whether they are indeed being delivered.

Faced with these perceptions, the corporate sector has worked through various phases of response, starting with a "deny and defend" position, moving to "paying penance" through donations and philanthropy, and currently settling on risk management through mitigation of the negative impacts of their business operations. This chapter will argue that if business is to retain its license to operate, corporations will need to move into a fourth phase of exploring alternative business models that have social and environmental responsibilities built into them.

RETHINKING THE MANAGEMENT OF ETHICAL STANDARDS: RETAIL-SECTOR CASE STUDY[1]

> We have overtime work till late every day. The price they pay us per piece is so low, there is no point working such long hours. If our income was higher, I would have no complaints. But all we have now is exhaustion and a low income. Some of us do not even have money to spend on food. It is more than we can bear. (A garment worker in a Chinese factory supplying well-known sports brands, quoted in Oxfam GB et al. 2004: 21)

Hit by an increasing number of anti-sweatshop campaigns in the 1990s, companies within the retail sector were among the first to adopt codes of conduct to police suppliers' adherence to labor standards. Implementation is largely through audits of workplaces conducted either in-house or through third-party commercial auditors. Yet, despite all the good intentions, improvements in working conditions have been limited. In 2003 and 2004, OI conducted extensive research with partners in 15 countries spanning the supply chains of more than 20 companies in order to understand why this is the case. We found that current sourcing strategies designed to meet just-in-time delivery (premised on flexibility and fast turnaround), combined with the lowering of unit costs, are significantly contributing to the use of exploitative employment practices by suppliers. Whereas companies have been putting resources into "fire-fighting" the problem of sweatshop labor by whipping suppliers into line with their codes of conduct, not one of them has adequately addressed the fact that their purchasing practices and sourcing strategies are not only a key cause of the problem but are ultimately undermining any efforts to secure decent working conditions (Dhanarajan 2004; ETI 2004).

Research conducted in the garment retail sector found that, although export-oriented industries are providing jobs, especially for women, the nature of those jobs is precarious: insecure, lacking proper labor protection or benefits, and unhealthy. Responding to retailer sourcing strategies, employment within global supply chains in this sector is typified by the following conditions:

- *Short-term rolling contracts* rather than permanent employment in order to accommodate buyers' demands for flexibility and uncertainty of orders, and to cut labor costs such as benefit payments and severance pay. Governments are increasingly confirming their acceptance of this type of employment as the norm in response to pressures to capture investment. For example, proposed labor reforms in Honduras would permit garment factories to hire up to 30 percent of their workers on temporary contracts (Raworth 2004a: 21).

- *Piece-rate payments* allowing the factory manager to determine the quantity that the worker must produce, a determination made in accordance with the order put in by the buyer rather than the time or effort required to do the work. When suppliers are given too little time to turn around the order, production targets become excessive. If targets are not achieved during the normal working day, workers are expected to work overtime on their own account and are not paid at all unless the set target is completed. Piece rates also allow the supplier to adjust to drops in unit costs by reducing the amounts paid per item. Workers at an Indonesian factory supplying six sportswear brands told researchers, "The usual target is 1000 pieces per lane, per day; but during export days, the target doubles to 2000 pieces. This doubling is very stressful for us and we often cannot reach it" (Oxfam GB et al. 2004: 42).
- *Low wages* to meet falling unit costs. At one Chinese factory, the owner reported that unit prices for a well-known UK brand of sports shoes were falling year on year. Workers from his factory interviewed in November 2003 complained that their wages had also fallen over the last three years. Whereas they used to be paid at least the minimum wage during the low season, that protection has since been removed. During a low season in 2003, workers in the sole department reported being paid between a mere RMB200 and RMB400 (€20–40) per month (Oxfam GB et al. 2004: 43). There has been an average drop in unit costs of 30 percent in three years in the garment sector. Conversely, production costs are rising for the factory. A Sri Lankan manufacturer supplying a U.S. sportswear company estimated that while his production costs had increased by approximately 20 percent in the last five years, unit prices paid by the company had dropped by 35 percent in the previous 18 months (Oxfam GB et al. 2004: 39). Threats to relocate are also often used as a means of bargaining down prices.
- *Excessive working hours and forced overtime* as the industry focuses on shortening lead times and fluctuating size and frequency of orders. On average, lead times have halved, from 90 days to 45 days. Workers at a Chinese factory producing for a UK sports brand alleged that they worked a total of 120 hours of overtime in

a month—three times in excess of Chinese labor legislation. One worker complained, "We have endless overtime in peak season and we sit working non-stop for 13 to 14 hours a day. We sew and sew without stopping until our arms feel sore and stiff" (Oxfam GB et al. 2004: 19). The "fast-fashion" phenomenon led by companies such as Zara and H&M that can take designs off the catwalk and into high-street stores at incredible speed—Zara can put together a range in 7–30 days—risks exacerbating the problem unless managed responsibly.

- *Restrictions on freedom of association* in order to prevent workers from challenging exploitative working conditions. Such restrictions range from simply not providing workers with time to organize to outright harassment, intimidation, and even violence against unionists.

Employment practices in the fresh-produce sector are similar, though breaches in labor standards here seem to result from what the UK Competition Commission terms as "coercive and abusive business practices" used by supermarket retailers. These fall into three categories:

- *Offloading of price and payment risks onto the farmer.* In most cases, supermarkets fix their profit margins and leave suppliers to bear price fluctuations. Payment for products is usually determined and made only after the product arrives rather than upon shipment. If the product is unsatisfactory or not needed, the farmer bears the cost of its being sold on the wholesale market. A South African–based apple packhouse manager supplying one of the UK's largest supermarkets told researchers, "They chop and change their minds constantly. It takes a month for us to get the fruit there, but it takes two minutes for them to change their minds . . . Then the only thing we can do is dump it somewhere else" (Raworth 2004a: 69).
- *Increasing specification costs but decreasing unit prices.* Product standards demanded by retailers have become highly specific—for example, Fuji apples must be 65 mm and not 63 mm—and these have raised costs in terms of both input and yield reduction. At the packhouse level, supermarkets have also become very prescriptive about the use of different types of bags, crates, boxes, and packaging, which has affected productivity because of the increase in complexity of the work. Although costs have risen, this increase has not been compensated with higher prices being paid by the retailer.

- *Discounting and fees.* Suppliers are often required to foot the bill for promotions whereby buyers discount products in order to boost sales. Further, suppliers are also asked to give "overrider" (in anticipation) discounts and upfront payments for the privilege of being on the retailers' list (Blythman 2003).

As one South African apple farmer supplying a number of UK supermarkets summed up, "The only ham left in the sandwich is our labour costs. If the supermarkets squeeze us, it's the only place where we can be squeezed" (Raworth 2004a: 7).

Failure to address the disparities between the commitments stipulated in the code of conduct on the one hand, and sourcing priorities on the other has meant that working conditions remain, by and large, exploitative. Both at the retailer end and at the supplier end, codes are viewed as something that can be derogated from in the normal run of the business. Code-compliance staff admit that in certain circumstances—for example, last-minute orders—excessive overtime is overlooked. From the supplier end, factory managers fake compliance during inspections. As one Chinese garment manufacturer said, "I know how to deal with the ethical code people from my many years of experience. I can judge the balance of power between the buying departments and those responsible for the codes to see where the real power lies" (Raworth 2004a: 37).

The OI research recommends four areas of change in policy and practice that would integrate the ethical and buying functions, which is necessary in order to better manage ethical standards:

- *Raise the status of ethical commitments within the business.* Such commitments are still being perceived and treated as a "bolt-on." Within the corporate hierarchy, ethical staff sit lower than buyers and have little mandate over sourcing decisions beyond either recommending who are the "good" and "bad" suppliers or making "bad" suppliers "good" so that buyers can source from them. They have little say in, or the ability to push for, more responsible purchasing practices. This needs to change in order to send out the right signals both within the company and throughout the supply chain.
- *Responsible negotiations with suppliers.* Retailers should be evaluating the impact of changes in lead-time strategies or pricing within a labor-standards framework. Production lead times need to be determined together with suppliers, and prices should be negotiated in the context of the supplier being able to meet labor standards.

- *Change the buying culture.* As a former fresh-food buyer from a leading UK supermarket reported, "Buyers are caught in a high-pressure culture of weekly reporting on their sales and profit margin targets. Ethical trade just doesn't fit neatly into numbers so it gets left out of the picture" (Raworth 2004a: 37, 2004b). Buyers within the retail industry operate in a business culture of performance targets and incentives that encourages them to squeeze suppliers on price and delivery. Many of those interviewed spoke of being given only 12–18 months in any given category before being moved to another, in order to prevent them from developing relationships with suppliers that might cause them to lose their edge in negotiations. Some retailers have conducted awareness-raising activities on their codes of conduct with their buyers, but none has gone so far as to change staff incentives and performance assessments so that they reward rather than undermine ethical purchasing.
- *Better critical-path management and improved forecasting.* Poor critical-path management and poor forecasting are seen as the key problems by retailing staff, especially within the apparel industry. There is little accountability at the retailer end of the production chain for changes or delays in decision making, which means that the supplier is expected to absorb them. Last-minute orders are very common. Efforts could be made to ensure that internal procedures for placing orders do not lead to excessive or unagreed time pressures for suppliers. Databases for logging internal decisions can improve accountability. Retailers can work with the supply bases to "multi-skill" suppliers so that orders can be spread to even out peaks and troughs, and they can be more thoughtful as to how orders are placed.

INTEGRATING THE ETHICAL WITH THE COMMERCIAL: UNILATERAL ACTION AND PUBLIC-POLICY INTERVENTIONS

Our research on the retail sector confirmed not just the desirability but also the absolute necessity of ensuring coherence and connectivity between ethical standards and core business operations. Simply mitigating negative impacts through castigating intermediaries or suppliers, or through philanthropic activities, neither placates the critics nor contributes to sustainable solutions. From a business perspective, keeping the CSR function separate means missing the opportunity to take a critical look at the direct impacts of irresponsible behavior upon the long-term profitability and survival of the business. As a parallel study conducted by Insight Investment, the asset manager of Halifax and Bank of Scotland Group (HBOS), which based its findings on interviews with the retailer end of the supply chain, concluded, breaches of labor standards are driven by failures that are also commercially undesirable (ACONA and Insight Investment 2004; HBOS 2004).

Take the coffee sector, for example. All four of the largest coffee roasters—Nestlé, Sara Lee, Proctor & Gamble, and Kraft—acknowledge that the current coffee crisis, which is destroying the livelihoods of 25 million farmers worldwide, is not in their own long-term interests. The impact that the crisis is likely to have on quality is significant; despite new technologies that allow roasters to mask the bitterness of lower-quality coffee, there is a bottom line that will be reached soon. Coupled with a general decline in coffee consumption—per capita consumption in the United States has more than halved in the last 30 years—this does not bode well. When interviewed in 2002, Nestlé conceded, "The present low price situation has a tremendously negative impact on the quality of the coffee produced, making it more difficult for Nestlé to find the quality we need for our product" (Gresser and Tickell 2002: 28) Yet despite the recognition, the industry—bar a few examples—has been slow to react and take responsibility for the part that it plays in contributing to the intractability of the crisis.

Research undertaken by OI in 2002 suggests that major roasters have been opportunistic in reaping short-term profit gains from the drop in prices. If roasters committed to paying prices that provide farmers with a decent income, ensured them greater security over future income through fixed contracts or supply agreements, and bought coffee that met basic quality standards, it would go some way toward alleviating the crisis. This call has resonated with a few. Starbucks, for example, has significantly boosted its purchase of fair trade coffee, is paying its suppliers around double the open market price, and has independent checks done to see that it carries out its own purchasing guidelines. Others have been less responsive. Kraft, when asked in 2002 for its views on the crisis, replied that "the market will find its own solution because countries and producers will be driven out of the market." Such a solution may be a long time coming. The cost of waiting as prices on world markets continue to hover around 50–60 cents per pound, the lowest in real terms over the past 100 years, is taking its toll on farmers, on their families, and on national economies. Mohammad Ali Idris, an Ethiopian coffee farmer, told OI researchers how bad this is for him:

> Five to seven years ago, I was producing seven sacks of red cherry [unprocessed coffee] and this was enough to buy clothes, medicines, services and to solve so many problems. But now even if I sell four times as much, it is impossible to cover all my expenses . . . Three of my children can't go to school because I can't afford the uniform. We have stopped buying teff [staple starch] and edible oil. The children's skin is getting dry and they are showing signs of malnutrition. (Quoted in Gresser and Tickell 2002: 10)

Further, simply waiting is not the solution for the industry: although it is true that eventually coffee production will go down as farmers simply cannot afford to continue to tend to their crop, and prices will correspondingly increase, the timescale that this involves might mean the end of the coffee industry as we currently know it. Coffee bushes take 10–15 years to be ready for harvesting; at present, farmers are still growing them because there are no alternatives, and in the hope that there will be a recovery.

A similar analysis can be applied to the pharmaceutical industry. For years, drug companies could rely comfortably on the fact that they produced medicines as evidence of their corporate social responsibility. This premise has been slowly eroded as evidence has emerged on, for example, unethical clinical trials. The AIDS crisis has, however, brought a definite end to that comfort. Against the backdrop of a public-health emergency of a global scale, the very pillars of the industry's operations—patenting and pricing—have been the subject of public outrage. Pharmaceutical companies have been accused of undermining poor people's access to medicines through two means: aggressively defending their patent rights through a variety of mechanisms so as to prevent the development of lower-cost generic medicines, and pricing medicines way beyond the means of poor people.

Many of the large firms have sought to mitigate these accusations through generous drug donations both unilaterally and through efforts such as the Accelerating Access Initiative. Only a few companies have met the challenge head-on by exploring differential pricing and voluntary licensing. Failure by others within the industry to address the health crisis in a meaningful way is serious: patenting and pricing of antiretrovirals continues to be a problem, despite donations. And looking to the future, the growing burden of noncommunicable diseases such as cancer, heart disease, and diabetes will take us to crisis point again if no real progress is made.[2] It is worrying, therefore, when the world's largest pharmaceutical company, Pfizer, rejects notions of tiered pricing. Interviewed in 2003, its vice president for corporate affairs was categorical: "We do pricing by markets" (quoted in Boseley and Pratley 2003).

Pfizer is also a member of the Industry Functional Advisory Committee, which advises the U.S. government on the intellectual-property aspects of its bilateral Free Trade Agreements (FTAs). Although the 2001 Doha Declaration confirmed the primacy of public health over patents, reaffirming the rights of countries to use all the public-interest safeguards in TRIPS, including compulsory licensing and parallel importation to promote "access to medicines for all," a number of U.S. FTAs—notably the Central American Free Trade Agreement (CAFTA)—have cut back on this safeguard facility by introducing longer patent periods, restrictions on compulsory licensing, and other provisions.[3]

A lack of progress by the pharmaceutical industry in addressing the impacts of its core operations on access to medicines is of concern to investors. Long seen as one of the best sectors in which to invest because of its high returns, pharmaceutical-industry stocks now come with the fear that continued public criticism of the industry for failing to act will start to pose material risks. A report issued in September 2004 by an international grouping of 14 institutional investors identified four potential risks connected with the industry's lack of response. First, damage to reputation would undermine belief in the patent system as a whole—and with it one of the key profit mechanisms for pharmaceutical companies. Second, damage to relationships with regulatory bodies that control intellectual property, pricing, and drug approval frameworks may lead to further calls even from mature markets for downward pricing. Third, it may hamper access to new markets. And fourth, the behavior of the pharmaceutical industry may lead to damage to staff morale, and to recruitment and retention problems (Pharmaceutical Shareowners Group 2004).

As demonstrated by the retail, coffee, and pharmaceutical sectors, when companies endeavor to apply their ethical responsibilities to core business operations, they can effectively and credibly manage their ethical standards. But the biggest threat to the CSR agenda is the fact that the market rewards irresponsible behavior (Tickell 2004). Look at any of those three sectors and you will see more irresponsible companies than responsible ones. Although the growth in the socially responsible investment (SRI) movement offers hope, far more work needs to be done to convince and convert mainstream investors and financiers to rethink current indicators of success, and to ask critical questions as to whether what constitutes growth in the short term translates into longer-term profitability. Business schools also must take up this challenge.

That the market is failing in this way also poses a real challenge to those who argue that CSR must continue to be a voluntary, self-regulatory regime. Although the voluntary mechanism is and will always be important in that it defines the norm and offers a competitive advantage to the leaders, it cannot drag up the laggards. It also fails properly to establish which activities are acceptable and which are not given that ultimately the company will respond to market imperatives. Take the retail sector: whether or not excessive overtime is seen as a breach of a code of conduct depends on whether it is peak or low season. The moral or ethical bottom line is tenuous.

Given this, the need to explore public-policy interventions becomes all the more crucial. What forms these take are up for debate. At one level, simply strengthening existing national laws—for example, labor legislation or consumer-protection laws—and their enforcement mechanisms will suffice. The complex nature of the TNC, in particular, has prompted calls for a corporate accountability framework of a more global nature that allows corporate veils to be pushed aside, jurisdictional barriers to be overcome, and access to justice to become more easily achieved. In the UK, civil society groups have tabled a Corporate Responsibility Bill that offers a regulatory combination of reporting, stakeholder consultation, access to information, directors' duties, and liability (including foreign direct-liability) mechanisms.

For their part, governments have been fairly reluctant to take on responsibility on this front. Going back to the DTI draft strategic framework, the main role that it carves out for government is essentially one of raising awareness and providing support to companies as they develop their own strategies voluntarily. Suggestions of introducing legally binding mechanisms on human rights have been met with unease on the anachronistic basis that international law conceives of the state and the state alone as an actor with obligations. Having said that, the British government has at least taken some steps to regulate how companies behave in their operations domestically and overseas: in July 2000, the UK Pensions Act was amended to require trustees of occupational pension plans to disclose their policy on SRI as part of their

Statement of Investment Principles (SIP). Belgium, France, Germany, and Sweden have adopted similar regulations. The Australian Financial Services Reform Act stipulates that all products with an investment component—including pension funds and mutual funds—must include disclosure of "the extent to which labour standards or environmental, social, or ethical considerations are taken into account in the selection, retention, and realisation of the investment." More recently, the Australian Securities and Investments Commission (ASIC) released Practice Statement 175, which requires advisers providing personal financial advice to enquire whether environmental, social, or ethical considerations are important to their clients.

It is to be hoped that the UK government's lead department on CSR will revisit its position and fulfill—as set out in the original draft—its "ambitious vision for Corporate Social Responsibility." In so doing, it should ensure that any policy or framework that it develops meets the imperative of making companies entrench social and environmental responsibilities within the core of their businesses and establishes a governmental role in ensuring that this happens. Indeed, unless governments start to take more ownership of the CSR agenda, it is unlikely that we will overcome what BP's CEO, Lord Browne, fears—that globalization will be perceived as "a new form of colonialism in which a tiny, self-perpetuating elite grow rich at the expense of everyone else."[4]

ACKNOWLEDGMENTS

This chapter is based upon a paper presented by the author on 1 October 2004 at the 2004 Transatlantic Business Ethics Conference organized by ESADE in Barcelona, Spain. The author wishes to thank Kate Raworth (case study on the retail sector), Henk Campher (coffee), and Mohga Smith and Ruth Mayne (pharmaceuticals) at OGB for their help with this text.

NOTES

[1] This section draws heavily on Raworth (2004a) and Oxfam GB et al. (2004).

[2] Patients in developing countries account for 59 percent of the 56.5 million annual deaths worldwide from noncommunicable diseases, including cardiovascular diseases, cancers, diabetes, and respiratory diseases.

³ This was followed by a decision by the WTO on 30 August 2003 to lift TRIPS restrictions on compulsory licensing for export of generic medicines to countries that lack the capacity to manufacture them themselves.

⁴ Lord Browne speaking at the Stanford Graduate School of Business Conference on Global Business and Global Poverty, Stanford University, 19 May 2003.

REFERENCES

ACONA and Insight Investment. 2004. "Buying Your Way into Trouble? The Challenge of Supply Chain Management." Available at http://www.insightinvestment. com/responsibility/project/responsible_supply_chain_management.asp (retrieved 18 January 2005).

Blythman, Joanna. 2003. "Lord of the Aisles." *Guardian* 17 May, available at http://www.guardian.co.uk/food/focus/story/0,956562,00.html (retrieved 29 September 2004).

Boseley, Sarah, and Nils Pratley. 2003. "In the Time It Takes You to Read This Article, Pfizer Will Make US$250,000. So Does It Have a Duty to Provide Cheap Drugs to the Poor?" *Guardian* 24 April.

Dhanarajan, Sumi. 2004. "Faster, Longer, Cheaper: The Nexus between Poor Labour Standards and Supplychain Management in the Apparel Industry." *European Retail Digest* 43(Fall):43–46.

Ethical Trading Initiative (ETI). 2004. "Purchasing Practices: Marrying the Commercial with the Ethical." Report from a round-table held in London, 7 July.

Gresser, Charis, and Sophia Tickell. 2002. *Mugged: Poverty in Your Coffee Cup*. Oxfam International Campaign Report, Oxford: Oxfam GB.

HBOS. 2004. *Taking Care of Tomorrow: The HBOS Corporate Responsibility Report 2004*. Edinburgh: HBOS plc.

Oxfam GB, Clean Clothes Campaign, and ICFTU. 2004. *Play Fair at the Olympics: Respect Workers' Rights in the Sportswear Industry*. Oxfam International Campaign Report, Oxford: Oxfam GB.

Pharmaceutical Shareowners Group. 2004. *The Public Health Crisis in Emerging Markets: An Institutional Investor Perspective on the Implications for the Pharmaceutical Industry*. London: PSG.

Raworth, Kate. 2004a. *Trading Away Our Rights: Women Working in Global Supply Chains*. Oxfam International Campaign Report, Oxford: Oxfam GB.

Raworth, Kate. 2004b. "The Supermarket Squeeze: How Fresh Produce Supply Chain Management Is Undermining Workers' Rights." *European Retail Digest* 42(Summer):81–84.

Tickell, Sophia. 2004. "Rethinking Corporate Responsibility." Unpublished paper. Oxford: Oxfam GB.

ELEVEN

Corporate Responsibility and CAFTA:

Are They Compatible?

CAROLINA QUINTEROS

INTRODUCTION

Central America is in the midst of a spate of free-trade agreements (FTAs), which are viewed as part of the strategy for lifting the region out of poverty. The assumption is that the opening up of markets will provide greater opportunities for export-oriented businesses. The growth of these businesses, which arc mainly small and medium-sized enterprises (SMEs) according to the official propaganda, could lead to more investment and more jobs. The official line makes no mention of the implications of the failure to protect local producers, in particular agricultural workers, when agreements are negotiated between highly asymmetrical economies, such as those of the tiny Central American countries as compared with the United States. Other issues ignored in the official discourse on FTAs include the reduction in tax revenue on imported goods and patent licenses, the pressing need to modernize national businesses in order to take advantage of access to new markets, and the fundamental inability to attract the kind of investment that would really benefit the countries and peoples of Central America.

Note: This chapter was translated from Spanish by Deborah Eade. It is based on an article published in 2005, shortly before the expiry of the Multi-Fibre Arrangement.

One of the sectors that supposedly benefits most from the Central American Free Trade Agreement (CAFTA) is the garment-manufacturing industry found in the assembly plants (*maquila*) and free-trade zones. Certainly, CAFTA has provided some advantages to this sector, and, in theory at least, this should give the *maquila* industry a clear competitive edge. However, the world market in the garment, apparel, and textiles industry is on the verge of major upheaval, which will mean that any benefits CAFTA might bring will be short-lived. In this case, corporate responsibility is not merely compatible with CAFTA but necessary to it.

This chapter examines why, despite CAFTA, the Central American *maquila* industry may not necessarily maintain its current success in the medium term. The chapter also argues that good business practices such as respect for employees' human rights and responsible behavior vis-à-vis the environment are not only a matter of personal or business ethics or altruism, but are also a question of remaining competitive and ensuring long-term business survival.

CAN CAFTA ENSURE THE FUTURE OF THE CENTRAL AMERICAN *MAQUILA* INDUSTRY?[1]

There is nothing new about the fact that members of the manufacturing sector in the industrialized countries feel seriously threatened by the competition they face from Asia, particularly China. Job losses in manufacturing have been significant in countries including the United States, where, according to the Chicago Federal Reserve, the percentage of workers in these industries dropped from 35 percent in 1947 to 12 percent in 2003 (*The Economist* 2003). Of course, this decline has been influenced by factors such as higher productivity, new management strategies, the business climate, and so on. Nonetheless, the exodus of jobs from the United States, notably to Asia, is a growing concern.

Whereas several US industries have been affected by this outflow of jobs (for example, the electronics and telephone industries, as well as those providing various administrative functions), the worst hit has been the manufacturing sector, especially in the labor-intensive industries, where wages represent a relatively large proportion of production costs.

The Wal-Mart phenomenon exemplifies the fears currently gripping the US manufacturing industry. Wal-Mart is the largest US corporation in terms of sales, income, and profits—outstripping even Exxon,

General Motors, and Ford (*Fortune* 2004). Wal-Mart is able to offer low retail prices because it can exert pressure on its suppliers to reduce their costs, who in turn exert the same pressure on the intermediary suppliers and primary producers. In order to cut their production costs, some suppliers have been forced to fire their workers and move their operations elsewhere, for example to China (where almost all the clothing sold in Wal-Mart stores is made). Labor activists in China have criticized the pressure to lower prices that Wal-Mart has brought on factory suppliers, who then lower pay or increase hours (Goodman and Pan 2004). In another case, reported in 2003 and 2004, Wal-Mart was taken to court by former immigrant employees working for a Wal-Mart contractor in stores in the United States, alleging appalling working conditions (Borger 2003; Greenhouse 2004).

If cost is the main criterion for being contracted as a supplier to a major chain, this leaves little room for considerations such as environmentally friendly production that also respects labor rights or is committed to providing decent jobs. The availability of low-cost basic consumer items is of concern the world over. However, when the pressure to push prices down whatever the consequences enters the global manufacturing sector, the effects could hardly be worse. This dynamic encourages a spurious form of competition. In other words, such pressure leads directly or indirectly to social dumping through wage cuts, violations of labor rights, and/or lack of respect for the environment, flexible or deregulated labor markets, authoritarian management styles, reduced social welfare spending, currency devaluations, and similar consequences.

If this scenario is worrisome for the United States, it is even more so for Central America. The race for the cheapest supplier disproportionately affects countries that are major suppliers of manufactured goods. Central America is highly dependent on exports to the United States, and the danger is that market pressures will lead to businesses relocating their factories to more "competitive" countries, with the obvious consequences in terms of job losses, and/or will allow the already poor working conditions in the *maquila* to worsen still further.

The Central American *maquila*, which mainly produces garments, was covered by the Caribbean Basin Initiative (CBI), and so was tax-exempt on agreed quotas of exports to the United States provided the fabric itself was produced in the United States. This will no longer be an option for the Central American garment industry, because the quota system that has governed the world market in garments, apparel, and textiles was set to expire January 1, 2005. After the expiry of the Multi-Fibre Arrangement (MFA), Central America will be competing with countries such as China in order to maintain its existing production levels. Central America is highly vulnerable to these changes, especially as it has no alternative industrial base to which to turn.

China has the world's largest capacity for garment and textile production, and is the main producer of cotton, synthetic fibers, and silk. The industry is highly productive and the products are of good quality, although costs are extremely low. Other countries have lower production costs (India, Indonesia, and Sri Lanka, for example), but China is the only one with all the conditions necessary to dominate most of the world market in this sector (Nathan Associates 2002). So why has it not yet done so?

The Multi-Fibre Arrangement on Textiles and Clothing

The world market in textiles and clothing was at the time of writing (2005) governed by a quota system under the Multi-Fibre Arrangement (MFA), according to which the main consumer countries or regions (the EU, Japan, and the United States) must restrict imports of such products to an agreed level. By the same token, producer countries know that they can export only to a given country to the agreed maximum. The MFA effectively favors the smaller producing countries by preventing larger countries from monopolizing the export market, and by encouraging the consumer countries to purchase from them.

Central America benefited from the quota system when China and other Asian countries had already met their quotas, and companies therefore set up in the region in order to take advantage of an unexploited opportunity. Even in 2003, Central America had yet to reach its MFA quota, which suggests that there is no additional production capacity to be released as soon as the MFA expires. By contrast, China has long overtaken its quota, with the result that about 60 percent of its current production is not on the world export market. It can safely be assumed that once the quota restrictions are lifted, China and other Asian countries will easily be able to invade the world market in textiles and apparel.

The situation poses serious threats to the Central American *maquila* industry, given that many companies will presumably look to relocate or outsource to low-cost areas. It will also affect their US counterparts and textile producers, as they too will have to compete with fabrics and garments from Asia penetrating their markets.

The MFA had already begun the gradual lifting of quotas. By 2002, certain barriers had come down and shortly afterwards Chinese linen products had swamped the US market, with the result that a million workers lost their jobs, and some factories have closed down. According to US textile producers, these products would control 75 percent of the market; they pressed the government to impose import quotas on them. By November 2003, the US administration announced that its commercial deficit had reached an all-time high, in part because of the massive rise in imports from China. This is just a taste of what is likely to happen after 2005, when the Asian garment industry could rapidly displace Central American products in the US market. Concern is so great that some businesses have already formed an alliance with the textile workers' union UNITE! in order to protect their jobs in the face of the threat posed by China.

The Central American *maquila* industry has no concerns about Chinese textiles as such, because the region itself no longer produces these. However, there is considerable fear that their products will be displaced by garments made in China and that the local factories will cease to be economically viable in the face of such competition, not only in terms of price but also in relation to the variety and quality of the materials available to the Chinese producers, their higher levels of productivity, and so on.

One possibility for the Central American assembly plants is that their manufacturing systems evolve in such a way that their products have greater value added, and that levels of productivity and quality also rise. One strategy is that of the "full package," whereby the manufacturers no longer merely assemble cut cloth, but purchase the fabric and send the finished product directly to the retailers. This would add value and improve prices as well as provide a more sustained relationship with their clients. The *maquila* workers believe that such an arrangement would also allow them to take advantage of the region's proximity to the United States, rather than losing everything to Asian competition. This, and the idea of establishing associations or clusters, has been the subject of much discussion among Central American *maquila* workers.

Free-Trade Agreements

To take full advantage of the geographical location and the "full package" idea, CAFTA would need to allow for textile imports as well as the abolition of quotas. This has been partially achieved. The CAFTA was relatively positive vis-à-vis the *maquila* sector in that it benefited from the CBI tax exemptions on garments produced in Central America as well as from exemptions in the free-trade zones. In the case of Canada, negotiations were broken off in 2003 because Canada refused to allow garments produced in Central America to be covered by CAFTA on the grounds that the *maquila* industry is subsidized. The WTO, however, has authorized the continuation of subsidies for the free-trade zones until 2009. Other advantages conferred by CAFTA on the *maquila* industry include the following:

- *Accumulation of origin*: Before the FTA, the US tax exemptions covered by the CBI applied only to garments manufactured from textiles made in the United States. With the FTA, the United States accepted tax-exempt imports of products made with "textiles in short supply" from countries with which the United States has signed some kind of free-trade agreement, with the definition of the place of origin of the textile determined by the yarn. Thus textiles can now be bought from trading areas such as CAFTA, CBI, NAFTA, the Andean Trade Preferences Act (ATPA), and the African Growth and Opportunity Act (AGOA). The quotas for purchasing such textiles depend on how much the country buys from the United States: a country purchasing more US textiles has a higher quota for purchasing textiles from elsewhere on the principle of accumulation of origin.
- *List of textiles in short supply*: If Central America needs a textile that is not produced in the United States, then it may be added, after a long administrative process, to the list of textiles in short supply. Textiles on this list are subject to special treatment. This list was extended appreciably under CAFTA in comparison with what had been allowed under the CBI.
- *Single transformation*: Garments in simple fabric assembled in Central America, such as boxer shorts and underwear, can be exported to the United States tax-free regardless of where the fabric originates.
- *De minimis clause*: The United States currently allows up to 7 percent of an item to be made from materials from outside the region without charging tax. Under CAFTA, this will rise to 10 percent.
- *Category 809:* In the past, garments had to have been cut in the United States in order for the assembled product to be tax-exempt. Under CAFTA, garments can be cut in Central America, but the exporting company has to pay value-added tax on the garments because they have been produced entirely outside the United States.

- *Administrative silence*: This is a procedure allowing textiles to be classified as being in short supply. If the United States does not make a ruling within a stipulated period (which has yet to be revealed), the classification is automatic.
- *Retroactive application*: CAFTA came into force in 2004, and companies that have complied with all the obligations can apply for tax rebates relating to 2004.

These new arrangements are certainly important, and the *maquila* industry has reason to feel optimistic. However, the benefits are still inadequate. For instance, the retroactive facility depends on reimbursement of taxes already paid, and is bound to be an administrative hassle. The notion of administrative silence might work quite well in contexts where bureaucratic process tends to be slow, as is the case in Central America, but not in countries such as the United States where such matters tend to be dealt with more rapidly. Clause 890 still applies value-added tax to garments made outside the United States; only a small increase was allowed under the *de minimis* clause. The accumulation of origin refers only to simple fabrics, and in the case of Mexico, for instance, refers exclusively to denim.

The most worrisome issue for the Central American *maquila* industry is that textiles from Asia are not included in the category of short supply. Only Costa Rica and Nicaragua will be allowed a quota for garments manufactured in certain of these textiles, although they are widely used in garments produced in the region (40 percent of Salvadoran production and 80 percent of Nicaraguan production). According to the Salvadoran Minister for the Economy, at least 18,000 jobs in El Salvador depend on being able to export garments made from Asian fabrics on a tax-exempt basis. In fact, the figure may be far higher (*La Prensa Gráfica* 2003b).

Finally, there is no incentive to upgrade the *maquila* industry beyond assembling garments. By allowing tax-exempt status only to simple finished products, Central America is condemned once again to the lowest point in the garment-manufacturing chain,[2] which in turn makes it still more difficult to see how it will fare after the MFA expires. Assembly plants command the lowest prices for their products, require little specialization or technical upgrading, and are therefore easily substituted and vulnerable both to pressure from their clients and to fierce competition from rival producers. Ultimately, it is the factory workers who have to face the competitive heat in the form of ever-increasing work pressures, as well as lower benefits than those enjoyed by employees in more stable factories.

In sum, although the Central American *maquila* industry has benefited from some important advantages, these will not be enough to protect it from the competition represented by China.[3] Preferential access to the US market might generate more exports in the short term, but ultimately would not compensate for the loss of benefits currently enjoyed under the quota system. The taxes paid on textiles and garments are relatively high, but not prohibitively so, and will easily be offset by Asia's low production costs (Nathan Associates 2002). For example, although Mexico saw a noticeable increase in garment exports to the United States with the establishment of preferential trading status, it is on the verge of losing its place as the second-largest exporter to the United States thanks to the increase in Chinese exports. It has been calculated that some 200,000 jobs have been lost in the Mexican *maquila* industry as a result of Chinese competition (Gilly 2003). Market losses such as these encourage companies to push down their production costs. Given that the garment industry is so labor intensive, this necessarily translates into a tendency to overexploit the workforce (Ross and Chan 2002).

Moreover, in addition to a declining market, and the temptation to reduce production costs by scrapping jobs and eroding labor standards, a massive influx of products into a market previously regulated by strict quotas could lead to oversupply and, eventually, a slump in world prices. This slump would hit the Central American producers twice: first, through losing their markets, and then through forcing them to sell at lower prices in the markets they do manage to keep.

What will the jobs be like in the *maquila* industry after 2005? Beyond any doubt, the expiry of the MFA will result in a major restructuring of the world market in textiles and garments. Even with CAFTA and the "full package," it will be difficult for Central America to recover from the impact of such changes. One might well anticipate a situation similar to what happened with the end of the quota system organized under the auspices of the International Coffee Organisation, which resulted in overproduction and oversupply and led to a reduction in world prices. Eventually, this downturn ruined many small farmers and others who depended on coffee production, while strengthening a small number of transnational companies involved in the coffee trade (Gresser and Tickell 2002; see also Chapter 12).

In the case of the coffee crisis, Central America seems to have come to terms with the fact that recovery will be difficult and that it is unlikely that the production and export of coffee beans will ever return to previous levels. Producers and others are working on various strategies for dealing with this blow, such as exploring the markets for specialty, organic, and fair trade coffee. Some have been more successful than others, but these options all basically revolve around the idea of "politically correct consumption." Might the garment industry follow suit?

Consumers in industrialized countries are increasingly opting for clothing labeled sweatshop-free, but Asia in general and China in particular are hardly conspicuous for offering good working conditions or respecting the needs of the workforce; the accounts of maltreatment of workers in China are too frequent to be ignored. It is widely acknowledged that one of the attractions China offers for investors in the textile and garment sector is precisely its low production costs, which are due to the poor wages and long working days for employees in these industries. Salaries are even heading downward. In the major industrial city of Guangdong, for instance, salaries are now at 1993 levels in real terms, and an employee earns an average of between US$50 and US$70 a month, which provides the same purchasing power as such workers had in the early 1990s. At the same time, China is experiencing an economic bonanza and unprecedented growth and has attracted more foreign investment than any other developing country in recent years.

The brand-name firms that source their products from these factories run the risk of damaging their own reputations, on which much of their marketing relies. It may not be possible to compete with Asian producers in terms of reducing production costs, but it may well be feasible to focus on encouraging businesses to improve their practices in relation to labor rights and to compete for the "politically correct consumer" market through production of "clean" or "sweatshop-free" clothes.

WHY DOES CAFTA NEED TO PRODUCE "CLEAN" CLOTHES?

Clothing retailers such as Liz Claiborne, Gap, or Phillips Van Heusen are just some of the many companies whose vast sales in the EU and North America are based mainly on promoting their brand name. These companies do not actually produce the clothing they sell, but they do control design and marketing. Production is outsourced to other firms, an arrangement that allows the brand-name companies to keep their own costs down and to avoid bearing the risks associated with primary production. It also allows these companies to focus instead on the more profitable activity of retailing, whether through their own stores (the approach taken by Gap, Levi's, and Nike), or through large chain stores such as JC Penny, Sears, or Wal-Mart.

In order to sell their goods, these companies need to know how to "position" them, which is where marketing comes in. Increasingly, companies are advised to exploit their brand as a concept, or lifestyle image. The vice president responsible for marketing at Starbucks, the US specialty coffee chain, argues that "consumers do not really believe that there is much difference between the different products, which is why brands have to establish an emotional relationship with their customers" (quoted in Klein 2001: 47–48).

The brand is thus sold not as a consumer item but as an experience or lifestyle option. Nike, for instance, has worked hard to present itself as a symbol of the healthy American way of life, in which sports offer a way to stand out from the crowd and to "belong." Benetton projects itself as being "alternative" and "committed" to causes such as nondiscrimination. Tommy Hilfiger seeks to embody the racial diversity of the United States, Adidas is associated with promoting football, and so on. In an advanced consumer society, people apparently don't buy products just because they are useful, but also because they represent an experience or lifestyle in which the consumer wishes to participate. The relationship with the purchased item thus takes on more abstract qualities, such as being healthy, rebellious, passionate about football, or even being an assertive woman.

This kind of consumerism is attracted to brand names rather than to consumer items as such, and some individuals (even those who are not particularly well off) will spend a small fortune on items that in all likelihood are barely distinguishable from lesser-known brands. In Central America, where most people are simply too poor to indulge themselves in this way, the markets are full of pirated versions of brand-name products, for example garments with false labels or produced without a proper license. Wearing a brand-name T-shirt is perceived as a different experience than wearing one that has no recognized label, even if the so-called brand is actually false. A brand-name item of clothing suggests that the wearer is fashionable, and confers status and identity, particularly among those who have traditionally been excluded and so see conspicuous consumption as a way to show that they "belong" (Sojo and Pérez Saínz 2002).

In conclusion, a company's ability to sell its products, which is the most profitable aspect of the clothing retail trade, is based on projecting an image of the company itself. Brand names are therefore both the cornerstone on which the major clothing companies build their marketing strategies, and also their Achilles heel, as the growing global labor-rights movement holds these companies to account for the conditions in which their suppliers work. And there is evidence that some companies are beginning to listen.

Labor Activism and Brand-Name Goods

Labor activists in the leading consumer countries have discovered that the way to get large companies more committed to resolving the problems relating to the *maquila* industries is precisely via the image they wish to project to their consumers, and hence through sales. Some companies, such as Nike, which has been the target of numerous campaigns denouncing working conditions among its suppliers, saw its sales fall significantly in 1995 (the peak year for such campaigns), and its quarterly profits dropped by some 70 percent until 1999, when they returned to former levels. According to Nike itself, even this recovery has apparently not been due to increased sales, but has been achieved through cuts in staff and contracts (Klein 2001: 436).

After 1995, the year in which anti-sweatshop protest campaigns hit the US media, many clothing companies began to get involved in the corporate social responsibility (CSR) agenda. They established or introduced corporate codes of conduct to be applied across the entire supply chain. To date, there are at least 125 such codes worldwide, and each company adopting such a code also (supposedly) has a system in place to monitor it.

The activist campaigns are increasingly focusing public attention on these issues, insisting that brand-name companies improve their compliance with their own codes of conduct. The response has not been uniform across the board, and some have responded better than others to these campaign pressures—particularly those that tend to promote their brands as an image, rather than relying on the attraction of low prices.

These companies are demanding that their suppliers comply with their codes of conduct, whether these are company codes or are voluntary or multisectoral in nature.[4] The adoption and observance of codes of conduct is increasingly seen as a risk-reduction strategy in terms of a company's public reputation and market performance. A supplier that fails to observe these standards jeopardizes the company's reputation, which may affect sales and its value on the stock market. In turn, the suppliers may come to see their observance of social standards as prerequisites to their continued place in the global supply chain for certain brands, especially those that have the largest public appeal. In some cases, a supplier that observes these standards may even increase its access to new retail companies, which are attracted by its relatively high commitment to the workforce in the form of more stable contracts and better wages.

Companies such as Nike and Adidas, for instance, now rate their suppliers according to their adherence to social and environmental standards, giving double points for doing so. The highest-scoring suppliers receive the best contracts, and those scoring poorly risk losing their contracts altogether. It is true that the monitoring is often done by the company itself, and that there is public wariness of in-house assessments. But the real point here is that compliance with such standards has become a real concern for brand-name companies and their suppliers (O'Rourke 2003). This trend has been reinforced by surveys undertaken in the United States that found that at least 80 percent of consumers would be willing to pay more for items guaranteed to have been produced under good working conditions. Consumers tend to avoid buying products from companies that are perceived as behaving badly or that have been implicated in scandals involving the violations of workers' rights. One poll found that 51 percent of US consumers claim to have actively "punished" or boycotted such companies (O'Rourke 2003).

Of course, there are those who question the importance to business of good social and environmental practices. Research undertaken by the World Bank found that hundreds of suppliers in the global garment-production chain do not regard the priority given to compliance with such codes as an incentive. These suppliers argue that the brand-name companies do not always guarantee contracts that allow them stable production targets, even when the need to comply with the various codes means that they will have to invest in upgrading their infrastructure, thereby incurring costs that will take them many years to recoup. Moreover, although the companies require them to adhere to the stipulations of the codes in respect of working hours and good employment conditions, they also impose their own production demands and often very tight schedules on the suppliers, while also expecting the suppliers to keep costs down. This situation places the suppliers in a dilemma, and raises questions about how important compliance with the codes really is to the companies contracting them (World Bank 2003). In view of the growing commercial success of companies not professing any CSR commitment, the World Bank also challenges surveys purporting to show that consumers are interested in sweatshop-free products.

Essentially, not all brands are equally sensitive to calls for better practices, and it is only to be expected that those companies whose marketing strategies are based more on low cost than on brand value or image will have less interest in maintaining high social and ethical standards. However, these are generally not the companies whose custom is most important to the suppliers. Producing goods for a well-known and respectable brand increases the supplier's business opportunities, given that such firms tend to pay better than do companies that are interested only in low-cost items, and that a supplier that is known to comply with more demanding standards will be in a better position to attract new clients. For some of the companies that are most committed to CSR, longer-term business partnerships (uncommon in the garment industry) tend to be established with suppliers that can both meet quality-control standards and also comply with codes of conduct and with good social and environmental practices.

Compliance with good social and environmental practices is relatively new to the garment industry, and the issue is now beginning to gather strength in other sectors. Activist pressure has begun to make the public more aware of what consumer power can do to bring about change. Obviously, such changes have been patchy, and not all companies are even convinced of the need to change at all. However, although in many cases the commitment to upholding human rights and other CSR goals remains little more than an ideal, market pressures and better-informed consumers clearly help to make change possible.

One notable example of how informed consumers have used their purchasing power to such ends is in the fair trade movement. The idea of fair trade is that small producers in developing countries are guaranteed a price that will both cover their costs of production and afford them a decent income. Fair trade has evolved as a form of cooperation that eliminates intermediaries (often the most obviously inequitable link in the supply chain, particularly in the international coffee trade, for example) between the producer and the market; ensures that the products will be purchased and distributed through small retail outlets; encourages producers to organize collectively; and seeks to educate public opinion in the countries where their products are eventually sold.

The basic criteria for fair trade products are that the selling price should ensure fair wages to the producers, that there should be no use of child labor, and that production systems should respect the natural environment, encourage gender equity, and respect labor rights (Intermón Oxfam 2003).

In the case of coffee, where low prices on the international market have pushed small producers further into poverty, fair trade has represented a window of opportunity for them to be assured a better price for their coffee and improve their livelihoods. Certain coffee retailers in the United States, including Starbucks, Dunkin' Donuts, Procter & Gamble, and Kraft Foods, now include fair trade coffee in their product lines, a small but growing niche within the global coffee market (see also Chapter 12; Utting-Chamorro 2005). The consumption of fair trade coffee grew by 12 percent in 2001, compared with overall growth in the sector of 1.5 percent (Gresser and Tickell 2002).

Returning to the garment and textiles market, the case of Cambodia is especially interesting. Cambodia is also in a disadvantaged position vis-à-vis the threat from Chinese competition from 2005. Throughout the 1990s, the Cambodian garment industry was developed mainly by manufacturers from East Asia (China, Hong Kong, Korea, and Taiwan) once their export quotas to China had been filled, in much the same way that the Central American industry evolved. In 2003, about 70 percent of Cambodian garment production was destined for the US market, and slightly over 25 percent to the EU. With the ending of US quotas in 2005, the Cambodian garment industry will lose its main *raison d'être*, again comparable to the situation facing Central America. But for Cambodia, this poses a real threat to the entire economy in that 80 percent of its export earnings are generated by the garment industry.

Cambodia knows that its industries will be unable to compete with China on the basis of low production costs (there is a 25 percent difference in China's favor), and so has opted to compete on other grounds—namely good working conditions. Ray Chew, former Secretary General of the Cambodian Association of Garment Manufacturers, has stated Cambodia's intention to develop a niche market for the Cambodian manufacturing industry as being reliable and able to guarantee that "this garment was produced in a country which respects workers' rights," a commitment affirmed by his successor, Ken Loo.

Cambodia signed a free-trade agreement with the United States, but included a rather more serious social clause than does CAFTA. The Cambodian treaty accords greater advantages as the country improves its compliance in respecting labor rights and working conditions. If the ILO reports advances in these areas, Cambodia's export quota rises accordingly. This converts adherence to decent standards into a business incentive, and also makes the ILO responsible for verification, along with local monitoring organizations. Furthermore, 70 percent of the costs associated with this initiative are met by the United States, 15 percent by the Cambodian government, and the remaining 15 percent by the manufacturers. If the manufacturers wish to benefit from the scheme, they must submit themselves to ILO and other inspections (Polaski 2003).

This effort has enjoyed the concrete support of certain key brand-name companies such as Gap and Nike, and has resulted in fourfold growth in the Cambodian garment industry in only five years, as well as more jobs. The reports have recorded important improvements in working conditions in Cambodian garment-manufacturing factories, and although poverty has not been eradicated, and there is still some way to go before production is entirely "clean" and based comprehensively on respect for labor rights, the workers have undeniably benefited from this scheme, particularly in areas such as forced labor, discrimination, and child labor. At the same time, it has given the Cambodian companies a competitive edge, and is therefore an important country for brand-name firms anxious to avoid possible conflicts arising from sourcing from factories in which labor rights are not taken seriously. Gap, for example, sources about 40 percent of its products from manufacturers that are part of the ILO monitoring scheme and is currently the largest purchaser of garments made in Cambodia.

CONCLUSIONS

Despite the propaganda surrounding the announcement of free-trade agreements in Central America, CAFTA does not hold out a promising future for the region's poorest. Even for the sectors that stand to benefit most, the supposed gains will not be enough to ensure their survival after the MFA quota system comes to an end, nor will they guarantee existing jobs.

Clearly, the underlying problem is that Central America opted to compete in the global market on the basis of low labor costs. In other words, the region chose to sell people's poverty as a productive resource, a strategy that can only spell disaster in the longer term as workers are rapidly losing their jobs to countries in which labor costs are even lower.

The huge changes taking place in the global garment and textiles industry are too important, and too far-reaching in their consequences affecting the lives of thousands of Central Americans, for it to be acceptable simply to ignore the need for innovative strategies to deal with this looming crisis. Preferential access to the US market and comprehensive adoption of the "full package" approach are good ideas, but not enough to change the underlying causes of the crisis. The clothing industry has a market niche, as yet unexploited, in the idea of "politically correct" consumption—the idea behind the fair trade movement. Guaranteeing respect for labor rights, improving working conditions, and adhering to good social and environmental practices would not only maintain their place in the market, but also make a major contribution to human and social development, and improve the quality of life of many thousands of people throughout Central America.

NOTES

[1] The *maquila* industry covers various sectors, but this chapter focuses only on industries in the textile, garment, and apparel manufacturing sectors.

[2] By virtue of allowing tax-exempt status only to garments assembled from materials produced in the United States, previous trade regimes, such as the CBI, had already tacitly condemned Central America to assembly-plant status, producing goods requiring little or no specialization.

[3] The United States managed to negotiate additional protection for its own textile industry. For example, by applying disincentives to imports of Asian textiles, it has ensured that Central American factories will continue to use US materials. This is the outcome that US entrepreneurs had been advocating. Jerry Cook, vice president of the international division of the Sara Lee Company, stated, "What is going to happen at the end of the day if the treaty isn't signed? My reply to that question is that the USA will be the big loser in international trade." Cook proposed that the trade agreement should allow a greater proportion of US inputs (cotton and yarn), which could be used with inputs from NAFTA, arguing, "If we start out like this, we shall have certain advantages in relation to China" (*La Prensa Gráfica* 2003a).

⁴ In the United States alone, there are three multisectoral or umbrella initiatives aimed at incorporating major companies in codes of conduct to improve the conditions of workers in their suppliers' factories: the Fair Labor Association (FLA), which is the oldest and brings together at least 10 of the most representative or iconic brands in US consumer culture (Liz Claibourne, Gap, Nike, etc.); Social Accountability International (SAI), which administers SA8000, a certification standard set up by human rights organizations, trade unions, and certain companies (including Human Rights Watch, the International Textile, Garment and Leather Workers' Federation, and Avon); and Workers' Rights Consortium (WRC), which is a university-oriented initiative set up by US students and the AFL-CIO to protest against sweatshop conditions in the *maquila* industry.

REFERENCES

Borger, Julian. 2003. "Migrant Workers Sue Wal-Mart: Conditions of Cleaners 'a Step from Slavery', Lawyer Alleges." *Guardian* 12 November 2003. Available at http://www.guardian.co.uk/international/story/0,1082840,00.html (retrieved 3 November 2004).

The Economist. 2003. "Panic over Manufacturing." 27 September–3 October. Available at http://www.economist.com/printedition/displayStory.cfm?Story_ ID=2087788 (retrieved 14 April 2006).

Fortune. 2004. "Fortune 500 Ranking 2002." Available at http://www.fortune.com/ fortune/global500 (retrieved 10 February 2004).

Gilly, Adolfo. 2003. "Tiempo de Escuchar." *La Jornada* 3 August. Available at http://www.lajornada.unam.mx/2003/ago03/030822/018alpol.php?printver=1& fly=2 (retrieved 18 February 2004).

Goodman, Peter J., and Philip P. Pan. 2004. "Chinese Workers Pay for Wal-Mart's Low Prices: Retailer Squeezes Its Asian Suppliers to Cut Costs." *Washington Post Foreign Service* 8 February: A01.

Greenhouse, Steven. 2004. "Wal-Mart Is Said to Be in Talks to Settle Illegal-Immigrant Case." *New York Times*, 5 August.

Gresser, Charis, and Sophia Tickell. 2002. *Mugged: Poverty in Your Coffee Cup.* Oxfam International Campaign Report. Oxford: Oxfam GB.

Intermón Oxfam. 2003. "Comercio Justo 2003." Available at http://www.intermon. org/page.asp?id=277 (retrieved 6 February 2004).

Klein, Naomi. 2001. *No Logo: El Poder de las marcas.* [Trans. Alejandro Jockl.] Madrid: Paidós Editorial.

La Prensa Gráfica. (2003a). "Invasión china obliga a E.U.A. a buscar acuerdo textil en TLC." 10 December. Available at http://archive.laprensa.com.sv/ 20031210/ecomonia/economia21.asp (retrieved 14 April 2006).

La Prensa Gráfica. (2003b). "Entrevista Miguel Lacayo, 'Se han mostrado agradecidos.'" 22 December. Available at http://archive.laprensa.com.sv/ 20031222/ecomonia/economia25.asp (retrieved 14 April 2006).

Nathan Associates. 2002. *Changes in Global Trade Rules for Textiles and Apparel: Implications for Developing Countries.* Research report submitted to USAID. Arlington, VA: Nathan Associates Inc. Available at http://www.nathaninc.com/nathan/files/ccPageContentdocfilename145825705546 TCB_Textiles_final.pdf (retrieved 20 January 2005).

O'Rourke, Dara. 2003. "Outsourcing Regulation: Analyzing Non-governmental Systems of Labor Standard Monitoring." *Policy Studies Journal* 31(1):1–29.

Polaski, Sandra. 2003. "How to Build a Better Trade Pact with Central America." Issue Brief, July. Available at http://www.ceip.org/files/publications/CAFTA-better-Polaski.asp (retrieved 24 January 2005).

Ross, Robert J. S., and Anita Chan. 2002. "From North-South to South-South: The True Face of Global Competition." *Foreign Affairs* September/October: 8–13.

Sojo, C., and J. P. Pérez Saínz. 2002. "Reinventar lo social en America Latina." In *Desarrollo Social en América Latina: temas y desafíos para las políticas públicas.* San José: FLACSO.

Utting-Chamorro, Karla. 2005. "Does Fair Trade Make a Difference? The Case of Small Coffee Producers in Nicaragua." *Development in Practice* 15(3&4):584–599.

World Bank. 2003. *Strengthening Implementation of Corporate Social Responsibility in Global Supply Chains.* Washington, DC: World Bank.

TWELVE

Partnering for Sustainability:

Business-NGO Alliances in the Coffee Industry

APRIL LINTON

A CRISIS IN COFFEE

A global coffee crisis has existed since the early 1990s. As Oxfam International's comprehensive report on the subject summarizes,

> There is a crisis affecting 25 million coffee producers around the world. The price of coffee has fallen to a 20-year low and long-term prospects are grim. Developing-country coffee farmers, the majority of whom are poor smallholders, now sell their coffee beans for much less than they cost to produce. The coffee crisis is becoming a development disaster whose impact will be felt for a long time. (Gressler and Tickell 2002: 6)

Since 1990, coffee production worldwide has increased by 15 percent, whereas consumption has increased by about 7 percent. This oversupply has resulted directly from a decline in industry regulation. The end, in 1989, of a quota system imposed under the International Coffee Agreement led to increased competition and production. Deregulation and temporary spikes in the price of coffee resulting from crop damage in Brazil encouraged overplanting of new trees, as well as new entrants into the market, notably Vietnam.

Two species account for virtually all coffee traded. *Coffea arabica* is the original coffee, native to the highlands of Ethiopia. *Coffea canephora* (generally known as robusta) originated in the lowland forests of West Africa. It did not enter the commercial market until after the Second World War, when it was introduced as low-grade filler used in blends. *Coffea arabica*, the tastier species, typically grows at higher altitudes than robusta, and is more vulnerable to poor soils and diseases. It thus commands a higher price, but is susceptible to price competition because much of it ends up as a flavor component in canned coffee blends. Cup quality reflects growing and harvesting conditions (e.g., altitude, soil quality, weather), as well as the way the coffee cherries are processed to yield green (unroasted) coffee beans for the market.

In the early 1990s, *C. arabica* accounted for about three-quarters of the world coffee supply. This figure is around 60 percent today. Production of *C. arabica* has declined, and robusta production has risen (almost all recently planted coffee is robusta) because new technologies such as steaming to mellow harsh flavors make it possible for roasters to use more robusta in their blends. Even European countries that used to import almost exclusively arabica beans are now buying robusta. Meanwhile, some arabica producers find that prices have fallen too low to sustain the more labor-intensive cultivation and harvesting that these coffees need. Because grocery store blends are still 35–40 percent arabica, their makers have started to worry about having a continued supply of their blends' flavor components. Even specialty roasters that buy the highest quality arabica beans at premium prices express concern that in the future they will not be able to locate enough of the coffees in which they are interested (Gressler and Tickell 2002).

The export price of coffee is pegged to futures contracts on the New York Stock Exchange. During the 1990s the "C" price for green arabica coffee declined from a high of US$2.71/lb to as low as US$0.48/lb. Currently it is about US$0.72/lb. Coffee producers, especially the small farmers who grow more than half the world's coffee, earn only a fraction of this export price because the typical pathway from producer to consumer involves several intermediaries. At such low price levels, farmers are borrowing against future harvests just to meet expenses. They cannot continue to produce at a loss, and usually lack the funds and technical support necessary for a transition to different crops or other income-generating activities.

The coffee crisis has left many farmers in poverty, damaging their families' health and their children's education prospects, while also encouraging migration to overcrowded urban areas where prospects are truly bleak. The crisis has also destabilized national economies that are largely dependent on coffee. In Central American countries, hardly a day goes by without a major newspaper story about economic and social fallout related to the dismal coffee market. For example, recent articles report the collapse of the Salvadoran government's fund to provide emergency loans to coffee growers (Cabrera 2003), and tell of farmers ceasing to harvest their coffee because the price of doing so exceeds what they would receive for their crop (Henríquez 2003). In Guatemala, aid agencies describe the situation as a national emergency, but government efforts to help families impoverished by the crisis have amounted to little more than empty promises (Garmendia 2003).

Coffee farmers and workers are suffering while Northern consumers continue to pay premium prices for the product they consume. This is ample reason for alarm. But the challenge facing the world coffee market also deserves our attention because these circumstances serve to illustrate current issues involving many commodities on which developing countries rely. Finding a solution to the coffee crisis is thus a test of whether trade liberalization can be made to work for poor people and poor countries. In part, the solution calls upon corporations and consumers in rich countries to act as global citizens rather than simply global marketers and global consumers.

In the wake of the coffee crisis, many nonprofit organizations are working to develop a market situation that is sustainable for workers and the environment. They seek to influence cultural and political values in such a way that consumers and corporations in the North will have to respond to them by incorporating the welfare of Southern workers and ecosystems into their purchasing decisions. This chapter discusses and evaluates current strategies to link producers, corporations, and consumers within this movement, highlighting the role that partnerships between NGOs[1] and corporations can play in broadening the market for coffee produced in a sustainable way. It describes the NGO-based movement to promote sustainable coffee and, against a backdrop of reasons why corporations and NGOs may benefit from collaboration, details the current state of NGO-corporate linkages in this domain. In conclusion, it presents challenges and opportunities that such partnerships create.

PROMOTING SUSTAINABLE COFFEE

The movement to certify and market coffee produced under environmentally and economically sustainable conditions is one of many
efforts aimed at linking social responsibility and globalization. Nonprofit fair trade labeling organizations such as TransFair promote Fair
Trade Certified coffee.[2] They aim to alter coffee's path from farmer to
consumer by making it possible for farmers to form cooperatives to process and market their own beans. Their goals include ensuring that
farmers earn a living wage for their produce, providing access to affordable credit, and encouraging practices that are sustainable for both
workers and the environment. The fair trade movement has done a good
deal to link together consumer activists, farmers, environmentalists,
development agencies, and industry leaders—many of whom see coffee
as one of the world's most powerful tools for social change (Rice and
McLean 1999). Fair traders seek to influence the values of the cultural
and political system in such a way that corporations—even the multinationals that purvey mass-market coffee—will have to respond to them.
For example, Hillary Abell, former Development Director of TransFair
USA, said in a 2001 interview that "norm change" was the group's
number one goal, and would be achieved by making "the fair trade
model as normal, unintentional, and universal as non-discrimination
and basic environmental responsibility are today" (quoted in Tarmann
2002).

Other NGO-based efforts to make coffee more sustainable prioritize
organic farming. Organic agriculture seeks to minimize environmental
damage and work within the natural environment to improve yields, disease resistance, and quality of a crop. In 1995, the International Federation
of Organic Agriculture Movements (IFOAM) published specific guidelines for organic coffee certification, stipulating that the coffee must be
produced using methods that preserve soil quality and prohibiting the
use of synthetic chemicals. The International Organic Accretion Service
(IOAS) works with IFOAM to certify organic farms.

Still other groups focus on maintaining shade trees around the coffee
plants. The trees provide bird habitat and often enhance coffee quality.
Shade trees are also "insurance" crops to the grower, providing fuel
wood, timber, and fruit. Furthermore, traditional shade farming
reduces farmers' dependence on expensive chemical applications,
safeguarding growers and their families from the potential harmful
effects of exposure to pesticides (Giovannucci and Koekoek 2003).

Although almost all organic coffee is shade grown, not all is certified as such. Shade-grown coffee initiatives are the youngest in the sustainable coffee movement, and currently have the smallest market share.

In 1995, Rainforest Alliance began to extend its ECO-OK (now Rainforest Alliance Certified) label to coffee. Shade growing is a criterion for this certification.[3] In late 1996, the Smithsonian Migratory Bird Center (SMBC) hosted the first Sustainable Coffee Congress, a working group that brings together representatives of conservation organizations and the coffee industry. Since then, the SMBC has played an important role in informing the shade-grown coffee movement. Since shade-grown coffee farms provide winter habitat to over 150 North American species of migratory birds, there is good potential for promoting SMBC's bird-friendly certified shade-grown and organic coffee among the estimated 60 million bird enthusiasts in the United States (Rice and McLean 1999). Conservation International (CI) also offers a shade-grown certification. Conservation Coffee identifies coffees that are "grown, processed, and marketed in a way that promotes biodiversity conservation while improving the lives of local people" (Conservation International 2001a).

A relatively new coffee certification comes from the Dutch NGO Utz Kapeh, whose code of conduct was developed in 2000 by a consortium of Guatemalan grower-exporters together with the Ahold Coffee Company. It is based on the EUREPGAP Protocol for Fruits and Vegetables, developed by the leading European retailers to provide basic assurance for food safety and environmentally and socially appropriate growing practices. In addition, it includes relevant criteria from ILO Conventions and the Universal Declaration of Human Rights. According to the Utz Kapeh Web site, the code

> is a 'decency' standard for coffee production that ensures good, efficient, responsible farm management and full traceability. Purchasing from these certified producers allows coffee brands to take direct responsibility for the source of [their] coffee. This will lead to better terms of trade for coffee producers, makes the coffee traceable for coffee brands, and creates long term relationships in the coffee chain. . . . As a complete package, Utz Kapeh provides a vehicle for public-private partnerships to channel support to certified farmers. The Utz Kapeh Foundation is the mainstream initiative for certified responsible coffee. (Utz Kapeh 2004, emphasis in original)

In the hopeful language of economist Michael Conroy (2001: 2):

> Advocacy-led certification processes represent an increasingly suc-
> cessful pursuit of alternatives to the downward pressure placed upon
> social and environmental responsibility by the refusal of the WTO to
> permit the use of production and processing methods (PPMs) as a
> basis for trade policy.

Certification introduces a positive, alternative system to laws,
which are often difficult or impossible to enact. It is "a carrot instead of
a stick" (Rainforest Alliance 1995), "a market-driven process designed
to encourage and reward firms that choose to produce or trade in products that use the highest social and environmental standards in their
production" (Conroy 2001: 4).

Of course, socially responsible production and procurement will
bring financial rewards only if it results in products that consumers
desire at prices they find reasonable. Fortunately, this does not require a
uniform definition of social responsibility, preferred product characteristics, or acceptable prices; customers make their own judgments about
these things. Like firms, NGOs play a role in shaping customers'
demands and expectations by providing *information* and *choice*. NGOs
advocating for policies and practices that promote sustainable coffee
aim to educate consumers about current issues concerning coffee production and the coffee crisis. Certified coffee offers a tangible alternative—a
way to be part of the solution.

WHY WOULD CORPORATIONS AND
NGOS COLLABORATE?

Businesses hold the key to capital, market share, and consumer influence. It is thus simple to understand why NGOs find business alliances
attractive as these can be a highly productive approach to reaching their
goals. But why might a business benefit from—or even form a partnership with—an NGO-based movement that seeks to monitor and/or
change its practices? Why might third-party certifications be attractive
to coffee importers, roasters, and retailers? Potential reasons concern
branding, vulnerability, risk reduction, and credibility (Conroy 2001).
These are discussed and illustrated in the following sections.

Branding

Businesses that sell coffee are in a good position to educate their customers about sustainability issues. In particular, the marketing infra-
structures and visibility of large corporations vastly exceed those of
NGOs, but difficulties that coffee roasters and retailers may face in
advertising certified coffee include confusion among certifications, sat-
urated markets, and increasing brand competition. This has led to a rise
in Cause-Related Marketing, also known as Societal Marketing—a strategic positioning and marketing tool that links a company or brand to a
relevant social cause or issue, for mutual benefit. Consumers are known
to be anthropomorphic about brands, choosing them for expressive as
well as practical reasons (Pringle and Thompson 1999). Corporations
can therefore promote brand attachment in a way that uses social and
environmental responsibility to add to their brand's "soul." Such integrated branding of coffee is somewhat challenging because various certifications are already "brands" to which competitors also have access,
but at the same time, a roaster or retailer can be negatively singled out
for not offering a certified product (Linton et al. 2004).

For corporations that already enjoy strong brand loyalty from their
customers, fair trade, organic, and/or shade-grown labels could become
"brand extensions" (David 2000:132). Starbucks' Commitment to Origins
campaign illustrates the use of certified coffee to retain brand loyalty. The
company's Web site states

> Purveying quality coffees means much more than selecting the finest
> beans on the market. It means protecting a way of life for our farmers
> by supporting social, economic and environmental issues that are cru-
> cial to their livelihood. Commitment to Origins is dedicated to creating
> a sustainable growing environment in coffee origin countries.
> (Starbucks Corporation 2003)

The Commitment to Origins campaign includes Fair Trade Certified,
organic, Farm Direct,[4] and various conservation (for example, shade-
grown) coffees, and encompasses collaborative relations with TransFair
USA and Rainforest Alliance, as well as a long-term partnership with
CI. Starbucks does not aim to single out one particular certification, but
rather to offer a whole line of products that have been produced and
obtained through socially responsible means.

Vulnerability

Corporations that do not proactively adopt socially conscious policies are likely to be targeted by NGO-driven boycotts, such as the US Labor Education in the Americas Project (US/LEAP) action against Starbucks in the early 1990s and Global Exchange's ongoing corporate campaigns. Until recently, these efforts were aimed almost entirely at the specialty coffee market, that is, at roasters and retailers that already pay top dollar for their coffee beans and favor sustainable practices for many reasons—a foremost one being that a reliable supply of premium coffee is essential for their businesses. Though it seems ironic, especially given that specialty coffee accounts for less that 20 percent of the total coffee market, the NGOs' strategy made sense because retail stores are a "sitting duck" target, and because specialty coffee shops cater to the younger, better-educated consumers known to be most receptive to messages about socially responsible consumption (Rice and McLean 1999; Linton et al. 2004). Thus, they offered the best possible audience for NGOs to spread their message to sympathetic consumers and challenge roasters to respond.

Risk Reduction

Partnerships with NGOs can and do help corporations achieve progressive goals. These partnerships can be a form of insurance against unsubstantiated criticism of a firm's practices and greatly reduce its risk of becoming the target of negative publicity, thereby making it more financially attractive to investors. The financial contributions and certification costs that these liaisons may entail are often offset by a shortened value chain. Certification schemes promote direct relationships between producers and buyers, eliminating several intermediaries along the way to market. Furthermore, working with groups that promote sustainable production of high-quality coffee helps coffee roasters ensure a future supply of their product. Of late, labeling organizations and other NGOs have worked harder to foster linkages between coffee producers and buyers, a potentially very productive strategy for all parties.

Credibility

First-party codes of conduct are not necessarily credible. For example, Gressler and Tickell (2002) note that the world's major coffee purveyors—Kraft (Philip Morris), Nestlé, Proctor & Gamble, and Sara Lee—all have statements of social responsibility that mention the countries and communities where their coffee is grown. They all acknowledge the coffee crisis and make contributions to development and aid programs in coffee-producing areas. Several have recently initiated small projects to improve coffee quality among growers in Mexico, Peru, and Vietnam. Yet these companies' high-profit, high-profile coffee brands rely increasingly on communication, transportation, and processing technologies that allow them to seek the lowest cost combination of coffees for their blends. Only one of the "big four" coffee companies, Nestlé, supports the reintroduction of a price-stabilization mechanism via the International Coffee Organization (ICO).[5] For these reasons, activists and informed consumers do not find the big four's claims of social responsibility convincing. By contrast, NGOs are perceived by the public as having greater credibility. They can exploit this and get corporations—even the giants—to seek their approval.

This process may work as follows. Activists spread a message to both consumers and corporations. In the case of the latter, pressure tactics such as boycotts may supplement information campaigns. Meanwhile, sympathetic consumers compel businesses to respond to their demands, and at least some businesses begin to market socially responsible products to their customers.

ON THE GROUND: NGO-BUSINESS PARTNERSHIPS IN THE COFFEE INDUSTRY

NGOs and businesses tend to discuss partnerships differently. For an NGO such as TransFair USA or Rainforest Alliance, a business partner may simply be a company that buys coffee that the group has labeled or certified, but when businesses publicize their partnerships with NGOs, they are talking about a relationship that includes joint, long-range goals and a commitment of financial support on the part of the company. Both types of partnerships are included in Table 12–1 and discussed here, though the examples lean toward long-term activities. The primary goals of these relationships fall into three main categories: promoting quality and fostering direct ties between producers and buyers; improving or sustaining the environment; and commitments to buy fair trade certified coffees.

Table 12–1. NGO-Business Partnerships in the Coffee Industry

Organization	Description/ Goals	Producer Partners	Business Partners
Groups that Provide a Label or Certification			
Conservation International (www.conservation.org)	Work with companies that have demonstrated a commitment to the environment	19 farms in Latin America	Green Mountain Coffee, Starbucks
Rainforest Alliance (www.rainforest-alliance.org)	Protect ecosystems and the people and wildlife that live within them by developing and implement-ing best management practices and standards for commodity crops, providing incentives to farmers to meet those standards, and encouraging the marketing industries and consumers to support farmers who are making on-farm improvements towards sustainability	Numerous farms and cooperatives in Central America and Mexico, often in partnership with a local conservation organization	Kraft Foods, DR Wakefield (UK importer), Coffee Enterprises (supplies coffee extract to Ben and Jerry's), Rodgers Family Coffee Companies, Green Mountain Coffee, Starbucks, Neumann Kaffee Gruppe, Volcafe Group, and more
Smithsonian Migratory Bird Center (http://nationalzoo.si.edu/)	Foster greater understanding, appreciation, and protection of migratory birds	Farms and cooperatives in Latin America	10 importers/ brokers and many roasters and retailers including Coffee Bean and Tea Leaf, Gillies, and Whole Foods

Table 12–1. NGO-Business Partnerships in the Coffee Industry *(Continued)*

Songbird Foundation* (www.songbird.org)	Raise public awareness about the importance of supporting sustainably grown coffees because of the direct impact coffee farming has on songbird habitat	Central American cooperatives	Small specialty roasters and retailers, Trader Joe's, and other grocery stores
TransFair USA (www.transfairusa.org)	Promote Fair Trade Certified coffee in the United States	40 cooperatives/ groups of cooperatives worldwide	Dunkin' Donuts, Millstone (P&G), Green Mountain Coffee, Peet's Coffee and Tea, Caribou Coffee, Starbucks, Seattle's Best Coffee, Thanksgiving Coffee, and more

Other Groups

National Wildlife Federation (www.nwf.org)	Protect wildlife and habitat	Cooperatives in Latin America	Green Mountain Coffee
Organic Coffee Association (www.orcacoffee.org/)	Promote the high standards of third-party certified organic coffee	13 farms in Latin America	18 specialty roasters, nine importer/ brokers, three retailers
TechnoServe (www.technoserve.org)	Help small-scale coffee growers in Latin America and Africa increase their incomes and living standards, link producers and consumers	Several farmer cooperatives in Nicaragua, El Salvador, and Tanzania; winners of Cup of Excellence awards	Proctor & Gamble, Peet's Coffee and Tea

*Note: The Songbird Foundation works in close collaboration with TransFair USA, Oxfam America, and Global Exchange.

Promoting Quality and Producer-Buyer Relations

In the past, coffee exporters sold their coffee under brand names. But the market has shifted in a generic direction, and thus there has been less emphasis on quality. Today it would be better to return to distinct brands and pursue quality. In an interview with the author (San Salvador, 15 July 2003), Miguel Valiente, director of ABECAFÉ (Asociación de Benefiadores y Exportadores de Café), El Salvador's largest coffee producer organization, noted that:

> . . . [r]elations between producers and buyers were much more personal before. They would see each other at least once a year. Now business takes place in a different way. . . . One way to revive the values of the past would be to promote client-producer relations with visits to the farms, and to encourage constant communication between producers and buyers.

Initially, sustainable coffee campaigns did not focus directly on producer-buyer relations. Growers often did not understand buyers' preferences and quality specifications; buyers did not necessarily know about the produce of smaller farms. In line with Miguel Valiente's wish, USAID has started to support initiatives to assist small and medium-sized coffee farms to improve the quality of their product and form business linkages with the specialty coffee roasters that pay top dollar for premium beans (USAID 2003).

The effort to raise quality and tap into exclusive market niches often includes the acquisition of organic, Fair Trade, and other certifications. Though the amount of coffee sold under these terms—at prices that are about double the current market rate—is very small, it is growing consistently. For example, the 11 cooperatives that form El Salvador's Fair Trade Association APECAFÉ (Asociación de Pequeños Productores de Café de El Salvador) increased their premium sales from 66,000 lb in 1999 to 198,000 lb in 2002. Their principal market is Japan, but the Neumann Group recently contracted to buy coffee from ten APECAFÉ cooperatives that participated in a Rainforest Alliance program (administered by the Salvadoran conservation group SalvaNATURA) to help farmers improve the quality of their coffee and undertake the transition to organic production (Asencio 2003; Belloso 2003).

Another group of Fair Trade cooperatives, *Manos Campesinas* in Guatemala, sold 528,000 lb of coffee at the agreed price of US$1.26/lb (or US$1.46/lb if organic) in the 2002/2003 harvest, up from 132,000 lb in 1998. The premiums from Fair Trade and organic sales have helped farm families stay on their land, improve their homes, send their children to school, invest in improvements to their farms, and in some cases contribute to collective social programs. *Manos Campesinas* credits its success in part to TransFair USA's efforts to promote its coffee to buyers, and to NGO support that has made it possible for the group to be represented at North American specialty coffee trade shows (Bollen 2003).

The NGO TechnoServe has launched an effort to help premium coffee growers in Latin America and Africa earn better prices, regardless of whether their coffee is certified by another NGO. Over the past few years, TechnoServe has played a key role in organizing Cup of Excellence competitions in Brazil, El Salvador, Guatemala, and Nicaragua. This is a tasting event designed to identify and promote the host country's best-quality coffees, with "blind cuppings" conducted by national and international judges. In July 2003, the 31 winning coffees from El Salvador were offered for sale to international importers and roasters during a special Internet auction. Father-and-daughter coffee growers Mauricio Batlle Mena and Aida Batlle broke international records, receiving US$14.06/lb for 2700 lb sold to bidders Solberg & Hansen. It was the highest price ever paid for coffee sold via the Internet. The Batlles have committed to continue paying their coffee pickers a wage 50 percent higher than the legal rate. All 31 lots of coffee were sold to specialty roasters and international buyers at an average price of US$3.44/lb—more than four times the "C" price (TechnoServe 2004). TechnoServe also works with large and small coffee growers to help them improve the quality of their coffee and to gain access to higher-paying markets.

Focusing on the Environment

Nineteen major coffee-growing areas are in what CI calls "biodiversity hotspots." Coffee is thus a central commodity in CI's efforts to conserve biodiversity, and its Center for Environmental Leadership in Business encourages coffee roasters to integrate environmental and social considerations into their purchasing. In partnership with Starbucks, CI developed the coffee industry's first global green coffee purchasing guidelines and began certifying Conservation Coffees. Presently, CI and Starbucks are working with the Colombian Coffee Federation to promote coffee production methods that "provide conservation opportunities, economic and social benefits for coffee farmers, and high coffee quality. In return, farmers receive a price premium for their coffee that is well above the local market price" (Conservation International 2001b, 2003).

More recently, Rainforest Alliance and Kraft Foods have entered into a partnership to promote coffee production that is sustainable for the land and for workers. In an unprecedented multiyear arrangement, Kraft Foods has committed to purchase more than 5 million pounds of coffee in the first year from farms in Brazil, Colombia, Mexico, and Central America that have been certified by Rainforest Alliance as managed in a sustainable manner. Ongoing monitoring and verification of compliance by these farms will be provided by Rainforest Alliance and members of the Sustainable Agriculture Network (SAN) (Kraft Foods 2003).[6]

This arrangement commits Kraft Foods to increasing purchases of certified coffee, paying more to farmers that employ sustainable farm-management practices, and extending the company's engagement with coffee-producing communities by supporting further development of the SAN, including the training of local specialists to help farmers achieve certification. Rainforest Alliance will continue to train local auditors and build alliances among farmers, NGOs, coffee associations, and agricultural research institutions. How much more than the "C" price Kraft will pay certified producers and how it will support the SAN are not publicly specified. Still, this partnership suggests that the broad-based concept of sustainability is entering the mainstream of the coffee industry.

BUYING INTO FAIR TRADE

In autumn 1999, Global Exchange approached then-CEO Howard Schultz about offering Fair Trade certified coffee in Starbucks stores. The company was hesitant, voicing concern about low quality. The NGO responded by organizing several peaceful protests in front of Starbucks stores in Seattle. A few months later, fair trade campaigners put their request to Starbucks stockholders at their annual meeting. The response was a drop in the bucket; the company announced a one-time Fair Trade purchase of 75,000 lb, or about 30 lb per store. Global Exchange's next step was to circulate an open letter, asking Starbucks to do more to see that coffee farmers get a fair price. Thirty demonstrations at Starbucks stores across the United States were scheduled for 13 April 2000. On 10 April, Starbucks announced an agreement with TransFair USA. Global Exchange called off the protests; Starbucks introduced a Fair Trade blend and agreed to develop educational materials for employees and customers. In October 2001, Starbucks promised to buy one million pounds of Fair Trade coffee in the next 12–18 months. The company still seems committed to maintaining Fair Trade certified coffee in its lineup, and has begun working with at least one Fair Trade coffee cooperative—PRODECOOP in Nicaragua—to help it to produce more coffee that the company will buy (James 2000; Levi and Linton 2003).

Now advocacy groups are targeting the "big four." In 2003, Proctor & Gamble agreed to begin offering Fair Trade certified coffee through Millstone, its specialty coffee division. The agreement came in response to a grassroots campaign by Global Exchange, Oxfam America, Co-op America, the Interfaith Fair Trade Initiative, and the corporation's shareholders. Thousands of people sent letters, faxes, and emails to Procter & Gamble demanding that it offer Fair Trade coffee. A press release reports that the agreement comes in response to dialogue with shareholders about the company's practices, as well as pressure from consumers, people of faith, human rights activists, and humanitarian organizations. When Proctor & Gamble announced that it would offer Fair Trade certified coffee through Millstone, the advocacy groups agreed to suspend their campaigns against the corporation and the shareholders withdrew the resolution they had filed on the issue (Orth 2003).

All in all, industry partners—especially the larger specialty roasters—are still very cautious about long-term links to fair trade groups. This is largely because fair trade criteria do not include a statement on quality. As Donald Schoenholt (2001), specialties editor for the *Tea and Coffee* trade journal, notes, "A guaranteed premium price without a guaranteed premium cup is not sustainable." Schoenholt asserts that although the fair trade movement is laudable, it does not always provide laudable coffee. Coffee of lesser quality is not interesting to specialty buyers. This issue is now fully on the agenda of fair trade promoters and is the focus of efforts to facilitate producer-buyer relations. But many specialty roasters are, justifiably, still wary of a certification system that detaches price and quality (Linton et al. 2004).[7]

Meanwhile, Fair Trade cooperatives and the second-tier organizations that represent them are fighting against the possibility that larger, owner-operated farms could qualify for Fair Trade certification. While the market for sustainable coffees seems to be growing, producers are well aware of its limits. As APECAFÉ's Coordinator of Small Producers put it,

> Big farms, especially the *beneficios* [that process their own coffee until it's ready for market], already have better access to credit and receive more of the export price. These producers could totally capture the fair trade market because it's easier for buyers to deal with a few big farms than with many small ones. What we really need is a social change much greater that certifying the big farms. (Quoted in Asensio 2003)

A SUSTAINABLE COFFEE INDUSTRY? CHALLENGES AND OPPORTUNITIES

The results of consultants Giovannucci and Koekoek's (2003: 69) survey of coffee purveyors and roasters indicate factors that the industry deems most important if the sustainable coffee market is to expand, namely consistent and reliable sources, quality, clarity between different types of certifications, and consumer awareness about these coffees. These issues frame the discussion that follows, which concludes by introducing a fourth actor: government.

Reliable Sources and Consistent Quality

All coffee roasters—from small specialty companies to industry giants—stake their future on being able to provide what their customers expect. For specialty roasters this means variety as well as high quality; for mass marketers it means consistency. The NGO-corporate partnerships described in this chapter all reflect efforts to incorporate a sustainable-production criterion into a company's purchasing decisions. The businesses clearly do not share a uniform definition of reliable supply or cup quality, and the resulting agreements are unique in terms of the commitments they encompass. Some may argue that certification schemes that allow farmers to receive less than the Fair Trade price or some use of chemical fertilizers and pesticides are watering down sustainability standards. Yet the introduction of such certifications (e.g., Rainforest Alliance Certified) has greatly increased corporate participation in the sustainability movement, as well as the potential for more individuals involved in production (e.g., large farm owners and landless plantation workers) to benefit.

These developments suggest that NGOs are wise to help producers grow the kinds of coffee that specialty buyers want and to foster connections between producers and buyers. More could be done to expand the variety of coffee that qualifies for a certification of sustainability. This means US-based NGOs expanding their focus to include coffee-producing regions in Africa and Indonesia, and/or strengthening their ties with the European NGOs that do work in these places. It also means additional efforts to include coffees that the makers of canned and instant coffee buy, including robustas.

Too Many Certifications?

Giovannucci and Koekoek (2003: 36) predict that

> the industry is clearly headed for a shakeout of the many initiatives. It is likely that the survivors will a) have true international credibility with farmers, their representatives, and consumers; b) be verified by independent certification; and c) will be simple and accessible enough to satisfy both the farmer's and the corporate bottom line.

On the other hand, Levi and Linton's (2003) interviews with coffee retailers did not yield evidence that multiple certifications confuse customers. No certifying agency claims to represent a mutually exclusive situation whereby only coffees with a particular label are protecting the environment, ensuring the existence of bird habitat, or guaranteeing the sustenance of small farmers (Lee 1999). Certification campaigns attract media attention and help people see some connection between their daily beverage and the producing country. In the words of coffee expert Timothy Castle (2001),

> Today the issues that consumers are asked to consider are becoming so numerous that the industry has started looking at all of these coffees as 'issue' coffees, and to some extent considering them interchangeable—as if there were some amorphous worry or concern on the part of the consumer that might be generically addressed by any of several anxiety-relieving certificates.

Whether or not businesses and NGOs will ever agree on and develop a "super seal" for sustainable coffee remains to be seen. But there is no evidence to date that activists or the industry are moving in this direction. That NGOs and corporations are taking multiple approaches to certification seems in line with the conclusion of management researcher Anja Schaefer and coauthors (Schaefer et al. 2003: 211) that "'greening' is only likely to persuade managers of the need and feasibility of change if it does not question the basic premises by which their enterprises operate."

Consumer Awareness

In order to change society's norms regarding the need for sustainable goods in the marketplace, the message must extend to consumers who as yet remain indifferent to concerns about workers and the environment in other countries. There still remain large consumer markets that are either unaware that they have the option of purchasing coffee produced in a sustainable way, or simply have not been persuaded to do so. Tapping into the coffee industry's resources to help promote a message of sustainability has certainly helped NGOs (with almost nonexistent advertising budgets) spread that message. In reaching out to Proctor & Gamble shareholders and consumers of brands such as Folgers, advocacy groups have begun to mainstream the demand for coffee produced in a sustainable way, but there is clearly much more to be done.

Activism in relation to coffee production and the NGO-corporate alliances emerging from it could eventually have cumulative norm-changing effects, to the extent that consumers would start to wonder about noncertified products. This has been the case for dolphin-safe tuna and cruelty-free cosmetics. "Certification systems offer the possibility of raising public awareness to the point that unlabeled products will be increasingly resisted by consumers and laws to curtail repugnant environmental and labor practices will be pressed upon governments" (Conroy 2001: 15).

The Role of Governments and Intergovernmental Organizations

In January 1999, UN Secretary-General Kofi Annan exhorted world business leaders to "embrace and enact" the UN Global Compact, whose nine principles covering human rights, labor, and the environment "unite the powers of markets with the authority of universal ideals" (Pike 2001). This is precisely the goal of third-party certification schemes. The Global Reporting Initiative (GRI), an organization dedicated to standardizing corporate sustainability reporting, estimates that more than 2000 companies voluntarily report their social, environmental, and economic practice and performance. But critical analysts are not ready to embrace this trend as a new model for global corporate governance. For example, Gary Gereffi et al. (2001: 57) argue that "certification remains a blunt and imperfect tool for augmenting the accountability of global firms."

One reason for their skepticism is that certifiers compete for legitimacy among advocacy groups (and, in some cases, consumers) as well as for adoption by multinationals. There is no guarantee that the best standards will win these battles. "Some observers even fear that certification driven by activists and corporations will pre-empt or supplant altogether the role of states and international organizations in addressing corporate accountability as free trade expands around the globe" (Gereffi et al. 2001: 57). It is possible that voluntary certification initiatives may allow entire industries to block the development of international labor and environmental laws directed at multinational companies.

Despite these deep reservations, Gereffi et al. (2001) believe that the strength and influence of certification initiatives are rising. In fact, certification is transforming traditional power relations in the global arena. Third-party certification and monitoring may soon become the norm in many global industries, including coffee. The challenge that activists now face is to avoid a situation in which market forces and the push towards standardization lead to lowest common denominator certification.

In the broader scheme of things, certification seems to work best in tandem with trade agreements like NAFTA and in countries with stringent labor and environmental standards, especially the countries of Northern Europe. In countries with relatively new or ineffective labor and environmental laws, certification can draw attention to uneven standards. "The challenge is for states to accept certification not as a threat but as an opportunity to reinforce labor and environmental goals within their sovereign territory and beyond" (Gereffi et al. 2001: 65).

Consumers and firms are key to meeting this challenge. Consumer action is political participation in that it mobilizes public opinion. This not only demands a new standard from businesses, but also puts an issue on the political agenda. In turn, firms are likely to lobby for appropriate government action (Smith 1990). In the future, the targets of sustainable coffee activism will be national governments, the WTO, and the World Bank. If human rights and environmental protection are to be supported, the burden falls upon the institutions that implement the market and its regulation (Tavis 2002).

CONCLUSION

The movement to ensure that coffee production is sustainable for workers and the environment is one of many efforts to "civilize" globalization, making it more responsive to social needs and to fill the social
void it has wrought. When consumers place pressure on corporations
to institute and maintain certain social and environmental standards,
new standards do emerge via self-regulation. In turn, corporations or
NGO-corporate partners may respond by lobbying governments or
inter-governmental bodies for laws applying to an entire industry
(Heldman 2002). To a large extent because of education and/or pressure
campaigns by NGOs, the specialty coffee industry has committed itself
to promoting sustainable coffee. Now the movement is starting to reach
the mainstream, a development that brings both opportunities and challenges. Although it is clear that coffee producers, consumers, and firms
all have reasons to care about sustainability, there is considerable
variation in *how much* they care—in the degree to which incentives
exist to prioritize sustainability above prices and short-term profits.
NGO-corporate partnerships are a step toward raising these incentives,
but they must work with governments and governmental organizations
to institutionalize sustainable practices.

NOTES

[1] I use "NGO" to refer to local, national, and international NGOs.

[2] The internationally accepted criteria for Fair Trade coffee are (1) purchase
directly from small farmers organized into democratically managed cooperatives, (2) guarantee a floor price when market prices are low, (3) offer farmers
credit (an obligation of the importer), and (4) promote long-term relationships
between importers and farmer cooperatives.

[3] As stated by the Rainforest Alliance (2003), "[t]he certification standards
guide farmers toward true sustainable agriculture and give independent auditors
a yardstick with which to measure improvements. Farms that meet the standards are awarded the *Rainforest Alliance Certified*™ seal of approval, which
is a prestigious badge that can be used to market farm products. This program
is unusual in that it includes both social and environmental standards and
unique in that it is managed by a coalition of local groups that understand their
culture, ecology, farming traditions and governments."

[4] "Starbucks exclusive single-origin coffees purchased directly from the
source" (Starbucks Corporation 2003).

⁵ This, Nestlé spokespeople told interviewers from Oxfam International, is because the company has incurred large fixed costs such as expensive processing plants and manufacturing technology for its instant coffee. When the price of green beans gets too low, it is difficult for Nestlé to compete with companies that have not made such sizeable investments (Gressler and Tickell 2002: 27).

⁶ The Sustainable Agriculture Network (SAN) encompasses more than 750 national and international subscribers and is closely associated with the US Department of Agriculture's Sustainable Agriculture Research and Education (SARE). The network includes producers, members' administrative councils and technical committees, and NGOs throughout the United States that are working to promote sustainable agricultural systems.

⁷ Some activists are also suspicious of large specialty roasters—let alone the "big four"—buying into fair trade. Laure Waridel (2002: 105), cofounder of the Canadian NGO Équiterre, remarks that "some roasters appear to be using fair trade to shield themselves against criticism from consumers and are making little effort to promote their fair-trade brands. Some appear to have adopted fair-trade coffee in order not to lose customers rather than as a means of assuming their responsibility towards coffee farmers. They talk about it as a new trend, like flavoured coffees. Some retailers show a serious lack of information in answering questions about fair trade."

REFERENCES

Asencio, Alfredo Rumaldo. 2003. Personal interview conducted by April Linton, APECAFÉ , San Salvador, 14 July.

Belloso, Guillermo E. 2003. Personal interview conducted by April Linton, SalvaNATURA, San Salvador, 11 July.

Bollen, Jerónimo. 2003. Personal interview conducted by David Holiday and April Linton, Quetzaltenango, 5 August.

Cabrera, Omar. 2003. "Colapso del fondo del café." *El Diario de Hoy* (El Salvador) 16 September.

Castle, Timothy J. 2001. "A Cup Fraught with Issues." *Specialty Coffee Retailer* 4:4 (November).

Conroy, Michael. 2001. "Can Advocacy-Led Certification Systems Transform Global Corporate Practices? Evidence and Some Theory." Working Paper, Political Economy Research Institute. Amherst, MA: University of Massachusetts.

Conservation International. 2001a. "Conservation Coffee™." Available at http://www.conservation.org/ImageCache/CIWEB/content/publications/coffee_2epdf/v1/ coffee.pdf (retrieved 8 January 2004).

Conservation International. 2001b. "Starbucks Coffee Announces New Coffee Sourcing Guidelines." Press release, 12 November. Available at http://www.celb.org/xp/CELB/news-events/press_releases/2001/11122001.xml (retrieved 8 January 2004).

Conservation International. 2003. "Partnership Profiles." Available at http://
www.conservation.org/xp/CIWEB/partners/profiles/corporate/starbucks.xml
(retrieved 8 January 2004).

David, Scott M. 2000. *Brand Asset Management: Driving Profitable Growth
through Your Brands*. San Francisco: Jossey-Bass.

Garmendia, Maite. 2003. "Crisis: medidas acordadas por el gobierno y la
plataforma agraria llegan tarde y a un ritmo lento." *Prensa Libre* (Guatemala)
7 October.

Gereffi, Gary, Ronie Garcia-Johnson, and Erika Sasser. 2001. "The NGO-
Industrial Complex." *Foreign Policy* (July–August):56–65.

Giovannucci, Daniele, with Freek Jan Koekoek. 2003. *The State of Sustainable
Coffee: A Study of Twelve Major Markets*. Cali: Feriva SA.

Gressler, Charis, and Sophia Tickell. 2002. *Mugged: Poverty in Your Coffee
Cup*. Oxfam International Campaign Report, Oxford: Oxfam GB.

Heldman, Caroline. 2002. "Consumer Activism in American Politics." Unpublished dissertation, Rutgers University.

Henríquez, José Luis. 2003. "El café perdió el año." *El Diario de Hoy* (El
Salvador) 11 October.

James, Deborah. 2000. "Justice and Java: Coffee in a Fair Trade Market."
Available at http://www. globalexchange.org/campaigns/fairtrade/coffee/
nacla1000.html (retrieved 16 June 2004).

Kraft Foods. 2003. "Kraft Foods to Serve Rainforest Alliance Certified Sustainable Coffee to Mainstream Market." Press release. Available at http://
164.109.16.145/newsroom /10072003.html (retrieved 6 February 2003).

Lee, Christopher M. 1999. "Sealed Fate? Seals Designating Certified-Organic,
Shade-Grown and Fair-Trade Coffees Battle for Market Share and Mind
Share. *Specialty Coffee Retailer* (August):6.

Levi, Margaret, and April Linton. 2003. "Fair Trade: A Cup at a Time? *Politics
and Society* 31(3):407–432.

Linton, April, Cindy Chiayuan Liou, and Kelly Ann Shaw. 2004. "A Taste of
Trade Justice: Marketing Global Social Responsibility via Fair Trade
Coffee." *Globalizations* 1(2):223–246.

Orth, Valerie. 2003. "Advocacy Groups and Shareholders Persuade Proctor &
Gamble." Press release, Global Exchange, 15 September. Available at http://
www.globalexchange.org/update/press/1043.html (retrieved 10 February
2004).

Pike, Alan. 2001. "Davos 2001—Management Sensitive to Ethical Concerns."
Financial Times 24 January. Available at http://specials.ft.com/davos2001/
FT3TYOIBIC.html (retrieved 16 June 2004).

Pringle, Hamish, and Marjorie Thompson. 1999. *Brand Spirit: How Cause
Related Marketing Builds Brands*. Chichester: John Wiley.

Rainforest Alliance. 1995. "ECO-OK Wins Drucker Award." *The Canopy*
(November–December). Available at http://www.rainforest-alliance.org/
news/canopy/can12-95.html (retrieved 15 January 2004).

Rainforest Alliance. 2003. "Rainforest Alliance Sustainable Agriculture Certification." Available at http://www.rainforest-alliance.org/programmes/cap/faq.html (retrieved 15 January 2004).

Rice, Paul, and Jennifer McLean. 1999. "Sustainable Coffee at the Crossroads." White Paper prepared for the Consumer's Choice Council, Washington, DC.

Schaefer, Anja, Andrea Coulson, Ken Green, Steve Naw, and Jim Skea. 2003. "Sustainable Business Organizations?" In Frans Berkhout, Melissa Leach, and Ian Scoones (eds.), *Negotiating Environmental Change*. Cheltenham: Edward Elgar.

Schoenholt, Donald N. 2001. "The Fair Trade Ideal: The Ultimate Answer for Sustainability?" *Tea and Coffee* 175(11). Available at www.teaandcoffe.net/1101/special.htm (retrieved 14 April 2006).

Smith, N. Craig. 1990. *Morality and the Market: Consumer Pressure for Corporate Accountability*. New York: Routledge.

Starbucks Corporation. 2003. "About Us." Available at http://www.starbucks.com (retrieved 15 November 2001).

Tarmann, Kevin F. 2002. "The Fair Trade Movement: Norm Change or Niche Marketing?" Unpublished dissertation, University of Virginia.

Tavis, Lee A. 2002. "Corporate Governance and the Global Social Void." *Vanderbilt Journal of Transnational Law* 35(2):487–546.

TechnoServe. 2004. "TechnoServe and the Coffee Industry." Available at http://www.technoserve.org/latin/ (retrieved 15 February 2004).

USAID. 2003. "USAID's Response to the Global Coffee Crisis." Press release, 24 February. Available at http://www.usaid.gov/about/coffee/ (retrieved 8 April 2003).

Utz Kapeh. 2004. "About Utz Kapeh." Available at http://www.utzkapeh.org (retrieved 15 January 2004).

Valiente, Miguel. 2003. Personal interview conducted by April Linton, San Salvador, 15 July.

Waridel, Laure. 2002. *Coffee with Pleasure: Just Java and World Trade*. Montreal and New York: Black Rose Books.

THIRTEEN

Reaching the Marginalized?

Gender Value Chains and Ethical
Trade in African Horticulture

ANNE TALLONTIRE, CATHERINE DOLAN, SALLY SMITH,
AND STEPHANIE WARE BARRIENTOS

INTRODUCTION

Ethical trading practices form an important part of the value chains for horticultural products sourced from Africa by major European buyers. For example, UK supermarkets require suppliers to comply with detailed codes of conduct covering employment conditions, and flower buyers in world market outlets such as the Dutch Auctions are increasingly demanding a product that meets strict environmental and sometimes social criteria. Codes thus comprise part of the governance of value chains that influence suppliers' production and employment strategies. Most employment in African horticulture is flexible and informal, with women predominant in insecure seasonal and casual work. Are codes able to reach the marginalized workers in these value chains?

This chapter explores the way in which codes are implemented in the value chains for African horticultural products. It draws on the findings of a two-year research project in the Kenyan flower, South African deciduous fruit, and Zambian flower and vegetable sectors.[1] We discuss the relationship between value chains in horticulture, the employment patterns of African producers, and the process of code implementation from a gender perspective. We ask whether, in the context of the gendered economy, codes alone can improve the working conditions for all workers. We argue that codes, implemented largely in a top-down manner, rarely reach beyond formal workers, and fail to address gender issues. There is, therefore, a need to consider other ways of addressing gender issues that are embedded at the local level.

We begin the chapter by providing an overview of the particular value chains found in African horticulture, highlighting the codes that are currently applied. This is followed by a discussion of the gender value-chain approach, and the nature of employment in the value chains. We explore the extent to which codes reach different categories of workers, and the concerns of workers in those chains. Sociopolitical factors that often affect the reach of codes, such as labor organization and legislation, are then discussed. Finally, we consider whether a focus on local-level implementation that is inclusive of all stakeholders can extend the reach of codes to cover more marginalized workers.

VALUE CHAINS IN AFRICAN HORTICULTURE

Global value-chain (GVC) analysis explores how the linkages between the production, distribution, and consumption of products are globally interconnected along value chains, and is an important framework for analyzing economic development in the context of globalization (Gereffi and Korzeniewicz 1994). Although GVC analysis was originally used to examine the international structure of production and trade, it has recently been extended to analyses of codes and standards in certain global industries (Ponte 2002; Dolan and Humphrey 2004).

A central concept within GVC is that of governance, which relates to the way in which producers engage in the chain and how the benefits of trade are distributed along it. Gereffi's original work on GVCs (Gereffi 1994) distinguished between two types of governance structures: buyer-driven and producer-driven. In a buyer-driven value chain, large retailers or brand-name companies make the key decisions about the nature of activities and actors in the chain without actually owning any manufacturing facilities. In a producer-driven value chain, large manufacturers/producers play the central role in coordinating production networks. As this chapter discusses, the concept of governance is helpful in understanding the way in which codes have been introduced in a top-down manner, and why certain value chains are characterized by significant levels of insecure and gendered employment.

Many African horticultural producers are linked to international markets through global value chains. This is most evident in the rapid growth of the Afro-European horticultural value chains. For example, Kenya, South Africa, and Zambia all rely heavily on European markets for their horticultural exports. In 1998/1999, 66 percent of all South African deciduous fruit exports, 94 percent of Kenyan flower exports, and 100 percent of Zambian vegetable and flower exports were sent to countries in the EU. These exports are routed through two types of value chains. The first are those controlled by supermarket buyers, particularly UK retailers, who source products through closely controlled supply chains. In the UK, supermarkets now account for approximately 75 percent of fruit and vegetable and 50 percent of cut-flower sales (Coote et al. 2003), giving them considerable buying power in their respective value chains.[2] These buyer-driven value chains are important for South African deciduous fruit and Zambian vegetables, and some Kenyan flowers.

The second type of value chain is that of flowers supplied to the Dutch Auctions, the most important world market outlet for cut flowers, where wholesalers purchase flowers for international re-export. Despite an increase in direct sales to retailers, the auctions remain the most significant way that cut flowers from sub-Saharan Africa reach European wholesalers and retailers. In Zambia, more than 90 percent of export-quality roses are sold via the auctions in the Netherlands. Similarly, in Kenya more than two-thirds of cut flowers are supplied to the auction halls. In contrast to the supermarket value chain, the auction is less strictly coordinated by buyers, and is characterized by relatively loose trading relationships.

Both value chains are shaped by the consumption practices of European consumers, including the recent trend toward ethical trade. However, the different characteristics and market orientation of the chains create different pressures, which influence the types of codes that are applied in each chain.

CODES OF CONDUCT IN AFRICAN HORTICULTURE

In our study, codes had been introduced from four different origins: dominant buyers such as supermarkets and importers (company codes); trade associations linked to the Northern fresh-produce industry (Northern sectoral codes); trade associations linked to the African horticultural sector (Southern sectoral codes); and independent bodies comprising a range of civil society organizations and companies (independent codes).

In buyer-driven value chains, such as South African deciduous fruit and Zambian vegetables, UK retailers introduced codes in order to protect themselves from a variety of consumer concerns, ranging from food safety to environmental damage to the exploitation of workers in developing countries. By the mid-1990s, all major UK supermarkets had developed company-specific codes and introduced detailed procedures for monitoring them (e.g., "Responsible Sourcing," developed by Waitrose, and "Sound Sourcing," developed by the Co-operative Group).[3] In response to this, many UK importers in these chains also developed their own codes to encompass the requirements of all the different supermarkets they supplied.

A second group of codes was developed by Northern trade associations to protect the image of the industry as a whole. These codes initially focused on environmental and food-safety issues. This group includes the environmental code of the Dutch organization Milieu Project Sierteelt (MPS), which now certifies between 70 and 80 percent of flowers in the Dutch Auctions. MPS certification can also include an optional "social qualification" (SQ) on worker welfare. The increasingly influential Euro-Retailers' Protocol on Good Agricultural Practice (EUREP GAP), developed by a network of European retailers to ensure best practice in the production and sourcing of fresh produce, and more recently flowers, is also a Northern sectoral code.[4]

There are also sectoral codes developed by producer and exporter organizations in Africa, which moved early to introduce their own standards as a way to protect their industries from criticism and to promote ethical production in the African horticultural sector. These tend to cover safe use of chemicals, food safety, and worker welfare, and include the following codes: Kenya Flower Council (KFC), Fresh Produce Exporters' Association of Kenya (FPEAK), and Zambia Export Growers' Association (ZEGA). Although Southern sectoral codes are not required by specific buyers, they have been used as benchmarks for other codes, and in some cases can facilitate access to Northern markets.

In contrast to company and sectoral codes, which are developed by industry, independent codes draw on wider stakeholder involvement. The most prominent of these in our case studies was the ETI Base Code, developed by a consortium of companies, trade unions, and NGOs that are members of the UK's Ethical Trading Initiative (ETI).

ETI member companies (including six UK supermarkets) are obliged to apply the Base Code to their own supply base, and thus the ETI code is now a prominent feature of buyer-driven fresh-produce chains to the UK. Another independent code is the International Code of Conduct for Cut Flowers (ICC), developed by a number of European NGOs and trade union organizations. The ICC is used by the German-based Flower Label Programme (FLP). In 2003, MPS's social chapter was also benchmarked against the ICC. Finally there is Max Havelaar Switzerland's Fair Trade flower program, which requires compliance with either MPS or ICC.

CODES AND GLOBAL VALUE CHAINS

Producers of export horticulture typically apply more than one type of code of conduct. This is because most producers are involved in more than one value chain, and the nature of the value chain determines, to some extent, the type of code that growers and producers adopt.

UK Supermarket Chains

There is considerable market pressure for producers supplying UK supermarkets to adopt codes. In Zambia, more than 80 percent of export-quality vegetables are sold to UK retailers, through importers who mediate their relationship with the supermarkets. In South Africa, all the employers in our study supplied different UK supermarkets, either as grower/packers, or through independent packing houses. Europe receives approximately 60 percent, and the UK 30 percent, of all South African fruit exports. In order to access and/or maintain this lucrative market, producers must now implement a number of codes, principally company codes governing employment conditions (often based on the ETI Base Code) and EUREP GAP (which has minimal social provision). Producers in our study reported that supermarkets demand compliance with codes, but offer no guarantee of buying the supplier's product in return for making considerable efforts to do so. This reflects classic buyer-driven chain relations, whereby lead companies (supermarkets) exert control over production without investing in production itself. Supermarkets acquire significant rewards by devolving code compliance upstream. For example, when retailers accept external codes such as EUREP GAP in lieu of their own codes (for food safety and protection of the environment), it allows them to reduce their own direct monitoring costs. Similarly, by adopting the ETI Base Code, which is endorsed by civil society organizations, retailers enhance their credibility in the eyes of consumers, and are thereby able to protect their market share (Dolan and Humphrey 2004). The onus in all cases, however, falls on producers to ensure compliance.

In contrast, the adoption of Southern sectoral codes in supermarket-driven chains has less to do with the dictates of buyers than with a desire to protect the national reputation of Southern industries in overseas markets. For example, the KFC code was initially developed by Kenya's largest producers to maintain the reputation of Kenyan flowers (as a brand) in the face of growing allegations of environmental damage. Until recently, some of the major UK supermarkets relied on KFC as a proxy for their own codes: Marks & Spencer and Tesco are both associate members of KFC. Similarly, as members of ZEGA, all Zambian companies in our study (both flower and vegetable growers) were using at least some parts of the ZEGA code, primarily as a training tool but with the hope that it will facilitate broad market access.

Dutch Auction Chains

Codes are not currently a requirement to access the Dutch Auction chain. In most cases, Northern and Southern sectoral codes are applied in these value chains, and occasionally independent codes under the FLP and Max Havelaar schemes are as well. For example, nearly 85 percent of Kenya's export flower business is certified as either MPS or KFC. In our study, MPS was used by two of the four Kenyan firms that sell a substantial proportion of their flowers through the Dutch Auctions, one of which is MPS-SQ.[5] Fewer Zambian flower producers were adopting Northern sectoral codes. Of the five flower farms in our study, only two had current MPS certification, one of which is MPS-SQ and also Max Havelaar certified. As noted, however, all Zambian producers are using the ZEGA sectoral code. Producers in Dutch Auction chains are, therefore, adopting codes largely on their own initiative, with few reporting market pressure to do so. They may gain access to certain (niche) markets through codes, but doing so is just one strategy open to them.

There is thus a strong association between the nature of the value chain and the motivations for adopting codes. In buyer-driven chains, codes form part of the governance structure operated by supermarkets, but in the market-oriented flower chain, codes are adopted as a way to access niche markets or as a management tool. When producers are embedded in both chains, they tend to apply several different codes, in some cases covering all four types.

GENDER VALUE-CHAIN APPROACH

Most codes aim to improve employment conditions within global value chains, either as their primary focus or as one of various objectives. The forms of employment found within different types of chain can vary, particularly in the ratio between permanent and more insecure temporary and seasonal employment. This relates partly to the type of chain and the production conditions of the specific product, but also to the gender context in which employment takes place.

A gender value-chain approach combines GVC analysis with a gendered economy perspective. This approach, which is explored in detail elsewhere (Barrientos et al. 2003), focuses on the intersection between value chains and employment at the production end of the chain, as well as the way employment is embedded within the social and institutional context in which value chains operate. Whereas GVC analysis allows us to trace the nature of power relations between key actors in a value chain, it has only recently been used to examine the employment strategies at the production end of the chain, where gender issues are most evident. By engendering the GVC approach, we are able to consider the extent to which codes implemented through the value chain can address the conditions of insecure and marginalized workers.

A gender value-chain approach takes as its starting point the concept of the gendered economy advanced by Elson (1999). The basic principle behind this concept is that the economy is not gender-neutral, and that it is necessary to consider both market-oriented activities and the "reproductive economy" as economic activity (Elson 1999). The latter includes unpaid domestic work and childcare that are typically undertaken by women rather than men, and underpins productive market-based activity, which is dominated by men. At its most basic, the gender division of labor that locates women in the reproductive economy differentiates the options of men and women to participate in market activity and conditions their subsequent experience of that employment (Barrientos et al. 2003).

Labor markets are embedded within, and constructed by, the gendered economy. They reflect the socially derived gender division of labor, and are situated at the intersection between productive (paid) and reproductive (unpaid) work (Elson 1999). Men tend to dominate in the productive, paid segment of the economy, often in permanent jobs with higher wages, whereas women, who bear the burden of domestic responsibilities, move between reproductive and productive work, the latter often in informal types of employment. The notion that women are secondary earners who can rely upon the earnings of men to buffer them against the risk of economic insecurity underpins this employment profile as well as most labor regulation (Elson 1999).

We have previously used the gender value-chain approach to analyze the gender sensitivity of the *content* of codes of conduct in the horticultural sector. Using a gender pyramid that distinguishes between three basic kinds of work—formal, informal, and reproductive—we analyzed the variable coverage of gender issues in the content of codes and the scope of their gender sensitivity (Barrientos et al. 2003). Figure 13.1 indicates the "reach" of codes. Most codes relate mainly to permanent workers, with some protection for part-time and temporary workers, and seasonal workers whose employment has been formalized (e.g., through contracts). They seldom reach workers who are informally employed.

Figure 13.1   The Reach of Codes

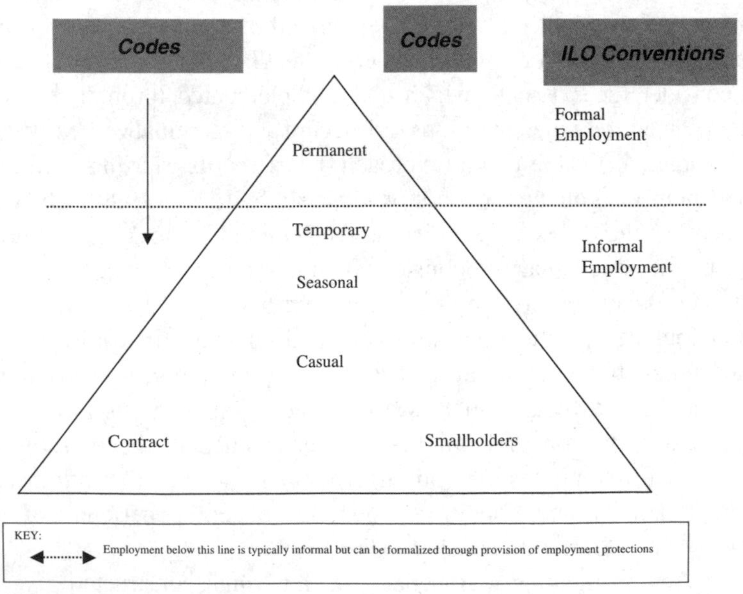

Source: Adapted from Dolan, Opondo, and Smith 2003.

Even where codes do reach informal workers, their coverage of gender issues is highly variable. Some codes formally address gender issues and integrate a number of international conventions relating to gender discrimination and inequality, whereas other codes make no mention of gender at all. Very few codes extend beyond working conditions to work-related issues such as the provision of housing, childcare, reproductive rights, parental leave, and transport. Given women's reproductive responsibilities, these issues are often of more significance to women than to men (Barrientos et al. 2003). The gender value-chain framework suggests, therefore, that existing codes of practice are unlikely to benefit all workers, especially female workers who are often in informal employment.

In this paper, we extend the gender value-chain approach to examine in more detail the implementation of codes in African horticultural value chains. Through in-depth research on 17 farms and packing houses in Kenya, South Africa, and Zambia, we analyze the extent to which codes are meeting the gendered needs and concerns of women and men workers in different types of value chains.

EMPLOYMENT IN AFRICAN HORTICULTURE

The African export horticultural industry employs a significant number of workers in production and post-harvest activities. In all three countries and industries that we studied, employment is highly gendered and informal. Women represent between 50 and 75 percent of total employment in Kenya, South Africa, and Zambia and are typically concentrated in the most labor-intensive forms of work, such as packing and harvesting. Companies perceive women as more "productive" in this kind of work, citing women's capacity to perform tedious and delicate work without complaint. The industry is also characterized by high levels of nonpermanent work (temporary, seasonal, casual, and contract), particularly for the tasks typically carried out by women. Thus women are often employed on a "flexible" informal basis, and are concentrated in the lower part of the employment pyramid depicted in Figure 13.1. Informal workers are typically excluded from trade union representation and lack employment benefits such as social security, maternity leave, housing benefits, or severance pay, which are of particular importance to women given their responsibilities for reproductive work.

Table 13–1. Key Employment Statistics from Case Study Firms

Country, Product	Nonpermanent Workers as % of All Workers	Female Workers as % of All Workers	Female Permanent Workers as % of Total Female Workers	Female Nonpermanent Workers as % of Total Female Workers
Kenya, flowers	35	61	65	35
South Africa, fruit	77	41	16	84
Zambia, flowers	24	43	66	34
Zambia, vegetables	81	70	13	87

Source: Study data collected between July and December 2002

However, despite these broad tendencies, there are some important differences in the employment patterns of the different products we studied.[6] The chains for Zambian vegetables and South African deciduous fruit employ high proportions of nonpermanent workers. The vast majority of these workers are women. Although it was not representative, the degree of informality among women workers was reflected in the sample we studied in our case studies, as shown in Table 13–1. The level of informality results from a number of factors. First, fruit and vegetable production is seasonal, requiring a large, flexible labor force that can be employed on a temporary basis. But the degree of informality is also related to the offsetting of risks by employers in buyer-driven value chains. Supermarkets' buying practices often transfer the risks of production to the producers, who face stringent supermarket demands and downward pressures on prices. Competitive pressures are intense; producers are squeezed in returns, and deflect this pressure onto the workforce, obliging employees to work longer and harder so that companies can maintain their UK clients (Dolan 2004; Raworth 2004).

In contrast, the cut-flower chains in both Kenya and Zambia, as shown in Table 13–1, display much higher levels of permanent labor. In the Kenyan case, women compose 61 percent of the workforce, of which nearly two thirds are on permanent contracts. In the case of Zambia, 66 percent of women workers are employed on permanent contracts. To some extent, this masks variation between farms. For example, in Kenya the ratio of permanent to nonpermanent labor varies from 9 percent permanent versus 91 percent nonpermanent on one farm to 81 percent permanent versus 15 percent nonpermanent on another. Nevertheless, the case studies suggest that there may be a departure from the traditional pattern of casual and seasonal employment on cut-flower farms.

Are the tendencies toward permanent labor linked to the structure of the value chain or to the codes that have been introduced into them? According to flower growers interviewed in Kenya and Zambia, employment has become more permanent for (at least) three reasons: less seasonality in production cycles; the need for a more stable, skilled workforce in order to maintain high quality; and, in a few cases, pressure to implement codes. Although these factors contribute to the shift toward permanent employment, they do not explain the role that buyers play in shaping the employment strategies of African producers. For example, the reluctance of fresh-produce suppliers to employ permanent workers is, somewhat paradoxically, linked to the nature of pressures coming down the value chain from supermarket buyers. These buyers have pursued a growth strategy based on price competitiveness. Suppliers who fail to deliver a quality product that meets the price, specification, and schedule that a retailer demands risk receiving fewer orders or being delisted from the chain altogether. The limited opportunities for African producers to access high-value markets mean that many are captive suppliers, locked into the buying practices of UK supermarkets in order to realize a return on their investments. This scenario places a strong imperative on producers to reduce costs, particularly labor, which constitutes a substantial portion of production costs in the fresh produce sector. By contrast, flower producers supplying the Dutch Auctions are not beholden to lead firms in the chain. The absence of dedicated customers dictating the terms of the trading relationship gives flower producers greater latitude to establish employment strategies that match production conditions (e.g., the annualization of production), while simultaneously maintaining their competitiveness. Hence, despite the fact that retailers place considerable pressure on African producers to adopt codes and improve working conditions, the countervailing pressure toward cost reduction inhibits a move in the direction of permanent employment.

Regardless of differences in the amount of informal work between value chains, our study found many commonalities in the experiences of nonpermanent horticultural workers across the three countries. Through undertaking a gender analysis of the key employment issues from the perspective of workers, we explored the extent to which code implementation is sensitive to the gendered needs of different types of employees. The following discussion presents some of the issues that were highlighted by a total of 261 workers during interviews and focus group discussions. We pay particular attention here to issues relating to the informality of employment, and the limitations of codes in reaching marginalized workers in a gendered economy.

Employment Status and Casualization

Many of the concerns raised by nonpermanent workers in our study related specifically to their employment status. Their lack of access to benefits such as maternity leave and sick pay had significant gender implications. They said they worried constantly about becoming pregnant, sick, or injured because of the loss of income, and the risk of losing their job. It was reported that many women resort to having abortions to avoid this happening. They were also less likely to have access to company childcare facilities, and struggled to afford private care. Nonpermanent workers were particularly vulnerable to sexual harassment and abuse, fearing being fired, or simply not being rehired, if they resisted or complained. Many workers felt safer if they kept their heads down; as one Zambian woman put it, "We just cry in our hearts because we cannot complain." Informal workers are rarely represented in workers' organizations and have few channels for communicating their grievances. These issues are reinforced by their exclusion from the protection of national laws, and often intensified by cultural norms that legitimate gender inequality.

Many codes stipulate that, as far as possible, producers should provide workers with regular employment, and caution against the use of fixed-term contracts as a strategy to avoid legal obligations to workers. However, in all three countries we found evidence of the use of repeated contracts such that a worker is effectively employed 12 months a year, but receives few of the benefits of permanent employment. In Kenya, three farms referred specifically to the use of rolling or repeated contracts, with all three employing high proportions of nonpermanent workers. In Zambia, of the 36 casual workers interviewed, 16 had been working for more than one year as a casual, and five had been working for more than two years. Although this is not illegal, it is cautioned against in most codes covering the sector. Yet as we have seen, the buyers that promote the use of codes often create pressures in their value chains that give rise to informal employment.

Working Hours and Overtime

Overtime work is an area in which the operation of value chains has a direct, gendered influence on employment. Long hours are typical as seasonality and events such as Christmas and Valentine's Day create peaks in demand. However, they are also a function of the production imperatives that filter through the supply chain from overseas buyers, who require exporters to respond swiftly to fluctuations in consumer demand. With low levels of wages generally, many workers were keen to work extra hours for the extra income it brings, so overtime as such may not be a problem for workers. There were, nonetheless, many complaints about compulsory or short-notice overtime, particularly from women with children who were unable to make alternative childcare arrangements and were forced to leave even small children unattended. However, from an employer's perspective, providing workers with advance notice of overtime is not always possible as the use of just-in-time supply means that orders can arrive suddenly, often during the same day that they are expected to be air freighted. Compulsory overtime at short notice is therefore not the producer's responsibility alone. The ability to uphold these standards is directly related to actors further up the value chain.

Wage Levels

Women's concentration in insecure forms of employment is also linked to social norms that legitimate the gendered allocation of tasks. Women are often recruited for jobs that are viewed as low-skilled and easily accomplished, involving repetition and stamina (for instance, the need to stand for long hours), such as sorting and bunching roses. Men are more likely to be hired in positions viewed as higher-skilled, for example as sprayers, irrigators, and tractor drivers. Jobs undertaken by men in the industry are more likely to be permanent and are paid higher wages. For example, in Zambia the average male wage in our case study was Kw150,669, compared to Kw137,554 for women. There was a similar disparity in Kenyan average wages, which were Ksh1138 for men and Ksh1065 for women. Men also tended to occupy more supervisory positions, due in large part to perceptions on the part of the management that women are less capable of performing senior jobs. As one manager in Zambia indicated, "All greenhouse supervisors are men because it would be very difficult for a woman to supervise men, unless she were very strong." Value-chain pressures for flexible labor strategies, combined with local assumptions about the kinds of tasks that women can and cannot undertake, therefore act to create and reinforce gender-based wage inequality.

Representation and Legislation

Another factor that reinforces gender inequality in the workplace is the lack of representation of women workers. Although half of the companies in the study were unionized, fewer than 50 percent of permanent workers were members in all but three cases. Nonpermanent workers were rarely unionized, especially casual and contract workers. Overall, women were underrepresented in unions, with more male than female shop stewards in all but two cases, despite the fact that women typically constituted most of the workforce. Workers' committees, which were quite common in Kenya and South Africa, similarly failed to give adequate representation to women workers.

In the countries we studied, national legislation also fails to prevent discrimination against women in the workplace, and often acts to reinforce local assumptions regarding the roles of men and women. In Kenya, the government has yet to enact the statutes that recognize equal pay for equal work, nor are there any specific legal protections against discrimination on the basis of sex. In Zambia, although the provisions in labor legislation are supposed to apply equally to men and women, the legislation does not define equal work. In contrast, South African postapartheid legislation is very progressive with respect to employment conditions, labor rights, housing rights, equal opportunities, and protection against racial and gender discrimination. However, enforcement of this legislation has been weak to date, particularly in rural areas.

Our discussion of patterns of employment, wage rates, working hours, representation, and legislation illustrates the gendered economy in which codes operate. Women are concentrated in insecure work and are therefore unlikely to have any knowledge of codes, or to be interviewed in the case of a social audit or assessment. They are also less likely to make a complaint for fear of losing access to future employment, and are vulnerable to abuse by supervisors who can exert their power over an insecure and vulnerable temporary workforce. It is critical that these underlying issues are tackled if codes are to bring improvements to female as well as male, and nonpermanent as well as permanent workers.

CONCLUSION: ENGENDERING CODE IMPLEMENTATION IN GLOBAL VALUE CHAINS

Our gender value-chain analysis of the implementation of codes in African horticulture demonstrates that, despite the fact that producers in buyer-driven chains are under more pressure to adopt codes, and social codes in particular, this has not necessarily led to better outcomes for women and informal workers. As long as codes fail to confront the local gendered economy, they are unlikely to improve the employment conditions of all workers.

The complexity of improving employment conditions through codes of practice is increasingly recognized. In particular, there is a growing awareness that long-term change in workplace practice necessitates an approach to code implementation that draws on multistakeholder participation (including the private sector, civil society, trade unions, and government), and emphasizes flexible application and local ownership (Dolan et al. 2003). Techniques such as participatory social auditing (PSA), used as part of a multistakeholder approach, are better able to address the complexities of local employment conditions and support code development on a sustainable basis (NRI 2002).

Participatory social auditing, which can be highly effective in identifying workers' concerns and the problems that underlie workplace issues (see Smith et al. 2004) can extend the reach of codes by bringing informal workers into the implementation process. However, to be effective in addressing gender issues, many of which are embedded in local employment practice and culture, PSA needs to be integrated into an ongoing process of code implementation, rather than be part of a one-off, snapshot approach. Our findings suggest that a process approach, accompanied by the establishment of a local multistakeholder initiative (in which all stakeholders work together), is more likely to address the issues of concern to marginalized workers, most of whom are women.

Local multistakeholder initiatives provide the basis for more sustained participation by different actors, especially trade unions and NGOs, in the process of implementing codes. The establishment of an autonomous body that represents different stakeholders provides a degree of independence and prevents any one group from dominating the process. It can also reflect the diverse interests of workers, including men and women, permanent and nonpermanent, unionized and nonunionized—and, importantly, allows organizations reflecting gender interests to participate. Such a body can provide guidance, oversee code implementation, and facilitate auditing on a basis that is mutually agreed among all stakeholders. In the South African wine industry, for instance, a local initiative (Wine Industry Ethical Trade Association, or WIETA) was established following an ETI pilot project. The Executive Committee of WIETA includes representatives from industry, trade unions, and NGOs, as well as government. It has developed its own code (incorporating international standards) and auditing process, both of which are sensitive to the needs of marginalized South African workers (such as women, black Africans, and nonpermanent workers). Membership includes some of the largest companies in the wine industry, and audits are now well underway (see also Nelson et al. 2005). Similarly, in Kenya a multistakeholder approach (the Horticulture Ethical Business Initiative, or HEBI) has emerged to guide social accountability in the sector through the development of a Kenyan Social Base Code and the engagement of local stakeholders in the auditing process (Dolan et al. 2003). HEBI has been particularly successful in ensuring that the interests of women and informal workers are identified in code implementation through the representation of NGOs reflecting women's interests on the steering committee, the inclusion of local female auditors in the auditing process, and the use of participatory methods to elicit the perspectives of marginalized workers.

It is hoped that such mechanisms will enable the voices of previously excluded groups, including women workers, to be heard and over time to challenge the gender inequality that is embedded in the workplace. However, there are significant challenges to developing a multistakeholder approach, including tensions among stakeholders and unequal power relations between groups. In Kenya, for example, unions have been reluctant to join HEBI, thus inhibiting the formation of a truly multistakeholder body. Furthermore, there is also a danger that local multistakeholder approaches may simply replicate and reinforce local gender norms. A key challenge for code initiatives that aim to institute multistakeholder processes is to ensure that the needs of *all* workers are incorporated into the process of code implementation, including those in less secure forms of employment, as well as local institutions in which workers have trust.

Ultimately, it is only by addressing the local gendered economy that working conditions are likely to improve through codes of practice. A top-down approach to code implementation will neither adequately address embedded gender inequality nor reach marginalized workers.

ACKNOWLEDGMENTS

This chapter is based on a research project funded by DFID (SSR project 8077, Ethical Trade in African Horticulture), coordinated by the Institute for Development Studies (IDS) at the University of Sussex. The views and opinions expressed are those of the authors alone.

NOTES

[1] This research was funded by DFID (SSR project 8077, Ethical Trade in African Horticulture). Unless otherwise specified, references to Kenya are from Dolan et al. (2003), to South Africa from Kleinbooi et al. (forthcoming), and to Zambia from Tallontire et al. (2004).

[2] UK supermarkets dominate the domestic fresh-produce market and some, such as Tesco, are significant in the global retail sector: Tesco was eighth in the world in terms of global retail sales in 2002 at US$39,517 million, compared to Wal-Mart at number one with US$229,671 million (Retail Industry 2003).

[3] UK supermarkets have been most active with regard to social codes. In other European countries retailers have relied on EUREP GAP. Interestingly, in the United States there is considerable activity on codes in the branded-clothing sector but relatively little on foods, beyond fair trade and environmentally friendly coffee.

[4] However, in contrast to other sectoral codes (whether Northern or Southern), EUREP GAP is retail driven.

[5] One farm was previously MPS certified, but withdrew from MPS when MPS and KFC announced their collaboration.

[6] The quantitative data presented in Table 13–1 are not representative of the industries as a whole, as we undertook a purposive analysis, aimed at identifying companies that were implementing social and/or environmental codes and supplying European markets. The companies can be regarded as some of the more progressive in the industry. Another problem is the comparability of the data due to the differing definitions of permanent, seasonal, and casual worker used between countries and even between firms in the same country.

REFERENCES

Barrientos, S., C. Dolan, and A. Tallontire. 2003. "A Gendered Value Chain Approach to Codes of Conduct in African Horticulture." *World Development* 31(9):1511–1526.

Coote, C., P. Greenhalgh, and J. Orchard. 2003. "High Value Horticulture and Organic Export Markets for Sub-Saharan Africa." Unpublished NRI report prepared for DFID. Chatham Maritime, United Kingdom: Natural Resources Institute.

Dolan, C. 2004. "On Farm and Packhouse: Employment at the Bottom of a Global Commodity Chain." *Rural Sociology* 69(1):99–126.

Dolan, C., and J. Humphrey. 2004. "Changing Governance Patterns in the Trade in Fresh Vegetables between Africa and the United Kingdom." *Environment and Planning A* 36(3):491–509.

Dolan, C., M. Opondo, and S. Smith. 2003 *Gender, Rights, and Participation in the Kenya Cut Flower Industry.* NRI Report No. 2768. Chatham Maritime, United Kingdom: Natural Resources Institute.

Elson, D. 1999. "Labor Markets as Gendered Institutions: Equality, Efficiency and Empowerment Issues." *World Development* 27(3):611–627.

Gereffi, G. 1994. "The Organization of Buyer-Driven Global Commodity Chains: How U.S. Retailers Shape Overseas Production Networks." In G. Gereffi and M. Korzeniewicz (eds.), *Commodity Chains and Global Capitalism.* Westport, CT: Praeger.

Gereffi, G., and M. Korzeniewicz (eds.). 1994. *Commodity Chains and Global Capitalism.* Westport, CT: Praeger.

Kleinbooi, K., S. Barrientos, D. Auret, and S. Smith. (in press) *Ethical Trade in South African Deciduous Fruit—Gender, Rights and Participation.* Stellenbosch, South Africa: Centre for Rural Legal Studies.

Nelson, V., A. Martin, and J. Ewert. 2005. "What Difference Can They Make? Assessing the Social Impact of Corporate Codes of Practice." *Development in Practice* 15(3&4):539–545.

NRI. 2002. "Building Multi-stakeholder Institutions for Developing and Managing National Codes of Practice." NRET Theme Papers on Codes of Practice in the Fresh Produce Sector (No. 2). Chatham Maritime, United Kingdom: Natural Resources Institute.

Ponte, S. 2002. "Standards, Trade and Equity: Lessons from the Specialty Coffee Industry." CDR Working Paper No. 02.13. Copenhagen: CDR.

Raworth, Kate. 2004. *Trading Away Our Rights: Women Working in Global Supply Chains.* Oxfam International Campaign Report, Oxford: Oxfam GB.

Retail Industry. 2003. "Top 100 Retailers Worldwide Realize Slow Growth." Available at http://retailindustry.about.com/library/bl/03q2/bl_rf100603. htm (retrieved 25 May 2004).

Smith, S., D. Auret, S. Barrientos, C. Dolan, K. Kleinbooi, C. Njobvu, M. Opondo, and A. Tallontire. 2004. "Ethical Trade in African Horticulture: Gender, Rights and Participation." *IDS Working Paper No. 223.* Brighton, United Kingdom: IDS.

Tallontire, A., S. Smith, and C. Njobvu. 2004. *Ethical Trade in African Horticulture: Gender, Rights and Participation. Final Report of the Zambia Study.* NRI Report No. 2775. Chatham Maritime: Natural Resources Institute.

PART 4

Resources

FOURTEEN

Development and the Private Sector:

An Annotated List of Selected Resources

JOHN SAYER AND DEBORAH EADE

This selected resources list provides further resources on the aspects of development and the private sector that have been addressed in this book, namely corporate social responsibility (CSR) and corporate accountability, different aspects of investing in development, issues relating to corporate codes of conduct and other mechanisms for regulating the private sector and monitoring compliance with legal and voluntary standards, and the development of alternative forms of trade that are based on social and ethical values. Even within these fields, there is a vast literature—some of it academic and research-based, some of it emerging from the minor industry that has sprung up to develop and monitor corporate codes, and some of it coming out of groups with a particular agenda to pursue or position to advocate.

Debates on corporate responsibility and more broadly the role of economic growth and public governance in eradicating poverty are very much alive, though some of these also have a long history. We have sought to reflect some of this variety by giving precedence to recent edited volumes and relevant journals and to authors whose work forms a touchstone in the field. Of the myriad organizations that work on these issues, we have highlighted a mixture of advocacy, campaigning, research, and other specialized agencies for which CSR in its broadest sense is part of their own "core business."

BOOKS AND REPORTS

Bais, Karolein, and Mijnd Huijser. *The Profit of Peace: Corporate Responsibility in Conflict Regions*. Sheffield: Greenleaf Publishing Ltd., 2005, ISBN 1-87471-990-X, 144 pp.

> Some 60,000 multinational companies work in more than 70 conflict regions worldwide. Many of these profit from conflicts, whether by trading arms, taking advantage of the absence of the rule of law, or exploiting the availability of cheap labor. Extensive and candid interviews with senior managers working in countries such as Afghanistan, Burma, and Rwanda show that most corporate managers recognize that the mere fact of investing in a conflict region inevitably influences the outcome of the conflict in some way. The authors set out a range of business practices that can help contribute to peace and stability.

Bendell, Jem (ed.). *Terms for Endearment: Business, NGOs and Sustainable Development*. Sheffield: Greenleaf Publishing Ltd., 2000, ISBN 1-87471-929-2, 280 pp.

> Many companies view engagement with their stakeholders as part of their strategy to improve social and environmental performance, and civil society organizations (CSOs) seek to define and monitor standards of good business behavior. The failure to pursue such standards will lead to public confrontation, with negative consequences for the company's profits and reputation. Contributors argue that the CSR agenda presents business with both a threat and opportunity in the pursuit of a social basis for global economic activity. See also David Murphy and Jem Bendell *In the Company of Partners: Business, Environmental Groups and Sustainable Development Post Rio* (Policy Press, 1997).

Commission on the Private Sector and Development. *Unleashing Entrepreneurship: Making Business Work for the Poor*. Report to the UN Secretary-General New York, NY: UNDP, 2004, 48 pp.

> This report, commissioned by the UN Secretary-General, considers how the private sector and entrepreneurship can be unleashed in developing countries, and how the existing private sector can be engaged in meeting that challenge. Employment in the formal or informal economy is the key link between growth and poverty alleviation, and many of the poor are themselves involved in the private sector. The Commission calls for a range of actions in the public, public-private, and private spheres; and for a focus on the agricultural sector and on "bottom of the pyramid" markets.

Commonwealth Business Council. *Corporate Citizenship in Action: Learning from Commonwealth Experience.* London: Commonwealth Business Council/ Commonwealth Secretariat, 2003, ISBN 1-903431-22-0, 76 pp.

> There are increasing demands on companies to play an active part in building a more equitable society. This volume offers examples of corporate citizenship in various parts of the Commonwealth. Companion volumes include *Commonwealth Insight 2003: Corporate Social Responsibility Report,* and *Commonwealth Insight 2003: Foreign Direct Investment Report.*

Crowe, Roger (ed.). *No Scruples?: Managing to Be Responsible in a Turbulent World.* London: Spiro Press, 2002, ISBN 1-904298-06-0, 188 pp.

> Contributors consider how the private sector should respond to so-called anti-globalization demonstrations, sharing insights from different perspectives on the call for business to be more socially accountable.

Danaher, Kevin, and Jason Mark. *Insurrection: Citizen Challenges to Corporate Power.* New York: Routledge, 2003, ISBN 0-415-94677-8, 350 pp.

> The authors examine the mass demonstrations at sessions of the World Bank, the IMF, the G-8, and the WTO, beginning with the 1999 "battle of Seattle." There is growing public disaffection with corporate malpractice, from the reliance of clothing and sportswear brands on sweatshop labor, to the links between some companies and governments that abuse human rights, or their role in environmental degradation and the decline of biodiversity. Danaher and Mark examine the background to and likely trajectories of global campaigns that challenge corporate behavior.

Department for International Development (DFID). *DFID and Corporate Social Responsibility: An Issues Paper.* London: DFID, 2003, ISBN 1-86192-565-4, 12 pp.

> This brief paper sets out the UK government's view that engaging the corporate sector through the social responsibility agenda is the best way to generate economic growth as a means of tackling poverty. See also *A Review of UK Company Codes of Conduct* (1998).

Demirag, Istemi (ed.). *Corporate Social Responsibility, Accountability and Governance.* Sheffield: Greenleaf Publishing Ltd., 2005, ISBN 1-87471-956-X, 378 pp.

> The "business case" argument for corporate social responsibility suggests that companies can increase their profits by observing high social and environmental standards. It is unclear, however, how nonfinancial stakeholders can use voluntary disclosures to hold companies accountable for the consequences of their actions.

A wide range of contributors expose the limitations of current reporting and accountability mechanisms, and the lack of effective regulatory control over multinational companies, and set out some emerging patterns of accountability and governance structures.

Dine, Janet. *Companies, International Trade and Human Rights*: *The Responsible Corporation*. Cambridge: Cambridge University Press, 2005, ISBN 0-521-82861-9, 354 pp.

The author examines the roles and motives of corporations within the global trading system, and the relationships between corporations, nation states, and international organizations. Trade regimes are failing to meet the objectives set out in international agreements, and poverty remains persistent and widespread. This book focuses on the role played by companies in these failures of global trade.

Elkington, John. *The Chrysalis Economy: How Citizen CEOs and Corporations Can Fuse Values and Value Creation*. Oxford: Capstone Publishing, 2001, ISBN 1-84112-14-2-8, 288 pp.

The author argues that two parallel trends are transforming corporate behavior: a younger and more networked generation of CEOs and business leaders is emerging at a time when the global economy is rendering previous ways of conducting business obsolete. Elkington describes the prevailing caterpillar and locust business models as degenerative, while butterflies and honeybees portray the regenerative or sustainable approach of the global future. These four types are distinguished both by how a company extracts value as it moves towards sustainability, and by the core values by which it operates. See also *Cannibals with Forks: The Triple Bottom Line of 21st Century Business* (1997) and (with Julia Hailes) *The Green Consumer Guide: From Shampoo to Champagne—High-Street Shopping for a Better Environment* (1998).

Fields, Gary, and Guy Pfeffermann (eds.). *Pathways out of Poverty: Private Firms and Economic Mobility in Developing Countries*. Washington, DC: World Bank, 2002, ISBN 0-82135-404-3, 280 pp.

In many developing countries, small agricultural family firms employ the largest numbers of people. These private firms can have a major role in reducing poverty, as seen in both China and Vietnam since the 1980s. Likewise, most workers in developing and transition countries are in the informal economy. Contributors underline the importance of the state and good public governance in fostering sustained development by, among other things, providing the infrastructure and investment in health, education, and other basic services upon which the private sector depends.

Hilton, Steve, and Giles Gibbons. *Good Business: Your World Needs You.* London: Texere Publishing, 2002, ISBN 1-587-99118-7, 255 pp.

> The authors contend that, rather than being an optional extra or a public-relations exercise, companies can improve their business by promoting public causes, and thus make capitalism an active force for social good. They argue that firms can use their brand to achieve social gain as well as increasing their own profits. For instance, a sportswear company could use its position in the market to convey anti-smoking messages to young people, and thus become more attractive also to the public-health lobby.

Hopkins, Michael. *The Planetary Bargain: Corporate Social Responsibility Comes of Age.* Basingstoke: Palgrave Macmillan, 1998, ISBN 0-312-21833-8, 247 pp.

> Arguing that poverty and unemployment can only be tackled by a combination of sustained economic growth and equitable distribution, Hopkins suggests that CSR is the way to create such prosperity and stability, and argues for a worldwide agreement or "planetary bargain" between the private and public sectors. This is illustrated by examples of international companies that have adopted socially responsible programs.

Hudson, Michael. *Global Fracture: The New International Economic Order.* London: Pluto Press, 2005 (2nd ed.), ISBN 0-7453-2394-4, 296 pp.

> The 1973 New International Economic Order (NIEO) was a demand by poor countries to improve the terms of trade for raw materials so they could build up agricultural and industrial self-sufficiency. Hudson argues that how the United States systematically undermined this initiative and instead pushed for its own financial supremacy through, for instance, trade embargoes and protectionism, coupled with increasing isolationism.

Jackson, Ira A., and Jane Nelson. *Profits with Principles.* New York: Random House, 2003, ISBN 0-385-50163-3, 400 pp.

> This book gives an overview of household-name companies such as Alcoa, Citigroup, Dell, Dupont, General Electric, Marriott, Proctor & Gamble, and Starbucks that are both increasing their markets and "doing the right thing" in terms of business ethics and wider corporate social responsibility. A growing number of companies are seeking to incorporate values into the way they work in order to benefit society as well as shareholders. Depicting such approaches as a new form of capitalism, the authors set out recommendations for policies that all companies can adopt.

Klein, Naomi. *No Logo: Taking Aim at the Brand Bullies*. London: Flamingo, 2001, ISBN 0-00-653040-0, 400 pp.

> Global brand-name goods rely on the image embodied by their logos, but this has also generated a global backlash against the dependence of sportswear and fashion companies on sweatshop labor, even as these firms charge exorbitant prices for their products. Likewise food, soft drink, and tobacco companies are accused of contributing to the rise in noncommunicable diseases. Klein examines contemporary consumer culture, highlighting the growing opposition to the power of the corporate sector to shape consumers' lives and values. See also *Fences and Windows: Dispatches from the Frontlines of the Globalization Debate* (Flamingo, 2002), a collection of articles and speeches written in the wake of the mass protests against the WTO, the G-8, and the international financial institutions that started in Seattle in 1999.

Korten, David C. *When Corporations Rule the World*. Bloomfield, CT: Kumarian Press (in association with Berrett-Koehler Publications), 2001 (2nd ed.), ISBN 1-88720-804-6, 208 pp.

> The revised edition of this classic work takes account of the role of CSOs and the new global citizens' activist movement (the Living Democracy Movement) in countering the negative impacts of corporate behavior in the global economy, and highlights efforts to develop more appropriate forms of global economic governance. See also *The Post-Corporate World: Life after Capitalism* (1999). Korten is the founding director of the People-Centered Development Forum.

Leipziger, Deborah. *The Corporate Responsibility Code Book*. Sheffield: Greenleaf Publishing, ISBN 1-87471-978-0, 512 pp.

> This comprehensive sourcebook is intended to help companies select, develop, and adopt social and environmental codes of conduct that are most appropriate to their business. It provides background information on universal principles and conventions that underpin specific international codes—for instance, on human rights, labor rights, the environment, and anti-corruption—and sets out the range of different approaches to the definition and adoption of codes and verification of workplace compliance, whether global or company-based. The book also includes how-to (or process) codes that focus on reporting and stakeholder engagement and assurance.

Daniel Litvin. *Empires of Profit: Commerce, Conquest and Corporate Responsibility*. London: Texere, ISBN 1-587-99192-6, 350 pp.

> The early multinational companies, such as the British East India Company, the British South Africa Company, the South Manchurian

Railway Company, and the United Fruit Company (UFC), were seldom benevolent in their motivation; for instance, in 1954, UFC assisted in toppling the elected president of Guatemala because it viewed his moderate land-reform plans as a threat to its extensive holdings. Litvin holds, however, that these companies also brought benefits, such as infrastructure, social facilities, and employment. Similarly, although some of the malpractices of their contemporary successors have rightly been exposed, he argues that they often offer relatively decent work as well as investment in developing countries.

Madeley, John. *Big Business, Poor Peoples: The Impact of Transnational Corporations on the World's Poor.* London: Zed Books, 1999, ISBN 1-856496-72-4, 192 pp.

Writing while the movement for corporate social responsibility was in its infancy, the author examines the negative impact on the poor of TNC activities in the areas of agriculture, forestry, fisheries, the extractive industries, manufacturing, and tourism. He illustrates how local communities are often dispossessed and marginalized as a result of such activities, and local governments often lack the power or the will to curb them.

McIntosh, Malcolm, Sarah Waddock, and George Kell (eds.). *Learning to Talk: Corporate Citizenship and the Development of the UN Global Compact.* Sheffield: Greenleaf Publishing, 2004, ISBN 1-87471-975-6, 432 pp.

The UN Global Compact complements other corporate citizenship initiatives by promoting dialogue on the relationship between business and society at a global level. It represents a set of principles that draws its moral and political legitimacy from the UN and that challenges businesses to align profitability with the common good. Contributors review the record to date of this initiative, drawing attention to the marked changes in international relations and global governance since it was established.

McIntosh, Malcolm, Ruth Thomas, Deborah Leipziger, and Gill Coleman. *Living Corporate Citizenship: Strategic Routes to Socially Responsible Business.* London: Financial Times and Prentice Hall, 2002, ISBN 0-273-65433-0, 320 pp.

The authors discuss how far the adoption of codes of corporate social responsibility serves as a public relations exercise that allows companies to make peripheral changes while carrying on their core business as usual. They argue, however, that genuine engagement with social and environmental issues will also enable companies to innovate and remain competitive. The book reviews eight major codes and includes case studies of their application by companies participating in the Global Compact.

Mamic, Ivanka. *Implementing Codes of Conduct: How Businesses Manage Social Performance in Global Supply Chains.* Sheffield: Greenleaf Publishing, in association with the ILO, 2004, ISBN 1-87471-989-6, 429 pp.

> Global value chains link workers, subcontractors, companies, retailers, and consumers across hugely different social and legal contexts and economies. This book addresses how voluntary corporate codes can be effective in ensuring that standards are observed in every link of the chain. Based on interviews with managers, government officials, workers and their representatives, and activists in the apparel, footwear, and retail sectors, the author identifies current approaches and sets out practical suggestions for how companies can best address social pressures in their daily business.

Moran, Theodore. *Beyond Sweatshops: Foreign Direct Investment and Globalization in Developing Nations.* Washington, DC: Brookings Institution Press, 2002, ISBN 0-81570-615-4, 196 pp.

> Moran compares the merits of enforceable and voluntary approaches to protecting labor standards, for instance through labeling, certification, and corporate codes of conduct, and the proposal to make a "living wage" part of the ILO core labor standards. He finds, however, that some 25 times more FDI in developing countries is in industrial sectors that employ relatively well-paid and protected trained workers, rather than in the garment, textile, and footwear plants, where workers are highly vulnerable to exploitation. See also Theodore Moran, Edward Graham, and Magnus Blomström (eds.), *Does Foreign Direct Investment Promote Development?* (2005), a compilation of recent research on the impact of FDI on the economic performance of the host countries.

Nelson, Jane, and Dave Prescott. *Business and the Millennium Development Goals: A Framework for Action.* International Business Leaders Forum: London, 2003.

> This briefing provides a framework for how companies and business coalitions can work with the UN system, governments, and CSOs to help achieve the Millennium Development Goals (MDGs). See also Jane Nelson *Business as Partners in Development: Creating Wealth for Countries, Companies and Communities* (The Prince of Wales Business Leaders Forum, 1996).

NGLS (UN Non-Governmental Liaison Service) and UNRISD. *Voluntary Approaches to Corporate Responsibility: Readings and a Resource Guide.* Geneva: NGLS, 2002, UNCTAD/NGLS/212, 211 pp.

> This book comprises two papers written under the auspices of an UNRISD research project on corporate social responsibility (CSR), and an extensive list of resources on the subject. Rhys Jenkins

examines the strengths and potential dangers of the proliferation of codes of conduct and the emergence of a minor industry to monitor them. Peter Utting examines the growing number of joint code-setting and monitoring arrangements, typically involving NGOs, concluding that international complaints procedures are generally weak and that many multi-stakeholder initiatives are dominated by Northern interests and perspectives.

Oxfam Australia. *The Mining Ombudsman Annual Report*. Melbourne: Oxfam Australia, annual publication.

This annual report compiles community complaints of human rights abuses and environmental degradation as the result of the operations of Australian mining companies in countries such as Indonesia, the Pacific Islands, Peru, and the Philippines. It calls for the industry to be subject to an independent complaints mechanism.

Picciotto, Sol, and Ruth Mayne (eds.). *Regulating International Business: Beyond Liberalization*. London, Macmillan Press in association with Oxfam GB, 1999, ISBN 0-333-7768-X, 277 pp.

This collection is based on research and advocacy work undertaken in response to the proposed Multilateral Agreements on Investment (MAI), broadening this to address the wider development concerns to be dealt with in any such regime. Contributors, who include academics, NGO researchers, legal specialists, and representatives of business organizations and labor unions, call for a positive regulatory framework for international business aimed at reducing poverty and promoting sustainable development.

Prahalad, C. K. *The Fortune at the Bottom of the Pyramid: Eradicating Poverty through Profits*. Philadelphia: Wharton School Publishing, 2004, ISBN 0-13-146750-6, 496 pp, plus CD-ROM.

Prahalad argues that private business can help to reduce poverty while also making a profit by creating new markets for products and services aimed at the poor—those at the bottom of the economic pyramid. He challenges misconceptions about the purchasing power, delivery infrastructure, and consumption habits of the poor that have discouraged companies from entering these markets. The book includes12 case studies of businesses that have become involved in this market ranging from the Aravind Eye Care System, the Indian prosthesis maker JaipurFoot, and the computer software conglomerate ITC in India, to the Mexican cement manufacturer CEMEX.

Raworth, Kate. *Trading Away our Rights: Women Working in Global Supply Chains*. An Oxfam International Campaign Report. Oxford: Oxfam GB, 2004, ISBN 0-85598-523-2, 112 pp.

> This report shows how companies' demands for faster, more flexible, and cheaper production in their supply chains are undermining the very labor standards they claim to be promoting, with particularly negative consequences for women workers. See also *Play Fair at the Olympics: Respect Workers' Rights in the Sportswear Industry* (Oxfam GB et al. 2004), Kevin Watkins and Penny Fowler *Rigged Rules and Double Standards: Trade, Globalisation, and the Fight Against Poverty* (Oxfam GB 2002), and *Beyond Philanthropy: The Pharmaceutical Industry, Corporate Social Responsibility and the Developing World* (Oxfam GB, Save the Children, VSO, 2002).

Schmitz, Hubert (ed.). *Local Enterprises in the Global Economy: Issues of Governance and Upgrading*. Cheltenham: Edward Elgar Publishing, 2004, ISBN 1-84376-974-3, 416 pp.

> Some argue that local relationships are central to the upgrading of local enterprises, but others maintain that the scope for upgrading is defined by the sourcing strategies of global buyers. This raises the questions of whether it is feasible to develop local upgrading strategies and whether global quality and labor standards help or hinder producers in developing countries. Based on theoretical and empirical research on local and regional clusters, global value chains, and global standards, contributors explore the interaction of global and local governance, highlighting power and inequality but also identifying scope for local action.

Schwartz, Peter, and Blair Gibb. *When Good Companies Do Bad Things: Responsibility and Risk in an Age of Globalization*. New York: John Wiley & Sons, 1999, ISBN 0-471-32332-2, 194 pp.

> Being socially accountable for their actions requires companies to go beyond ethical behavior, and to anticipate the demands of public opinion before being forced into action by regulatory means. The failure to do so can quickly expose a company to international opprobrium and threaten its prosperity. The CSR agenda has gained global momentum largely as a result of public pressure on individual companies. The authors argue that know-how and integrity are mutually reinforcing, and that social value can therefore translate into business value.

Sullivan, Rory (ed.). *Business and Human Rights: Dilemmas and Solutions*. Sheffield: Greenleaf Publishing, 2003, ISBN 1-874719-70-5, 336 pp.

> Contributors analyze the relationship between companies and human rights in the context of globalization. Part I maps the reasons

(financial, ethical, regulatory) why human rights have become a business issue. Part II looks at the practical experiences of companies in responding to specific human rights issues in their own operations, in their supply chains, and in specific countries. These case studies provide insights into how companies organize themselves to respond to human rights challenges, and what their experiences have been to date. Contributors also examine the roles of non-business actors, such as governments, labor unions, and NGOs, and address the question of the limits to responsibility.

UNDP. *Human Development Report 1996: Economic Growth and Human Development.* New York: Oxford University Press, 1996, ISBN 0-19-511158-3, 229 pp.

This issue of the annual Human Development Report focuses on the relationship between economic growth and development, arguing that if it is not properly managed, growth can be "jobless, voiceless, ruthless, rootless and futureless, and thus detrimental to human development." It concludes that growth and equity are mutually reinforcing, and thus the quality and sustainability of growth and policies to ensure the distribution of its benefits are just as important as its quantity.

UNIFEM. *Women, Work, and Poverty.* New York: UNIFEM, 2005, ISBN 1-932827-26-9, 112 pp.

Published to mark the tenth anniversary of the Beijing Platform for Action, this book urges governments and policy makers to pay more attention to employment and its links to poverty, in particular to women's informal employment. It provides data on the size and composition of the informal economy and compares national data on average earnings and poverty risk across different segments of the informal and formal workforces in seven countries.

Utting, Peter. *Rethinking Business Regulation: From Self-Regulation to Social Control.* Technology, Business and Society Programme Paper 15. Geneva: UNRISD, 29 pp.

This paper examines contemporary aspects of business regulation associated with corporate social responsibility (CSR) in order to understand its influence in business, government, multilateral, and civil society circles, and assess its potential to counter the perverse effects of globalization and neoliberal policies. Utting cautions against broad generalizations about the future trajectory of CSR and corporate accountability, pointing out the major political and structural challenges to be faced, which will largely depend on effective and broad-based alliances to promote the CSR agenda.

Warner, Michael, and Rory Sullivan (eds.). *Putting Partnerships to Work: Strategic Alliances for Development between Government, the Private Sector and Civil Society.* Sheffield: Greenleaf Publishing, 2004, ISBN 1-87471-972-1, 336 pp.

> This book is based on the 1998–2002 research conducted under the auspices of Business Partners for Development (BPD), which aimed to enhance the role of the extractive industries in international development. The program included partnerships in Asia, Africa, and Latin America that were involved in conventional projects and also in areas such as conflict prevention, regional development, and managing oil-spill compensation. Recording failures as well as successes, the book shows that well-founded partnerships with governments, civil society, and local communities offer major mutual benefits and argues that all parties should therefore view these as an integral part of how companies work.

Zadek, Simon. *The Civil Corporation: The New Economy of Corporate Citizenship.* London: Earthscan, 2001, ISBN 1-85383-997-3, 258 pp.

> The author explores how far businesses can and should improve their social and environmental performance, arguing that corporate citizenship emerges from the New Economy dynamics and relating this to learning, knowledge, and innovation. The book sets out practical issues for business, including goal and boundary setting, measurement, dialogue, and trust building. See also Simon Zadek, Richard Evans, and Peter Pruzan (eds.), *Building Corporate Accountability: Emerging Practices in Social and Ethical Accounting* (1997); Simon Zadek, Niels Hojensgard, and Peter Raynard (eds.), *Perspectives on the New Economy of Corporate Citizenship* (2001); and Simon Zadek *Tomorrow's History: Selected Writings of Simon Zadek 1993–2003* (2004).

JOURNALS AND MAGAZINES

Business Ethics: The Magazine of Corporate Responsibility. Published quarterly by New Mountain Media. No ISSN. Editor: Marjorie Kelly

www.business-ethics.com

> BEM covers the subjects of business ethics, corporate social responsibility, and socially responsible investing and seeks to promote ethical business practices and help to create financially healthy companies in the process. The magazine hosts annual corporate awards, socially responsible investing awards, and lists the 100 best corporate citizens. Its website offers comprehensive information on CSR-related issues.

CSRwire—The Corporate Social Responsibility Newswire Service.

www.csrwire.com

CSRwire seeks to promote corporate responsibility and sustainability through providing information and positive examples of corporate practices in the form of press releases, publications, links to corporate reports, and CSR events. Its *CSR Directory: Resources for Promoting Global Business Principles and Best Practices* (edited by Michael Kane and originally published by the US Environmental Protection Agency), is an interactive, web-based tool providing real-time contact information for over 700 relevant organizations.

Corporate Social Responsibility and Environmental Management. Published quarterly by John Wiley and Sons. ISSN: 1535-3958. Editor: Richard Welford.

www.interscience.wiley.com/journal/csr

CSR focuses on the development of practical tools, case studies, and the assessment of the relative merits of different approaches to the incorporation of social and environmental responsibilities into an organization's business. There is a strong focus on methodology, principles, practice, science, technology, and law.

Development. Published quarterly by Palgrave Macmillan for the Society for International Development. ISSN: 1011 6370. Editor: Wendy Harcourt.

www.palgrave-journals.com

Development often addresses issues concerning the impact of the private sector on development. Among recent issues, Volume 47(3) (September 2004) on Corporate Social Responsibility includes articles that are skeptical of the CSR movement's attempt to harness business to a social justice agenda, while others are more positive about initiatives such as the Global Compact and public-private partnerships.

Electronic Journal of Business Ethics and Organization Studies. Published annually by the Business and Organization Ethics Network (BON). ISSN: 1239-2685. Editor: Anna-Maija Lämsä.

www.ebjo.jyu.fi

EBJO is an online journal available free of charge. It covers both theoretical and empirical approaches to enhancing the field of business ethics, and seeks to be a web-based communication medium for academic institutions, industries, and private consulting firms.

Ethical Corporation Magazine. Published monthly by Ethical Corporation. No ISSN. Editor: Tobias Webb.

www.ethicalcorp.com

Ethical Corporation is the monthly print magazine of the Ethical Corporation, dedicated to analyzing the key trends and events in global corporate responsibility. Articles from the magazine and other materials are also published online and are available on the organization's website.

Journal of Business Ethics. Published seven times a year by Springer Netherlands. ISSN: 0167-4544 (print), 1572-0697 (electronic). Editor-in-Chief: Alex C. Michalos; Editor: Deborah C. Poff.

www.springerlink.com

JBE defines "business" as including all systems involved in the exchange of goods and services, and holds that "ethics" encompasses all human action aimed at securing a good life. Systems of production, consumption, marketing, advertising, social and economic accounting, labor relations, public relations, and organizational behavior are analyzed from a moral viewpoint. The journal is aimed at the business community, universities, government agencies, and consumer groups.

The Journal of Corporate Citizenship. Published quarterly by Greenleaf Publishing. ISSN: 1470 5001. Editor: Malcolm McIntosh.

www.greenleaf-publishing.com /jcc/jcchome.htm

A multidisciplinary journal publishing contributions by researchers and practitioners involved in public policy, organizational behavior, economic history, strategic management, citizenship, human rights, corporate governance, sustainability management, responsible supply-chain management, stakeholder management, poverty, gender, and globalization.

Transnational Corporations. Published three times a year by UNCTAD. ISSN: 1014 9562. Editor: Karl P. Sauvant.

www.unctad.org

TC publishes policy-oriented articles and research notes that provide insights into the political, economic, legal, social, and cultural impacts of transnational corporations (TNCs) and foreign direct investment in an increasingly global economy and the resulting implications for policy.

ORGANIZATIONS AND WEBSITES

AccountAbility: The Institute of Social and Ethical AccountAbility, Unit A, 137 Shepherdess Walk, London N1 7RQ, UK.

www.accountability.org.uk

An international membership organization dedicated to promoting ethical accountability for sustainable development through the development of innovative tools and standards, most notably the AA1000 Series; undertaking research on best practice for practitioners and policy makers in organizational accountability; and promoting accountability competencies across the professions.

African Institute of Corporate Citizenship, PO Box 37357, Birnam Park, 2015 South Africa

www.aiccafrica.com

An NGO dedicated to contributing to responsible growth and competitiveness in Africa by changing the way businesses operate in the continent. It has a number of subsidiary organizations that focus on particular issues, and maintains an extensive publishing program.

Ashridge Centre for Business and Society, Berkhamstead, HP4 1NS, UK

www.ashridge.org.uk

An international authority on corporate, government, and community relations, the Centre's research focuses on the development of global business ethics; social accounting and reporting; and the changing nature of corporate community involvement and investment. It also conducts surveys, for instance into the number of leading companies that have statements of business principles or codes of ethics and how many of these actively incorporated issues of human rights.

Business & Human Rights Resource Centre

www.business-humanrights.org

An independent website in partnership with Amnesty International, business groups, and academic institutions containing information from the UN and ILO, companies, human rights, development, labor, and environmental organizations, governments, journalists, and other organizations that serves as an "online library" to provide links to a wide range of materials and to promote informed discussion of important policy issues.

Business for Social Responsibility (BSR), 111 Sutter Street, 12th Floor, San Francisco, CA 94104, USA

www.bsr.org

Through providing a wide range of training and advisory services, BSR seeks to help companies achieve commercial success in ways that respect ethical values, people, communities, and the environment. Founded in 1992, BSR is a global nonprofit membership organization of companies who together employ more than 6 million workers around the world. BSR works with its members and collaborates with other organizations in promoting more responsible business practices.

Business in the Community (BITC), 137 Shepherdess Walk, London N1 7RQ, UK

www.bitc.org.uk

BITC is a movement of companies in the UK committed to improving their positive impact on society as well as making corporate social responsibility a part of their business principles. It is made up of 650 companies, including 75 percent of the FTSE 100. In association with The Prince of Wales Business Leaders Forum, BITC provides key considerations and methods for companies wanting to incorporate human rights standards into their business processes. Its report, "Winning with Integrity—A Guide to Social Responsibility" (2000), offers practical guidelines for businesses to measure and manage the impact of corporate social responsibility.

The Business Humanitarian Forum, 7-9 chemin de Balexert, 1219 Châtelaine, Geneva, Switzerland

www.bhforum.ch

The Business Humanitarian Forum brings together major humanitarian agencies and international business executives to promote cooperation in fostering stable, prosperous, and democratic societies in areas of real or potential crisis or conflict.

Caux Round Table (CRT), Amaliastraat 10, 2514 JC The Hague, The Netherlands

www.cauxroundtable.org

CRT is an international network of principle business leaders working to promote a moral capitalism through which business can flourish on a sustainable and socially responsible basis and long-term prosperity can become the foundation for a fair, free, and transparent global society. It works with global business leaders, international institutions, and policy makers to improve investment environments in selected developing countries and promoting the adoption of 12 core standards for the transparent management of national financial institutions. It has secretariats in Europe, Japan, Mexico, and the United States.

Centre for Social Markets (CSM), 1 Trafalgar Avenue, London SE15 6NP, UK, and 39 Hindusthan Park, Kolkata 700 029, India

www.csmworld.org

CSM is a nonprofit organization that works for social justice, human rights, and sustainable development through promoting responsible entrepreneurship and the effective use of economic institutions. CSM seeks holistic and integrated solutions to sustainability crises such as global poverty and climate change by harnessing the power of markets and entrepreneurship. CSM works through a global network of associates and specialists in diverse fields. Although international in scope, CSM has a particular focus on the private sector in developing countries and countries in transition.

Clean Clothes Campaign (CCC) International Secretariat, Postbus 11584, 1001 GN Amsterdam, The Netherlands

www.cleanclothes.org

CCC is a coalition of consumer organizations, labor unions, researchers, solidarity groups, and other activists that informs consumers about the conditions in which their garments and sportswear are produced and pressures retailers to take responsibility for these conditions. Its code of labor practices for the apparel industry is based ILO standards. CCC also provides information on Codes of Conduct and Independent Monitoring and comments on specific corporate codes, as well as publishing a wide range of reports. There are CCC affiliates in many countries worldwide.

Codes of Conduct

www.codesofconduct.org

A web-based resource that offers links to codes of conduct that have been either formulated or adopted by companies, industries, governments, unions, and universities.

Co-op America, 1612 K St NW, Suite 600, Washington, DC 20006, USA

www.coopamerica.org

Co-op America is a membership organization that seeks to harness the economic strength of consumers, businesses, investors, and the market place to create a just and environmentally sustainable society. Its programs include Green Business; Green Energy; Responsible Shopper; Shareholder Action; Social Investing; and Sweatshops. The Co-op America Business Network provides business tools, undertakes research, gives information on energy efficiency, and shows how businesses and governments can work together. Publications include the National Green Pages, the consumer magazine

Co-op America Quarterly, and a range of consumer action guides. Co-op America belongs to the NGO Taskforce on Business and Industry (ToBI), an international NGO network created to develop a unified perspective on global issues such as corporate accountability and responsible entrepreneurship and investment.

Copenhagen Centre for Corporate Responsibility (TCC), Porcelænshaven 24A, DK2000 Frederiksberg-C, Denmark

www.copenhagencentre.org

Established in 1998 by the Danish government to respond to the growing interest in corporate social responsibility and social partnerships, the Centre's main purpose is to conduct research and bring together business leaders and policy makers to debate the changing role of business in society. Its numerous publications and research papers are available via its website.

Corporate Watch, 16b Cherwell Street, Oxford OX4 1BG, UK

www.corporatewatch.org

Corporate Watch undertakes research and public education on the social and environmental impacts of large corporations, particularly multinationals. It publishes a quarterly magazine, *Corporate Watch*, as well as specific reports and information on the following industries: arms, construction and property, finance, food, forestry, leisure, media, mining, nuclear power, oil and gas, public relations, lobbying, security, and utilities.

CorpWatch, 1611 Telegraph Avenue, Oakland, CA 94612, USA

www.corpwatch.org

An online information and research service that exposes and campaigns on the negative social, political, economic, and environmental impacts of transnational corporations, CorpWatch grew out of *The Corporate Planet: Ecology and Politics in the Age of Globalization* (Sierra Club Books, 1997) written by its founder, Joshua Karliner. It maintains an extensive database on specific companies and sectors, the most recent of which is the War Profiteers website launched in the wake of the US-led invasion of Iraq.

CSR Europe (formerly European Business Network for Social Cohesion), Rue Defacqz, 78-80, Brussels 1060, Belgium

www.csreurope.org

Founded in 1995, CSR Europe is the leading European business network for corporate responsibility, whose membership includes more than 60 leading TNCs. Its goal is to help companies to prosper in ways that stimulate job growth, increase employability, and prevent social exclusion, thereby contributing to a sustainable economy and a more just society. Its publications include *CSR Magazine* and reports on topics such as corporate performance in relation to human rights and cause-related marketing.

Ethical Trading Initiative (ETI), Cromwell House, 14 Fulwood Place, London WC1V 6HZ, UK

www.ethicaltrade.org

ETI is an alliance of companies, NGOs, and trade unions committed to working together to identify and promote good practice in the implementation of codes of labor practice, including the monitoring and independent verification of the observance of code provisions. Members are expected to adopt the Base Code of labor practice, and the ETI encourages the use of a widely endorsed set of standards that can be used by large and small companies alike.

Fair Labor Association (FLA), 1505 22nd Street NW, Washington, DC 20037, USA

www.fairlabor.org

FLA is nonprofit organization that brings together industries, NGOs, and academic bodies concerned to protect the rights of apparel and footwear workers worldwide. The FLA grew out of the Apparel Industry Partnership (AIP), a voluntary initiative supported by the White House in 1996. Its Workplace Code of Conduct is part of the FLA Charter Agreement, a pioneering industry-wide code of conduct and monitoring system. The FLA accredits independent monitors, determines whether companies are in compliance with its standards, and issues public reports that enable consumers to make responsible purchasing decisions.

Fairtrade Foundation 16 Baldwin's Gardens, London EC1N 7RJ, UK,

www.fairtrade.org.uk

The Fairtrade Foundation was formed by a group of British development NGOs in response to concerns about the negative effects of conventional international trade on poor producers and on Third World economies. It undertakes campaigning and consumer education work aimed at promoting fair returns to producers within a more sustainable trade regime and also seeks to influence the retail and catering trades as well as individual consumers through its imports of bananas, coffee, chocolate, cocoa, and tea. The Foundation is the UK branch of Fairtrade Labelling Organizations International and licenses the FAIRTRADE Mark to products that meet internationally recognized standards.

Fairtrade Labelling Organizations International (FLO), Bonner Talweg 177, D-53925 Bonn, Germany

www.fairtrade.net

FLO is the worldwide Fairtrade standard-setting and certification organization. Products that bear its label enable over 1 million disadvantaged producers, workers, and their dependants in 50 countries to be covered by Fairtrade standards.

Forestry Stewardship Council (FSC), FSC International Center, Charles-de-Gaulle 5, 53113 Bonn, Germany

www.fsc.org

FSC is an international network comprising regional offices and national initiatives in 34 countries to promote responsible management of the world's forests, which it defines as being environmentally appropriate, socially beneficial, and economically viable. FSC certification assessments are carried out by accredited bodies, and the FSC trademark is a guarantee that timber has been produced from well-managed forests.

Global Exchange 2017 Mission Street, San Francisco, CA 94110, USA

www.globalexchange.org

Global Exchange is a nonprofit research and action centre that promotes environmental, political, and social justice around the world, with a focus on US corporations. As part of its Global Economic Rights' Initiative, Global Exchange has developed a list of corporate accountability campaigns on major brands through which it hopes to convince corporations of the need to include social, labor, and environmental concerns in their core business agenda.

Global Reporting Initiative (GRI), Keizersgracht 209, PO Box 10039, 1001 EA Amsterdam, The Netherlands

www.globalreporting.org

GRI is an international, multistakeholder effort to develop and disseminate globally applicable Sustainability Reporting Guidelines. These guidelines provide a common framework for organizations to report voluntarily on the economic, environmental, social impact of their activities, products, and services. GRI incorporates the active participation of businesses, accountancy, human rights, environmental, labor, and governmental organizations and is an official collaborating centre of the United Nations Environment Programme (UNEP).

Global Witness, PO Box 6042, London N19 5WP, UK

www.globalwitness.org

Global Witness conducts research and campaigns to expose the links between natural resource exploitation and human rights abuses, with a particular focus on armed conflict. It has published reports on Angola, Burma, Cambodia, Cameroon, the Democratic Republic of the Congo (DRC), Liberia, and Zimbabwe, many of which are available in French and Portuguese.

Interfaith Center on Corporate Responsibility (ICCR), Room 1282, 475 Riverside Drive, New York, NY 10115, USA

www.iccr.org

ICCR is an international coalition of faith-based institutional investors such as denominations, religious communities, pension funds, healthcare corporations, and dioceses who believe in ensuring a social as well as a financial return. The social and environmental portfolio of the companies in which they invest are therefore scrutinized, while ICCR members also use their influence to urge corporations to change their business practices rather than simply taking their investment elsewhere. ICCR produces a range of publications, including its regular magazine *The Corporate Examiner*, all of which can be purchased from its website.

International Centre for Trade Sustainable Development (ICTSD) International, Environment House 2, 7 chemin de Balexert, 1219 Châtelaine, Geneva, Switzerland

www.ictsd.org

ICTSD is an independent NGO that seeks to contribute to a better understanding of development and environmental concerns in the context of international trade. With a wide network of governmental, nongovernmental and inter-governmental partners, ICTSD provides nonpartisan reporting and facilitation services at the intersection of international trade and sustainable development and seeks to build bridges between sectors with seemingly disparate agendas.

International Federation of Alternative Trade (IFAT), Prijssestraat 24, 4101 CR Culemborg, The Netherlands

www.ifat.org

IFAT serves to bring together "alternative" and fair trade organizations in order to benefit small food producers and artisans worldwide. IFAT promotes fair trade through market development, monitoring, and advocacy programs that include public education, campaigns and lobbying, and the provision of technical and business support. The website provides access to resources on fair trade and links to relevant organizations.

International Business Leaders Forum (IBLF), 15-16 Cornwall Terrace, Regent's Park, London NW1 4QP, UK

www.iblf.org

IBLF is a nonprofit organization that promotes responsible business practices in order to achieve development that is socially, economically, and environmentally sustainable. Its members include more than 60 multinational companies. IBLF engages with leaders in business, civil society, and the public sector in transition and emerging economies and encourages them to form geographic or issue-based partnerships as a means of fostering a climate of corporate responsibility.

International Confederation of Free Trade Unions (ICFTU), 5 Boulevard du Roi Albert II, BP 1, 1210 Brussels, Belgium

www.icftu.org

ICFTU is by far the largest confederation of trade union centers, with 221 affiliated organizations from 148 countries and territories. Apart from representing its affiliates, it provides research, education, training, and information services. Regular publications include the annual *Survey of Trade Union Rights*, which details over 100 countries that violate basic trade union rights, and the monthly magazine *Trade Union World* (also available as *Le Monde Syndical* and *El mundo sindical*).

International Labour Organization (ILO), 4 route des Morillons, 1211 Geneva, Switzerland

www.ilo.org

The ILO is the UN specialized agency advocating social justice and universal human and labor rights. Its tripartite structure is comprised of workers, employers, and national governments. ILO Conventions and Recommendations set minimum standards across the entire spectrum of work-related issues. Its publications include technical manuals and reference works, training materials, the annual *World Labour Report*; two journals (published in English, French, and Spanish), *International Labour Review* and *Labour Education*; and the magazine *World of Work*, which covers health and safety issues.

Investor Responsibility Research Center (IRRC), 1350 Connecticut Avenue NW, Suite 700, Washington DC, 20036-1702, USA

www.irrc.org

IRRC provides services relating to corporate governance and social responsibility including proxy research and analysis, benchmarking products, and proxy voting services to institutional investors and a wide range of other clients in order to enable them to make informed decisions. It publishes a quarterly journal, *Corporate Governance Bulletin*, as well many reports on issues such as remuneration practices for corporate directors, the representation of women and ethnic minorities on US corporate boards, human rights in China, and records on social investment and shareholder voting.

Marine Stewardship Council (MSC) Unit 4 Bakery Place, 119 Altenburg Gardens, London SW11 1JQ, UK

www.msc.org

The MSC promotes sustainable fisheries and responsible fishing practices by means of a certification program that is appropriate to all sizes of fishing enterprise; and by encouraging consumers to choose products bearing the MSC label. The certification standards take into account relevant laws, ecological sustainability and ecosystem integrity, sound management systems, and social benefits deriving from the fishery.

New Economics Foundation (nef), 3 Jonathan Street, London SE11 5NH, UK

www.neweconomics.org

nef is a "think and do tank" that challenges orthodox economics and seeks to combine rigorous research with practical approaches to addressing economic, environmental, and social concerns. With a focus on the needs of those who are disadvantaged in the mainstream economy—economics as if people mattered—nef works on issues such as time banks, urban renewal, access to finance, and new ways of understanding and measuring progress. Its extensive publishing program covers issues ranging from the economics of the US-led invasion of Iraq to how to set up a social investment fund. Many of its publications are available free of charge.

Philippine Business for Social Progress (PBSP), PO Box 3839, Manila, Philippines

www.pbsp.org.ph

Established in 1970, PBSP is the first non-profit consortium of corporations in SE Asia that both advocates and practices corporate social responsibility and corporate citizenship. It believes not in philanthropic welfare but in releasing human potential and achieving better socioeconomic equity as the most effective and sustainable approach to reducing poverty.

Public Services International Research Unit (PSIRU), Business School, University of Greenwich, Park Row, Greenwich, London SE10 9LS, UK

www.psiru.org

PSIRU conducts empirical research into privatization and the restructuring of public services worldwide, with a particular focus on water, waste management, energy, and healthcare. PSIRU houses an extensive database on the economic, political, financial, social, and technical experience of privatization, and on the multinational companies involved. Its reports are available free of charge.

Social Accountability International (SAI), 220 East 23rd St. Suite 605, New York, NY 10010, USA

www.sa-intl.org

SAI (formerly the Council on Economic Priorities Accreditation Agency) seeks to promote workers' human rights as an organization that sets standards, licenses independent auditors to verify workplace compliance, and as a resource on ethical supply chains. Social Accountability 8000 (SA8000) is based on ILO standards and UN conventions on human rights and is designed to ensure compliance with high ethical standards by integrating management tools that serve both the needs of business and the rights of workers. SAI also offers training and certification for auditors as well as training and technical assistance to workers, managers, and suppliers. More broadly, SAI seeks to educate the public about the importance of social performance standards.

SustainAbility, 20–22 Bedford Row, London WC1R 4EB, UK

www. sustainability.com

SustainAbility is a strategy consultancy and think tank specializing in the business risks and market opportunities of corporate responsibility and sustainable development. Its ultimate goal is to foster a market system that rewards business for wider social, economic, and environmental excellence. Its monthly newsletter, *Radar*, reviews and interprets key events relating to sustainable development, business, and the triple bottom line, and its Issue Briefs cover emerging topics, such as nanotech, offshoring, and emission trading.

Sweatshop Watch, 1250 So Los Angeles Street, Suite 212, Los Angeles, CA, 90015, USA

www.sweatshopwatch.org

Sweatshop Watch is a coalition of organizations concerned with labor, community, and civil rights as well as religious and women's issues. It was formed in response to the discovery of inhumane conditions in sweatshops employing Thai immigrant workers in El Monte, California, for whom it won US$4 million in overtime compensation and damages. The coalition seeks to inform garment workers about their rights, and educate consumers about their responsibilities.

Trade Union Advisory Committee to the OECD (TUAC), 15 rue Laperouse, 75016 Paris, France

www.tuac.org

TUAC is an interface for labor unions at the OECD on all issues relating to workers, and focuses in particular on the implementation of the OECD Guidelines for Multinational Enterprises and Corporate Governance and on OECD relations with non-member countries.

Transparency International (TI), Alt Moabit 96, 10559 Berlin, Germany

www.transparency.org

TI, which comprises an international secretariat and 85 national chapters, seeks to curb the demand and supply of corruption at every level, raising awareness about its damaging effects, advocating policy reform, and working towards compliance with existing conventions. TI publications include the Bribe Payers Index, which ranks the industrialized countries by the propensity of their companies to pay bribes abroad, and the Corruption Perceptions Index, which ranks countries by experts' perception of corruption among public officials and politicians. The Global Corruption Barometer surveys public attitudes to corruption in a range of countries. These and many other publications are available free of charge, most of them in Chinese, English, French, German, Spanish, and Russian.

United Nations Conference on Trade and Development (UNCTAD), Palais des Nations, 8-14 avenue de la Paix, 1211 Geneva, Switzerland

www.unctad.org

UNCTAD seeks to assist the integration of developing countries into the world economy in ways that promote global development in three main ways: by acting as a forum for intergovernmental deliberations and consensus building; by undertaking research, data collection, and policy analysis; and by providing technical assistance to developing countries and donors. Its extensive publications, reports, and statistical data are available via its website, most of them free of charge and many also in French and Spanish.

United Nations Industrial Development Organization (UNIDO), Wagramerstrasse 5, PO Box 300, A-1400 Vienna, Austria

www.unido.org

UNIDO helps developing countries and transition economies to pursue sustainable industrial development as one means to relieve poverty. It focuses on productive employment, a competitive economy, and a sound environment. UNIDO acts as a global forum for information exchange and policy debates on all matters relating to industrial development, and provides technical advice and assistance to support industrialization efforts. In addition to its annual *Industrial Development Report*, UNIDO has an extensive list on private-sector development, agro-industries, investment and technology production, environmental management, and sustainable energy and climate change. These are all available via UNIDO's website, many of them free of charge.

UN Global Compact, The Global Compact Office, United Nations, Room S-1881, New York, NY 10017, USA

www.unglobalcompact.org

The Global Compact is a voluntary initiative that brings together CSOs including labor unions and NGOs, the UN, and business to support 10 universal environmental and social principles, particularly in the areas of human rights, labor, and anti-corruption. The overall goal of this network is to harness corporate power to foster a sustainable and inclusive global economy.

Verité, 44 Belchertown Road, Amherst MA 01002, USA

www.verite.org

Verité is a nonprofit social auditing and research organization dedicated to ensuring that people worldwide work in safe, fair, and legal conditions. It works with like-minded groups to assess and monitor factory conditions, and provides customized services for individual companies to ensure that goods sold under their trademark are produced under acceptable conditions. It produces a number of publications on labor rights and the magazine *Verité Monitor.*

Women in Informal Employment: Globalizing and Organizing (WIEGO), Carr Center for Human Rights at Kennedy School of Government, Harvard University, 79 John F. Kennedy Street, Cambridge, MA 02138, USA

www.wiego.org

WIEGO is a worldwide coalition concerned with improving the status of women in the informal economy, which is where women workers, particularly the poorest, are concentrated. This work and its economic contribution remain largely invisible in official statistics and policies. WIEGO seeks to redress this imbalance through compiling better statistics, conducting research, developing programs and policies, and promoting the organization and representation of workers in the informal economy.

World Business Council on Sustainable Development (WBCSD), 4 chemin de
Conches, 1231 Conches, Geneva, Switzerland

www.wbcsd.ch

WBCSD is a coalition of 175 companies that believe that sustainable development and business are mutually reinforcing. It therefore seeks to provide business leadership as a catalyst for sustainable development and to promote eco-efficiency, innovation, and corporate social responsibility. Its key projects include accountability and reporting, energy and climate, sustainable health systems, sustainable livelihoods, sustainable mobility, and water. A number of publications and guides are available on its website.

About the Contributors

Stephanie Ware Barrientos is a Fellow at the Institute of Development Studies at the University of Sussex, where she specializes in gender and development, with a particular focus on globalization, agribusiness, ethical trade, corporate responsibility, and international labor standards.

Jem Bendell is a Visiting Fellow at Nottingham University Business School in the UK and Adjunct Professor at the Auckland University of Technology in New Zealand. He has been involved in and published extensively on corporate responses to development challenges.

Catherine Dolan is Assistant Professor of Anthropology at Northeastern University. A specialist on Eastern Africa, her research focuses on the political economy of food and agriculture, development theory, gender and employment, and the social relations of commodities.

Sumi Dhanarajan is a Policy Adviser on the private sector for Oxfam GB. Trained as a barrister, she has served as Human Rights Officer to the Malaysian Bar Council and as Legal Adviser to the Secretariat of Legislative Councillors of the Hong Kong Democratic Party.

Deborah Doane is an Associate of the New Economics Foundation (nef) in London, and Chair of the Corporate Responsibility Coalition (CORE) coalition, which campaigns for laws that will ensure corporate social responsibility.

Deborah Eade worked in Mexico and Central America from 1982 to 1991, where she served for eight years as Oxfam GB's Deputy Regional Representative. Editor of the journal, *Development in Practice*, she has published widely on international developmental and humanitarian issues.

Niamh Garvey was, at the time of writing, working with the ELDIS information dissemination service at the Institute of Development Studies at the University of Sussex. She is currently Policy and Advocacy Officer at Christian Aid Ireland.

David Hall is director of the Public Services International Privatisation Research Unit (PSIRU) at the University of Greenwich, specializing in water, energy, and healthcare, and the design and maintenance of the database and website. Previously at the Public Services Privatisation Research Unit, he has published on public expenditure and labor law.

April Linton is Assistant Professor of Sociology at the University of California, San Diego. Her work encompasses many aspects of globalization including international migration, transnational social movements, and the effects of policies on trade, development, and the environment.

Lienda Loebis is Deputy Director for Marketing and Promotion in the Department for Small and Medium Enterprises at the Ministry of Industry and Trade of the Republic of Indonesia, and was for many years in charge of the Department's international cooperation.

Emanuele Lobina specializes in water at the Public Services International Privatisation Research Unit (PSIRU) based at the University of Greenwich. He studied political science and international trade law at the universities of Florence and Turin, and has collaborated with IDHEAP at the University of Lausanne.

Robin de la Motte works on WaterTime at the Public Services International Privatisation Research Unit (PSIRU) based at the University of Greenwich, and previously worked at the European Commission in Brussels.

Ben Moxham is a researcher at Focus on the Global South, a research and advocacy organization based in Bangkok.

Julian Oram was, at the time of writing, a senior research analyst at the New Economics Foundation (nef), and is currently a Policy Officer in the Food Rights Team at ActionAid in London.

Peter Newell is Senior Research Fellow at the Centre for the Study of Globalisation and Regionalisation at the University of Warwick and has published widely on the politics of corporate regulation and accountability.

Carolina Quinteros is a Salvadoran sociologist and teaches Political Science at the Universidad Centroamericana José Simeón Cañas (UCA) in San Salvador. She is the founder and principal researcher of the Independent Monitoring Group for El Salvador (GMIES).

Leopoldo Rodríguez-Boetsch is Assistant Professor of Economics and International Studies at Portland State University, Oregon. His areas of specialty include Latin American political economy and economic development.

John Sayer was a farmer in Wales before moving to Asia in 1976, where he became Co-Director of the Asia Monitor Resource Centre (AMRC), working with the region's labor movements on information systems, new technology, occupational health and safety, and labor rights. From 1991, he headed the program department of Oxfam Hong Kong, later becoming its director and subsequently interim director of Oxfam International. He resumed the directorship of Oxfam Hong Kong in 2006.

Hubert Schmitz is a Professorial Fellow at the Institute of Development Studies at the University of Sussex, where he led its work on the collective efficiency of small firms and on local upgrading in global chains. He is currently developing value-chain analysis for policy makers.

Sally Smith is a Research Officer at the Institute of Development Studies at the University of Sussex, where she focuses on fair trade and the impacts of ethical trade for workers in global value chains.

Anne Tallontire leads the Enterprise, Trade and Finance Group at the Natural Resources Institute at the University of Greenwich and is a core member of the Natural Resources and Ethical Trade Programme where her research focuses on fair trade, ethical sourcing, corporate responsibility, international trade, and gender issues.

Peter Utting is Deputy Director of the United Nations Research Institute for Social Development (UNRISD) where he coordinates an international research program on corporate social responsibility and development.

Index

Accountability: development policy and, 33–34; in private versus public sector, 128; *See also* Corporate accountability (CA)

AccountAbility: The Institute of Social and Ethical AccountAbility, 281

Adidas, 214, 216

African horticulture: codes of conduct in, 249–251; Dutch Auctions and, 252–253; employment in, 255–260; gender issues in, 255–260; implementing codes of conduct in, 261–262; nonpermanent workers in, 258; permanent labor in, 256–258; value chains in, 248–249

African Institute of Corporate Citizenship, 281

Agriculture: employment practices in, 196–197; monopolies in; 151–152; organic, 226

Agrochemical corporations, vii

Airline industry, 152–153

Alliance for a Corporate-Free UN, ix

Allied Signal Seat Belt Company, 87

Annan, Kofi, 240

Anticapitalist movement, 6

Anti-privatization campaigns: actors in, 112–113; alternative positions of, 116–118; countries with, 111, 112, 114–116; against energy privatization, 108–110; impact of, 104–105; by international organizations, 113; through legal battles, 115–116; political support for, 113–115, 120–121; success of, 115; support for, 112–115, 120–121; against water privatization, 105–108

Argentina: anti-inflationary program in, 134; Convertibility Plan in, 140; debt in, 132–133; dependence on international capital flows, 135; economic crisis in, 125–144; economic reforms in, 125–138; evaluating privatization in, 132–133; foreign direct investment (FDI) in, 130; Law of Convertibility in, 143; privatization in, 129–132, 144; privatization in theory in, 127–129; Privatized Public Service Enterprises (PPSEs) in, 138–144; recession in, 135–136, 137; trade balance with Brazil, 136, 137; trade surplus in, 137; unemployment rate in, 132

Ashridge Centre for Business and Society, 281

Australia, 113–115

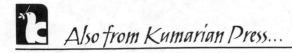 *Also from Kumarian Press...*

Of Related Interest:

Globalization and Social Exclusion: A Transformationalist Perspective
Ronaldo Munck

Development NGOs and Labor Unions: Terms of Engagement
Edited by Deborah Eade and Alan Leather

Feeding the Market: South American Farmers, Trade, and Globalization
Jon Hellin and Sophie Higman

New and Forthcoming:

A World Turned Upside Down: Social Ecological Approaches to Children in War Zones
Edited by Neil Boothby, Mike Wessells, and Alison Strang

Non-State Actors in the Human Rights Universe
Edited by George Andreopoulos, Zehra Arat, and Peter Juviler

Piecing a Democratic Quilt: Regional Organizations and Universal Norms
Edward McMahon and Scott Baker

Transnational Civil Society: An Introduction
Edited by Srilatha Batliwala and L. David Brown

Cinderella or Cyberella? Empowering Women in the Knowledge Society
Edited by Nancy J. Hafkin and Sophia Huyer

Kumarian Press, located in Bloomfield, Connecticut, is a forward-looking, scholarly press that promotes active international engagement and an awareness of global connectedness.

Visit Kumarian Press at www.kpbooks.com or call toll-free 800.289.2664 for a complete catalog.